T0230016

Lecture Notes in Computer Science 706

Edited by G. Goos and J. Hartmanis

Advisory Board: W. Brauer D. Gries J. Stoer

H. Dieter Rombach Victor R. Basili
Richard W. Selby (Eds.)

Experimental Software
Engineering Issues:

Critical Assessment and Future Directions

International Workshop
Dagstuhl Castle, Germany, September 14-18, 1992
Proceedings

Springer-Verlag
Berlin Heidelberg New York
London Paris Tokyo
Hong Kong Barcelona
Budapest

H. Dieter Rombach   Victor R. Basili
Richard W. Selby (Eds.)

Experimental Software Engineering Issues:

Critical Assessment and Future Directions

International Workshop
Dagstuhl Castle, Germany, September 14-18, 1992
Proceedings

Springer-Verlag
Berlin Heidelberg New York
London Paris Tokyo
Hong Kong Barcelona
Budapest

Series Editors

Gerhard Goos
Universität Karlsruhe
Postfach 69 80
Vincenz-Priessnitz-Straße 1
D-76131 Karlsruhe, Germany

Juris Hartmanis
Cornell University
Department of Computer Science
4130 Upson Hall
Ithaca, NY 14853, USA

Volume Editors

H. Dieter Rombach
Fachbereich Informatik, Universität Kaiserslautern
Postfach 3049, D-67653 Kaiserslautern, Germany

Victor R. Basili
Department of Computer Science, University of Maryland
College Park, Maryland 20742, USA

Richard W. Selby
Department of Information & Computer Science, University of California
Irvine, CA 92717, USA

CR Subject Classification (1991): D.2, K.6

ISBN 3-540-57092-6 Springer-Verlag Berlin Heidelberg New York
ISBN 0-387-57092-6 Springer-Verlag New York Berlin Heidelberg

© Springer-Verlag Berlin Heidelberg 1993
Printed in Germany

Typesetting: Camera ready by author
45/3140-543210 - Printed on acid-free paper

Preface

Experimental Software Engineering Issues:
Critical Assessment and Future Directions

Context

Since its inception in 1968, software engineering has struggled to find its identity. Today, we can identify three different approaches to study of the discipline of software engineering in the research community: the mathematical or formal methods approach, the system building approach, and the empirical studies group. Within the mathematical or formal methods group, the emphasis is on finding better formal methods and languages and software development is viewed as a mathematical transformation process. Within the system building group, the emphasis is on finding better methods for structuring large systems and software development is viewed as a creative task which cannot be controlled other than through rigid constraints on the resulting product. Within the empirical studies group, the emphasis is on understanding the strengths and weaknesses of methods and tools in order to tailor them to the specific goals of a particular software project.

The purpose of this workshop was to gather those members of the software engineering community who support an engineering approach, based upon empirical studies, to provide an interchange of ideas and paradigms for research.

Software engineering based upon empirical studies is made difficult when one observes that in practical software organizations, project contexts (i.e., project goals and environmental characteristics) vary from project to project. Thus, no single technology or method can be expected to work well in all contexts, and observing software phenomena out of context seems to be doomed to fail. As part of the learning process, we need to characterize and understand the project context and understand the various phenomena relative to that context and learn in an incremental and evolutionary manner. We need to replicate experiments in different contexts to fully understand the nature of the various phenomena and be able to build models to facilitate learning.

Improvement oriented approaches that take into account the evolutionary and experimental nature of software have recently been suggested as a framework for studying the relationships between product and knowledge engineering. This framework bears the potential of integrating the efforts of the formal methods, system building, and empirical studies approaches in a promising way. These improvement approaches are based on the use of empirical technology for building models. Formal methods as well as system building technology can be elevated to the level of useful technology from an engineering perspective if augmented with knowledge of their effectiveness based on empirical evidence. Other frameworks with similar objectives have been suggested too.

After twenty-five years of software engineering it seemed appropriate to rethink its scientific and engineering basis. Based on the increasing demands imposed on our field by the ever-increasing complexity and criticality of software related applications, a move towards an engineering view of our field is needed. Such a move must not be construed as a competition between the mathematical, system building, and empirical studies approaches. Instead, it suggests that all three are necessary, but that we cannot ignore the nature of our field, which requires more than devising new languages and techniques and more than just building systems which can be judged at the end. We need to do all of this in a framework which enables us to understand all existing and new technologies, and use them in a controlled fashion to develop the systems required by our customers.

Objectives

We have only begun to understand the experimental nature of software engineering, the role of empirical studies and measurement within software engineering, and the mechanisms needed to apply them successfully. Workshop discussion was focused on assessing past accomplishments within the experimental software engineering community and proposing necessary future steps. The topics of discussion included several of the most eminent challenges within experimental software engineering:

(1) Identifying the appropriate paradigm for software engineering:
Should we adapt the mathematical approach or the experimental approaches used in physical or social sciences? For what purposes do we need empirical studies in experimental software engineering? What are software-specific constraints or requirements for empirical studies?

(2) Understanding the range of different contexts for empirical studies in software engineering:
Why do we measure? What is it we want to know? How do the changing project contexts affect our ability to measure?

(3) Devising the appropriate procedures and mechanisms for empirical studies:
How should we perform empirical studies? How should we specify the objectives and context of studies? How should we determine the appropriate measures for a given objective? How should we design the appropriate experiments or case studies? How should we collect and validate product and process data?

(4) Guiding the use of empirical data to build or improve existing software models:
What are the appropriate analysis procedures for software engineering data? How can these procedures help us create models of software processes and products? What alternatives exist to model building based on empirical data?

(5) Identifying appropriate concepts and mechanisms for packaging existing models for reuse across projects:
What makes models reusable? How do we determine the needs for reuse? How should we organize and build up reusable model libraries? What mechanisms are needed to support reuse of models across projects?

(6) Proposing appropriate means of distributing experimental ideas to practitioners and students:

How do we make improvement happen in practice? What organizational structures are needed to support technology transfer, especially what roles can universities and industry play? How can we change our university curricula in order to instill ideas of empirical studies into students early on? How can we train practitioners in the experimental paradigm of software engineering?

Session Organization

In order to address all these challenges, an international workshop on the topic "Experimental Software Engineering Issues" was organized and held at the International Conference and Research Center for Computer Science (IBFI) at Dagstuhl Castle in the Federal Republic of Germany. The motivation for this workshop was to provide a forum for a relatively small but representative group of leading experts in experimental software engineering with an emphasis on empirical studies from both universities and industry to meet and reflect on past successes and failures, assess the current state-of-the practice and research, identify problems, and define future directions. An organizing committee identified key topics and key people to participate in the workshop. The six challenges above were chosen for discussion along with people to present keynote presentations and chair those sessions. A final session was aimed at devising an agenda for the future.

After the selection of discussion topics, keynoters and session chairs was made, approximately thirty more participants were invited to submit position papers on one of the selected topics. The participants came from Europe, the United States and Canada, Asia and Australia. During each session, a keynote presentation was followed by a number of position statements and extensive discussion. The materials contained in this volume include for each session the keynote address, position papers, and a discussion summary.

This workshop was scheduled to run from Monday, September 14, through noon on Friday, September 18. Six half-day sessions (Monday, Tuesday, Thursday) were devoted to the topics listed. Each session was organized by a session chair, and introduced by a keynote presentation intended to provide a critical assessment of the topic at hand and to make provocative statements to stimulate discussion. The keynote was complemented by a number of position statements. The major portion of each session was reserved for lively discussion. Wednesday was reserved for sightseeing in the city of Trier. The wrap-up session on Friday morning was intended to synthesize the results of a week-long discussion into a statement of where we stand as a field (i.e., what we agree on, what we don't agree on) and devise an agenda for future progress in our field.

Results

The results of the workshop can be summarized in terms of what has been achieved in the past in terms of measurable benefits from the software practitioner's perspective, what lessons have been learned regarding experimental software engineering in general and empirical studies in specific, what are remaining key points of dissent, and what are the important topics for future work. The following summaries reflect the consensus achieved in the discussion sessions complemented by the written opinions collected from the workshop attendees via a questionnaire.

(A) Past Achievements (Practitioners' Perspective):

Each workshop attendee was in a position to report about empirical studies and/ or measurement programs and subjective results ranging from increased understanding of certain software engineering phenomena or the improvements of real-world software processes. Most of these achievements are not well documented or documentation is company-confidential. Most of the achievements are based on empirical studies in very specific contexts and cannot be generalized due to the variability in contexts across different organizations.

The workshop attendees felt that in order to live up to the theme of the workshop, we needed to come up with documented results which could be analyzed by others and could be used to convey the potential value of empirical work in terms of measurable benefits. One outstanding example was reported by Frank McGarry from the Software Engineering Laboratory at NASA's Goddard Space Flight Center and will be mentioned here as an example. Frank McGarry reported the following practical SEL achievements which had been achieved through and demonstrated via empirical studies:

- People oriented technologies are most effective (e.g., inspections, Cleanroom) as opposed to automated tools

- Commonly accepted complexity measures are not very meaningful in our domain

- Ada software costs more to develop; less to deliver because of reuse (multiple experiments)

- Inspections by stepwise abstraction reading are the most effective and most cost effective testing method

- Models/relationships developed are incorporated into management process (e.g., manager's handbook) and supported (e.g., SME)

- The error rates in development projects were reduced significantly through the use of Cleanroom (e.g., 33% on a series of 3 projects)

- Environmental heritage/context/legacy is the dominant impact on processes and products (e.g., use of Ada over time)

- Productive reuse is driven by process reuse and packaging of design - *not* by code packaging (e.g., Ada/OOD experiments)

- Some commonly accepted processes assumed to be beneficial are inappropriate for the SEL (e.g., IV&V)

- Personnel variation in productivity are tremendous (factors of 3 or 4 for large systems; factors of up to 15 in small systems)

- Design structure (strength/coupling) is an excellent predictor of module defects

Examples from other local environments have been provided but cannot be reported in this brief summary.

(B) **Past Achievements** (Researchers' Perspective):

The most important lessons learned about empirical studies and measurement include a broad agreement regarding the experimental nature of software engineering. This experimental nature requires empirical studies as a driver for learning and improvement. Empirical studies need to be performed with a goal and hypothesis in mind and the context characteristics need to be taken into account when interpreting measurement data. A variety of approaches for improvement and goal orientation were surveyed in Vic Basili's keynote address.

The most frequently occurring themes during the discussion and on the questionnaires were:

- Software engineering research needs to be driven by empirical studies

- Metrics and data in isolation (i.e., without context) are useless

- No single set of metrics is universally best

- Sound empirical approaches are essential

- Empirical studies have produced results in local contexts; but we have not been able to generalize local results

As an example, Vic Basili and Frank McGarry from the Software Engineering Laboratory at NASA's Goddard Space Flight Center reported the following research lessons they had learned about the application of empirical studies and measurement over the past fifteen years:

- The purpose of experimentation is for self-improvement and self-understanding rather than inter-organization and inter-country comparison

- Expectation/provision of N to 1 improvement in productivity over finite time (5 to 10 years) is baseless and won't happen!!!

- We are most effective when using multiple processes based on context (e.g., we are using Fortran/Functional-Decomposition-based design/reuse-oriented waterfall, ADA/OOD/reuse-oriented waterfall, and Cleanroom)

- Each of the above technologies and processes had to be tailored to our environment

- Understanding (baselining) is absolutely mandatory as a first step (before planning/controlling, technology transfer)

- Process definition/clarification of the empirical process is mandatory for successful experimentation/measurement (i.e., Doctor heal thyself)
- The process improvement paradigm is equally important for the software development task and the experimentation/data collection task
- The process for empirical studies has to be well defined and improved
- There must be a goal/rationale for data collection
- Data by itself provides minimal, most likely erroneous or detrimental insights
- The measurement data has intrinsic imprecision, inconsistency, and incompletely represented context and it always will. This drives the need to study trends not absolute facts.
- Packaging of experience is key to success - but is rarely done effectively
- Packaging (i.e., development of local standards) needs to be experience driven (e.g, 2167A is an incomplete approach)
- Effective cookbooks can be developed for particular domains (e.g., SEL measurement handbook, SEL management handbook)
- More data does not necessarily mean better results (i.e., national databases for measurement data are a waste of time and resources)
- Experimentation requires two identifiable, separate (but cooperating) organizational infrastructure components, which both involve cost
  - overhead to project (noise -- < 2%)
  - analysis and synthesis of data (8-10%)
  - support (quality assurance, databases, ...)
- Developers treat data collection/experimentation as an annoyance only, not as significant impact
- Infusion of significant process change (e.g., Ada, Cleanroom, OOD) requires 5 to 10 years

(C) Key Points of Dissent:

Although, all workshop participants agreed on the need for employing empirical studies and measurement in order to introduce engineering discipline into the field of software engineering, several points of dissent remained.

Examples of dissent explicitly voiced by participants included:

- Are large-scale, real-world experiments feasible from a scientific point of view? The majority opinion was that large-scale experiments (better: case studies) are feasible. They serve the purposes of observing trends rather than absolute facts and are needed for scaling up statistically significant observations from controlled experiments. In any engineering discipline such large-scale experiments are a useful and necessary. The minority opinion was that large-scale experiments can never be sound from a pure scientific perspective and, therefore, are not helpful.

- What are the right kinds of goals for measurement and empirical studies to begin with? The majority opinion was that there is no general answer to this question. The only rule of thumb is to start with goals oriented towards understanding, to continue with goals oriented towards better management and prediction, and ultimately address goals aimed at change/improvement. The specific goals depend on the needs and characteristics of the organization at hand. The minority opinion was that one should always start with micro-level goals (e.g., understand a testing process) before moving towards macro-level goals (e.g., understand the entire development process).

- Is the Hawthorne effect crucial? Some viewed the impact of the Hawthorne effect as so crucial that they concluded measurement of people could/should not be performed at all; others viewed it as non-critical. Again, there seemed to be a difference of opinion depending on the purpose of empirical studies and measurement. The majority opinion was that the Hawthorne effect can be tamed using appropriate statistical designs/analyses.

- How can empirical studies and measurement be introduced in teaching curricula? The majority viewed it as essential to train students from the beginning in evaluating the effects of methods and tools. A minority suggested postponing the topic to advanced software engineering classes.

(D) **Important Topics for Future Work:**

Future work needs to emphasize both the development and assessment of better infrastructure technology (i.e., principles, methods, tools) for experimentation and measurement, the application of that infrastructure for empirically investigating existing software evolution aspects in order to build better models of the basic building blocks of our discipline, and the infusion of empirical studies ideas into the educational system (i.e., teaching and training) and the real world.

As far as the development and assessment of infrastructure technology for experimentation and measurement is concerned, there was widespread agreement that the most significant need for research exists in technologies for modeling software engineering aspects, feeding back empirical data to improve those models, and organizing models for reuse, as well as in the availability of more laboratory environments for empirical studies. Specific suggestions included:

- Better approaches for scaling up empirical results from small, controlled environments to large, real-world environments

- Infrastructure for software measurement, spanning metrics specification, collection, analysis, visualization and predictive guidance

- Alternate approaches for validating software models based on small sets of data points

- A taxonomy of study types depending on the purpose of study

- Formal approaches for hypothesis formulation

- Processes for creating baselines for different domains and environments

- An expanded notion of study context to include different processes and organizational structures in different business domains

- Investigation of the use of better graphical, animated methods for presenting and analyzing experience models

- Demonstration of practical benefits of measurement and risk (based on data)

- More real laboratories for conducting empirical research (Existing examples include the Software Engineering Laboratory at NASA's Goddard Space Flight Center and the Software Technology Transfer Initiative Kaiserslautern (STTI-KL) at the University of Kaiserslautern.)

- Communication networks enabling individual research groups and companies to cooperate in the sense that empirical studies are being replicated across environment boundaries to improve the believability of local findings or understand the impact of different contexts (An existing example is the International Software Engineering Research Network (ISERN) founded by Prof. Basili, USA, Prof. Cantone, Italy, Dr. Oivo, Finland, Prof. Rombach, Germany, Prof. Selby, USA, and Prof. Torii, Japan.)

As far as the empirical investigation of existing software evolution aspects are concerned, major efforts are needed in the following areas:

- Characterization of naturally occurring software artifacts

- Analysis of process-product relationships

- Measurement of (Derivation of measures for) the evolution of software

- Measurement of (Derivation of measures for) integration aspects of software

- Documentation and publishing of results and achievements in objective terms (see the SEL example under (A) and (B))

- Promotion of existing knowledge via software engineering handbooks (!! Don't be afraid of incompleteness at this stage !!)

- Development of social and economic models for software evolution

As far as the infusion of empirical studies ideas into education and practice are concerned, major efforts are needed in the following areas:

- Development of undergraduate software engineering courses stressing engineering aspects (e.g., problem solving using heuristics) supported by appropriate textbooks

- Development of graduate software engineering courses stressing the basic principles, methods and tools for measurement and empirical studies supported by appropriate textbooks

- Development of technology transfer programs based on measurement (i.e., first, quantitative baselines of the state of affairs need to be developed; second, changes for the purpose of improvement can be introduced)

In summary, the workshop served as an important event in continuing to strengthen empirical software engineering as a major subdiscipline of software engineering. The deep interactions and important accomplishments from the meeting documented in this proceedings have helped identify key issues in moving software engineering as a whole towards a true engineering discipline. By the end of the workshop, most of the attendees acknowledged that they feel part of a true community of empirically oriented software engineers. In order to foster that sense of community, the empirical software engineering community intends to hold a continuing series of conferences and meetings that build on this workshop. Furthermore, an e-mail list for communication and exchange of information among people interested in empirical software engineering research was suggested.

NOTE: Such an e-mail list "empirical-se@informatik.uni-kl.de" now exists! Requests to join should be sent to "empirical-se-request@informatik.uni-kl.de".

Acknowledgements

It would have been difficult to organize a workshop like this without help and financial support from a variety of organizations. First, we would like to thank all the workshop participants for their effort in submitting position papers and participating in the discussions. Next, the session chairs and keynoters deserve a special thanks for their contributions to the success of the workshop.

Clearly, an effort such as this could not have been successful without financial support. We would like to acknowledge and sincerely thank the IBFI for supporting lodging and providing excellent meeting facilities, and the University of Kaiserslautern for additional general purpose funds. Our special thanks go to Alfred Bröckers, Chris Lott, and Martin Verlage from the University of Kaiserslautern for having taken notes of all discussion sessions and to Mrs. Kilgore from the University of Kaiserslautern who did a splendid job in providing secretarial support and arranging the social events. Last but not least, we acknowledge the tremendous amount of work by Mr. Martin Verlage in editing these proceedings.

Kaiserslautern   H. Dieter Rombach
May 1993   Victor R. Basili
                                                      Richard W. Selby

Contents

Contents

Session 3: Procedures and Mechanisms for Measurement/Experimentation

Session 4: [Measurement-Based] Modeling

Session 5: Packaging for Reuse / Reuse of Models

Session 6: Technology Transfer, Teaching and Training

Session 1:

The Experimental Paradigm in Software Engineering

Session Chair:	William W. Agresti
Keynote:	Victor R. Basili
Position Papers:	William W. Agresti
	Les Belady
	Norbert Fuchs
	Jochen Ludewig
	Walt Scacchi
	Walter F. Tichy

The Experimental Paradigm in Software Engineering

Victor R. Basili

Institute for Advanced Computer Studies
and
Department of Computer Science
University of Maryland

What is software and software engineering?

Software can be viewed as a part of a system solution that can be encoded to execute on a computer as a set of instructions; it includes all the associated documentation necessary to understand, transform and use that solution. Software engineering can be defined as the disciplined development and evolution of software systems based upon a set of principles, technologies, and processes.

We will concentrate on three primary characteristics of software and software engineering. Its inherent complexity, the lack of well defined primitives or components of the discipline, and the fact that software is developed, not produced. This combination makes software engineering quite different than anything we have dealt with before.

One important characteristic about software is that it can be complex; complex to build and complex to understand. There are a variety of reasons for this. For example, we often choose software as a part of the solution, rather than hardware, because it is the part of the solution we least understand; or it is something new, or there is a requirement for change and evolution of the function or structure. In all of these cases complexity is introduced, the development increases error prone, estimation is difficult and there is a lack of understanding of implications of change.

However, the primary reason software is complex is probably the lack of models, especially traceable models of the product, process and any other forms of knowledge required to build or understand software solutions as well as the interaction of those models. Software is not very visible, i.e., we do not have satisfactory models of the various aspects of the software, e.g., the functionality, the structure, etc. In fact we do not even have intuitive models in many cases. This leaves us with a poor understanding of processes, requirements, etc. and products.

Lastly, software is created via a development process, not a manufacturing process. This really means software is engineered. We have learned a great deal about manufacturing in the past few decades but we have not learned much about development/engineering.

So given the nature of this discipline, how does one begin to analyze the software product and process?

The Experimental Paradigm in Software Engineering

Victor R. Basili

Institute for Advanced Computer Studies
and
Department of Computer Science
University of Maryland

What is software and software engineering?

Software can be viewed as a part of a system solution that can be encoded to execute on a computer as a set of instructions; it includes all the associated documentation necessary to understand, transform and use that solution. Software engineering can be defined as the disciplined development and evolution of software systems based upon a set of principles, technologies, and processes.

We will concentrate on three primary characteristics of software and software engineering; its inherent complexity, the lack of well defined primitives or components of the discipline, and the fact that software is developed, not produced. This combination makes software something quite different than anything we have dealt with before.

One important characteristic about software is that it can be complex; complex to build and complex to understand. There are a variety of reasons for this. For example, we often choose software for a part of the solution, rather than hardware, because it is the part of the solution we least understand, or it is something new, or there is a requirement for change and evolution of the function or structure. In all of these cases complexity is introduced, the development becomes error prone, estimation is difficult, and there is a lack of understanding of implications of change.

However, the primary reason software is complex is probably the lack of models, especially tractable models of the product, process and any other forms of knowledge required to build or understand software solutions as well as the the interaction of these models. Software is not very visible, i.e., we do not have satisfactory models of the various aspects of the software, e.g., the functionality, the quality, the structure. In fact we do not even have intuitive models in many cases. This leaves us with a poor understanding of processes, requirements, and products.

Lastly, software is created via a development process, not a manufacturing process. This really means software is engineered.We have learned a great deal about quality manufacturing in the past few decades but we have not learned much about quality development/engineering.

So given the nature of this discipline, how does one begin to analyze the software product and process.

What are the available research paradigms?

There is a fair amount of research being conducted in software engineering, i.e., people are building technologies, methods, tools, etc. However, unlike in other disciplines, there has been very little research in the development of models of the various components of the discipline. The modeling research that does exist has centered on the software product, specifically mathematical models of the program function.

We have not sufficiently emphasized models for other components, e.g., processes, resources, defects, etc., the logical and physical integration of these models, the evaluation and analysis of the models via experimentation, the refinement and tailoring of the models to an application environment, and the access and use of these models in an appropriate fashion, on various types of software projects from an engineering point of view. The research is mostly bottom-up, done in isolation. It is the packaging of a technology rather than the solving of a problem or the understanding of a primitive of the discipline.

We need research that helps establish a scientific and engineering basis for software engineering.

To this end, the research methodologies required involve the need to build, analyze and evaluate models of the software processes and products as well as various aspects of the environment in which the software is being built, e.g the people, the organization, etc. It is especially important to study the interactions of these models. The goal is to develop the conceptual scientific foundations of software engineering upon which future researchers can build. This is often a process of discovering and validating small but important concepts that can be applied in many different ways and that can be used to build more complex and advanced ideas rather than merely providing a tool or methodology without experimental validation of its underlying assumptions or careful analysis and verification of its properties.

There are several example methodologies used in other disciplines [7,8]. These consist of various forms of experimental or analytic paradigms. The experimental paradigms require an experimental design, observation, data collection and validation on the process or product being studied. We will discuss three experimental models; although they are similar, the tend to emphasize different things.

Before discussing these paradigms, we will offer some definitions of terms that are used when discussing experimentation. A **fact** is information obtained through direct observation. A **hypothesis** is an educated guess that precedes an experiment. An **experiment** is a test, trial or tentative procedure policy; an act or operation for the purpose of discovering something unknown or of testing a principle, supposition, etc. ; an operation carried out under controlled conditions in order to discover an unknown effect or law, to test or establish a hypothesis, or to illustrate a known law. A **theory** is a possible explanation based upon many facts and reason. A **law** is a description/observation of behavior used for prediction and based upon facts and reason. A **model** is a simplified representation of a system or phenomenon with any hypotheses required to describe the system or explain the phenomenon, often mathematically. A model can be a theory or a law. A **paradigm** is conceptual filter that determines how we perceive and interpret. A **truth** is what really is.Experimentation does not provide truth, it only provides models in the form of theories or laws.

1) The scientific method: observe the world, propose a model or a theory of behavior, measure and analyze, validate hypotheses of the model or theory, and if possible repeat the procedure.

In the area of software engineering this inductive paradigm might best be used when trying to understand the software process, product, people, environment. It attempts to extract from the world some form of model which tries to explain the underlying phenomena, and evaluate whether the model is truly representative of the phenomenon being observed. It is an approach to model building. An example might be an attempt to understand the way software is being developed by an organization to see if their process model can be abstracted or a tool can be built to automate the process. Two variations of this inductive approach are:

1.1) The engineering method: observe existing solutions, propose better solutions, build/develop, measure and analyze, and repeat the process until no more improvements appear possible.

This version of the paradigm is an evolutionary improvement oriented approach which assumes one already has models of the software process, product, people and environment and modifies the model or aspects of the model in order to improve the thing being studied. An example might be the study of improvements to methods being used in the development of software or the demonstration that some tool performs better than its predecessor relative to certain characteristics. Note that a crucial part of this method is the need for careful analysis and measurement.

1.2) The empirical method: propose a model, develop statistical/qualitative methods, apply to case studies, measure and analyze, validate the model and repeat the procedure.

This version of the paradigm is a revolutionary improvement oriented approach which begins by proposing a new model, not necessarily based upon an existing model, and attempts to study the effects of the process or product suggested by the new model. An example might be the proposal of a new method or tool used to perform software development in a new way. Again, measurement and analysis is crucial to the success of this method. Proposing a model or building a tool is not enough. There must be some way of validating that the model or tool is an advance over current models or tools.

It is important to note that experimentation must be guided; there must be a rational for collecting data. Experiments must be designed to acquire information useful for the building of a suitable description (or model) of the systems under study. Experimentation alone is of no value if there is no underlying framework where experimental results can be interpreted. Other issues involved in these inductive, experimental methods include the types of experimental design appropriate for different environ-

5

ments, whether the experiment is exploratory or confirmatory, the validation of the data, the cost of the experiment, the problems of reproducibility, etc.

On the other hand, an analytic paradigm is:

2) The mathematical method: propose a formal theory or set of axioms, develop a theory, derive results and if possible compare with empirical observations.

This is a deductive analytical model which does not require an experimental design in the statistical sense but provides an analytic framework for developing models and understanding their boundaries based upon manipulation of the model itself. For example the treatment of programs as mathematical objects and their analysis of the mathematical object or its relationship to the program satisfies the paradigm.

Unfortunately, many projects and proposals that claim to be research are simply developments. These paradigms serve as a basis for distinguishing research activities from development activities. If one of these paradigms is not being used in some form, the study is most likely not a research project. For example, building a system or tool alone is development and not research. Research involves gaining understanding about how and why a certain type of tool might be useful and by validating that a tool has certain properties or certain effects by carefully designing an experiment to measure the properties or to compare it with alternatives. The scientific method can be used to understand the effects of a particular tool usage in some environment and to validate hypotheses about how software development can best be accomplished.

How do you do experiments?

There are several different approaches to experimenting in the software engineering domain. One set of approaches can be characterized by the number of teams replicating each project and the number of different projects analyzed, as discussed in [6]. It consists of four different experimental treatments, as shown in Table 1: blocked subject-project, replicated project, multi-project variation, and single project case study.

The approaches vary in cost, level of confidence in the results, insights gained, and the balance between quantitative and qualitative research methods. Clearly, an analysis of several replicated projects costs more money but provides a better basis for quantitative analysis and can generate stronger statistical confidence in the conclusions. Unfortunately, since a blocked subject-project experiment is so expensive, the projects studied tend to be small. To increase the size of the projects, keep the costs reasonable, and allow us to better simulate the effects of the treatment variables in a realistic environment, we can study very large single project case studies and even multi-project studies if the right environment can be found. These larger projects tend to involve more qualitative analysis along with some more primitive quantitative analysis.

Because of the desire for statistical confidence in the results, the problems with scale up, and the need to test in a realistic environment, one approach to experimentation is to choose one of the treatments from below the line to demonstrate feasibility (statistical significance) in the small, and then to try one of the treatments above the line to analyze whether the results scale up in a realistic environment - a major problem in software engineering research..

Scopes of Evaluation

		# Projects	
		One	More than one
# of Teams per Project	One	Single Project (Case Study)	Multi-Project Variation
	More than one	Replicated Project	Blocked Subject-Project

Table 1: ANALYSIS CLASSIFICATION: SCOPES OF EVALUATION

Given these research paradigms and experimental approaches, how do we apply them to the study of software and software engineering in practice? That is, software as an artifact does not exist in nature, it exists only where it is created. Therefore, it must be studied where it exists - in industrial and government environments. Under these circumstances, we need to provide proper motivation for organizations to allow researchers to "interfere" with their software development.

What is the relationship between software research and development in practice?

From a research perspective, we need to establish a scientific and engineering basis for software engineering. That is, we need industry based laboratories that allow us to understand the various processes, products and other experiences and build descriptive models understand the problems associated with building software, develop solutions focused on the problems, experiment with them and analyze and evaluate their effects, refine and tailor these solutions for continual improvement and effectiveness and enhance our understanding of their effects, and build models of software engineering experiences.

From a business perspective, we need to develop products and processes that will help us build quality systems productively and profitably, e.g., estimate the cost of a project, track its progress quantitatively, understand the relationships between models of cost, calendar time, functionality, various product qualities, etc., and evaluate the quality of the delivered product. These models of process and product should be tailored based upon the data collected within the organization and should be able to continually evolve based upon the organizations evolving experiences.

That is, a successful business must understand the process and product, define process and product qualities, evaluate successes and failures, feedback information for project control via closed loop processes, learn from our experiences so we can do business better, package successful experiences so we can build competencies in our

7

areas of business, and reuse successful experiences. It requires a closed loop process that supports learning, feedback, and improvement. Key technologies for supporting these needs include modeling, measurement, and the reuse of processes, products, and other forms of knowledge relevant to our business. This is, feedback loops are the development view of an experimental paradigm.

Thus the research and business perspectives of software engineering have a symbiotic relationship. That is, from both perspectives we need a top down experimental, evolutionary framework in which research and development can be focused, logically and physically integrated to produce and take advantage of models of the discipline, that have been evaluated and tailored to the application environment.

We can create experimental laboratories associated with the creation of software artifacts from which we can develop and refine models based upon measurement and evaluation and select the appropriate models to aid in development. Each such laboratory will help the business organization be more successful. However, since each such laboratory will only provide local, rather than global models or truths, we need experimental laboratories, at multiple levels. These will help us generate the basic models and metrics of the business and the science.

Can this be done?

There has been pockets of experimentation in software engineering but there is certainly not a sufficient amount of it [7]. One explicit example, with which the author is intimately familiar, is the work done in the Software Engineering Laboratory at NASA/GSFC [4]. Here the overriding experimental paradigm has been the Quality Improvement Paradigm [1,5], which combines the evolutionary and revolutionary experimental aspects of the scientific method, tailored to the study of software, i.e., the development of complex systems that need to have models built and evolved to aid our understanding of the artifact. It involves the understanding as well as the evolutionary and revolutionary improvement of software. The steps of the QIP are:

> **Characterize** the current project and its environment.
>
> **Set** the quantifiable **goals** for successful project performance and improvement.
>
> **Choose** the appropriate **process** model and supporting methods and tools for this project.
>
> **Execute** the **processes**, construct the products, collect and validate the prescribed data, and analyze it to provide real-time feedback for corrective action.
>
> **Analyze** the **data** to evaluate the current practices, determine problems, record findings, and make recommendations for future project improvements.

8

Package the experience in the form of updated and refined models and other forms of structured knowledge gained from this and prior projects and save it in an experience base for future projects.

To aid in the setting of goals, the guiding of the experiment, the rational for collecting data, the building of models, and the underlying framework for interpretation, the Goal/Question/Metric (GQM) paradigm was developed and had been evolving. The GQM is

"a mechanism for defining and interpreting operational, measurable software goals. It combines models of an **object of study**, e.g., a process, product, or any other experience model, and one or more **focuses**, e.g., models aimed at viewing the object of study for particular characteristics that can be analyze from a **point of view**, e.g., the perspective of the person needing the information, which orients the type of focus and when the interpretation/ information is made available for any **purpose**, e.g., to characterize, evaluate, predict, motivate, improve, specifying the type of analysis necessary to generate a **GQM model** relative to a **particular environment**." [3]

To help create the laboratory environment to benefit both the research and the development aspects of software engineering, the Experience Factory concept was created. The Experience Factory represents a for of laboratory environment for software development where models can be built and provide direct benefit to the projects under study. It represents an organizational structure that supports the QIP by providing support for learning through the accumulation of experience, the building of experience models in an experience base, and the use of this new knowledge and understanding in the current and future project developments.

The Experience Factory concept supports a software evolution model that takes advantage of newly learned and packaged experiences, a set of processes for learning, packaging, and storing experience, and the integration of these two sets of functions. As such, it requires separate logical or physical organizations with different focuses/ priorities, process models, expertise requirements. It consists of a **Project Organization** whose focus/priority is delivery and an **Experience Factory** whose focus is

"to support project developments by analyzing and synthesizing all kinds of experience, acting as a repository for such experience, and supplying that experience to various projects on demand. The **Experience Factory** packages experience by building informal, formal or schematized, and productized models and measures of various software processes, products, and other forms of knowledge via people, documents, and automated support." [2]

What kinds of experience has been packaged in the SEL? There are a great variety of experiences that have been organized, including resource models and baselines, e.g., local cost models, resource allocation models; change and defect baselines and models, e.g., defect prediction models, types of defects expected for the application; product models and baselines, e.g., actual vs. expected product size, library access, over time; process definitions and models, e.g., process models for Cleanroom, Ada waterfall model; method and technique evaluations, e.g., best method for finding interface faults; products, e.g., Ada generics for simulation of satellite orbits; quality models, e.g., reliability models, defect slippage models, ease of change models; lessons learned, e.g., risks associated with an Ada development.

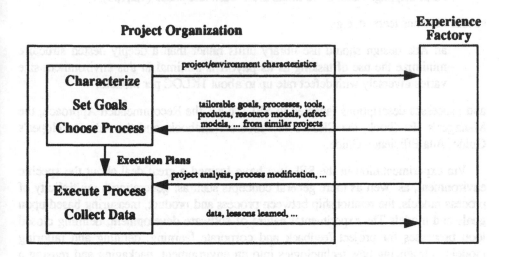

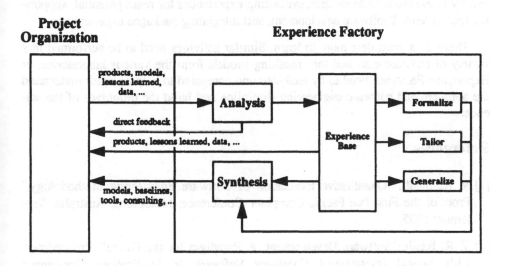

These experiences have been packaged in a variety of forms. There are equations defining the relationship between variables, e.g.,

$$\text{Effort} = 1.48 * \text{KSLOC}^{.98} \quad \text{or} \quad \text{Number of Runs} = 108 + 150 * \text{KSLOC};$$

histograms or pie charts of raw or analyzed data, e.g.,

Classes of Faults: 30% data, 24% interface, 16% control,
15% initialization, 15% computation

Effort Distribution: 23% design, 21% code, 30%test, 26% other;

graphs defining ranges of "normal", e.g.,

Fault Slippage Rate: halve faults after each test phase (4,2,1,.5);

specific lessons learned, e.g.,

an Ada design should use library units rather than a deeply nested structure
minimize the use of tasking as its payoff is minimal in this environment size
varies inversely with defect rate up to about 1KLOC per module;

and processes descriptions (adapted to SEL), e.g., the Recommended Approach, the
Manager's Handbook, the Cleanroom Process Handbook, and the Ada Developer's
Guide, Ada Efficiency Guide.

Via experimentation in the SEL, we have learned a great deal about the specific
environment, as well as more general concepts such as: generating a multiplicity of
process models, the relationship between process and product, measuring based upon
goals and models The experimental nature of software development, defining closed
loop processes for project feedback and corporate learning, defining and tailoring
models, introducing new technologies into an environment, packaging and reusing a
variety of experiences as models, evaluating experiences for reuse potential, supporting reuse oriented software development, and integrating packaged experiences.

There is a great deal more to learn. Similar activities need to be performed in a
variety of environments and the resulting models form the various laboratories, or
Experience Factories, need to by analyzed and compared to help us better understand
the software and software engineering discipline and build the primitives of the science.

References

[1] V. R. Basili, "Quantitative Evaluation of Software Engineering Methodology,"
Proc. of the First Pan Pacific Computer Conference, Melbourne, Australia, September 1985.

[2] V. R. Basili, "Software Development: A Paradigm for the Future", Proceedings,
13th Annual International Computer Software & Applications Conference
(COMPSAC), Keynote Address, Orlando, FL, September 1989

[3] V. R. Basili, "The Goal/Question/Metric Paradigm", white paper, University of
Maryland, 1990.

[4] V. R. Basili, G. Caldiera, F. McGarry, R. Pajerski, G. Page, S. Waligora, "The Software Engineering Laboratory - an Operational Software Experience Factory",
International Conference on Software Engineering, May, 1992, pp. 370-381.

[5] V. R. Basili, H. D. Rombach "The TAME Project: Towards Improvement-Oriented Software Environments," IEEE Transactions on Software Engineering, vol. SE-14, no. 6, June 1988, pp. 758-773.

[6] V. R. Basili, R. W. Selby, Jr., "Data Collection and Analysis in Software Research and Management," Proc. of the American Statistical Association and Biomeasure Society Joint Statistical Meetings, Philadelphia, PA, August 13-16, 1984.

[7] V. R. Basili, R. W. Selby, D. H. Hutchens, "Experimentation in Software Engineering," IEEE Transactions on Software Engineering, vol.SE-12, no.7, July 1986, pp.733-743.

[8] NSF Report on Research in Software Engineering - unpublished.

Profile of an Artifact Assessment Capability

William W. Agresti

The MITRE Corporation
7525 Colshire Drive
McLean, Virginia 22102

Abstract

The features of an emerging artifact assessment capability are outlined. Experience developing this capability has led to speculation about the role and practice of experimental software engineering. The objectives of identifying leading indicators and enabling us to "speak with data" are discussed. Viewing our industrial software projects as naturally occurring experiments (and possibly using them in a large, simple trials study) is suggested.

Introduction

Building an artifact assessment capability has sharpened our vision of software measurement and analysis as an empirical science. In this paper, we sketch the artifact assessment capability; we highlight two of the purposes for experimental software engineering -- the search for leading indicators and the obligation to speak with data; and we speculate on perceiving large industrial software projects as constituting naturally occurring experiments and as enabling large simple experimental trials.

An Artifact Assessment Capability

Artifact assessment is the critical evaluation of software designs and code to determine their quality, including the degree to which they reflect the use of sound software engineering principles. Artifact assessment is not an end in itself; during an ongoing development, it provides information to make specific and supportable recommendations for improving the system being developed. Also, it plays an essential role in reuse, re-engineering, prototype evaluation, and software modernization.

We have been growing an artifact assessment capability over the past four years to meet a need that is widely shared by our customers faced with the acquisition and modernization of very large software-intensive systems. To diagnose the health of their ongoing projects, we have traditionally evaluated milestone reviews and documents. However, as software projects grow in size and complexity, reviews become longer and documents thicker; they are increasingly inadequate as a basis for assessment.

An artifact assessment capability addresses the need for more systematic and more incisive evaluation of software as it is being developed. The foundation of our capability is the tool-supported analysis of Ada designs as they become increasingly more detailed during development. Currently, our artifact assessment capability provides static profiles of design characteristics; visualization of design structure; and prediction of size, reliability, maintainability, and flexibility. Prediction is achieved by applying a set of multivariate models based on software structural attributes.

Recently we reported on empirical studies involving 21 Ada subsystems and 183,000 lines of code [1,2]. We hypothesized that design complexity would help explain variation in measures related to software quality. Using data extracted from error and change reports, we found variation indeed existed in the dependent variables for the 21 observations:

- Defects per thousand source lines of code varied from 1.4 to 17.0

- The percentage of "easy fixes" (i.e., defects requiring less than one hour to correct) varied from 26% - 89%

Explanatory variables in the models highlighted characteristics such as interconnection among design units and the import/export of declarations. The models explained 50-75% of the variation in quality.

We regard the validation and refinement of our tools, methods, and models as continuing exercises. As we examine large artifacts, we identify new design patterns leading to new hypotheses; see the influence of design methods on design structure; and learn what assessment information will help developers. Our objective is to improve all aspects of the capability while fairly characterizing the confidence that should be associated with the information it provides.

Leading Indicators

Because large system developments take an extended period of time, we have a keen interest in analyzing the evolving artifact for leading indicators: that is, characteristics related to a later outcome or condition . Managers, several months into development, may still be relying on pre-development estimates of system size and cost; ways to refine the estimates based on early development activities are absent. While maintainability is a design characteristic, it is only during maintenance that we discover a system is difficult to enhance. Our artifact analysis includes watching the system take shape over time, seeing evidence of design decisions in the early structure of the artifact. The intention with our models is to identify design features worth noting early, to refine an earlier estimate or to intervene so the system is not built on a problematic foundation. The models have shown that measures of context coupling, visibility, and locality in Ada designs appear to be useful leading indicators of software quality [1].

Speaking with Data

In Japanese Quality Control, Kaora Ishikawa has written, "We should talk with facts and data." [3] Experimental programs aim to do so. Too often in software engineering, we are able only to parrot claims about the consequences of actions, without being able to cite quantitative support for our remarks. In our case, recommendations on

14

improving a project are clearer and more convincing when the artifact analyses provide supporting quantitative evidence. Consider observations that are generally accepted -- such as the tendencies for schedules to slip, code to grow, and planned reuse to vanish. Making the same observations by using empirical data assists planning (by determining the magnitude and timing of the phenomena) and process improvement (by identifying starting points for root-cause analysis).

As an example, the Software Engineering Laboratory at the National Aeronautics and Space Administration's Goddard Space Flight Center provides its managers with quantitative guidelines for estimating size, cost, and schedule at five estimation points during a project [4]. The guidelines are based on 15 years experience collecting and analyzing data on flight dynamics software development. Managers in the SEL environment are advised, for example, to plan for a 40% increase in estimated system size from preliminary design review to the end of the project.

Field Studies of Naturally Occurring Experiments

Bill Curtis has been a leader in helping us see large-system development as a behavioral process. His field research treats ongoing industrial development projects as opportunities to learn more about social and organizational processes that underlie development (e.g., [5]). If we look to the social sciences for views on experimentation, we find the economist Milton Friedman observing, "Unfortunately, we can seldom test particular predictions in the social sciences by experiments explicitly designed to eliminate what are judged to be the most important disturbing influences. Generally, we must rely on evidence cast up by the 'experiments' that happen to occur." [6,7] In software development, with the most important influences being individuals and teams, field studies to understand these influences are precisely what are needed.

Large, Simple Experimental Trials

Another aspect of viewing industrial projects as "naturally occurring experiments" is the approach being pursued (not without controversy) in the medical field: the use of large simple experimental trials to learn the effects of treatments on patients. Instead of exercising control by using very selective clinical trials and collecting extensive data at considerable expense, the large simple trials approach calls for use of practicing physicians' patient populations and the recording of a very few, easily obtained data or outcomes. While the applicability to software projects is speculative, it seems possible that certain questions, with meaning across a wide range of projects, may be amenable to this strategy. A clear parallel is that software project managers, like physicians, are extremely busy; yet engaging them in recording a very few outcomes or data items for a large number of "trials" is appealing.

In summary, through our artifact assessment work, we have begun learning about the evolving structure of industrial software systems. One route to making progress in our research community is to make maximum use of our naturally occurring experiments: large-systems development and modernization projects.

References

1. W. W. Agresti and W. M. Evanco: Projecting Software Defects from Analyzing Ada Designs. IEEE Transactions on Software Engineering SE-18 (1992)

2. W. W. Agresti, W. M. Evanco, and M. C. Smith: Early Experiences Building a Software Quality Prediction Model. Proceedings of the Fifteenth Annual Software Engineering Workshop, NASA Goddard Space Flight Center, Greenbelt, Maryland (1990)

3. M. Imai: Kaizen. New York: McGraw-Hill (1986)

4. Software Engineering Laboratory: Manager's Handbook for Software Development (Revision 1), NASA Goddard Space Flight Center, Greenbelt, Maryland (1990)

5. B. Curtis, H. Krasner, and N. Iscoe: A field study of the software design process for large systems. Communications of the ACM 31, 1268-1287 (1988)

6. M. Friedman: Essays in Positive Economics. Chicago: University of Chicago Press (1953)

7. I am grateful to W. M. Evanco for discussions on relationships to economics and econometrics.

Experiments and Measurements for Systems Integration

L. A. Belady

Mitsubishi Electric Research Laboratories Cambridge, Massachusetts, USA

Abstract

The engineering of sytems integration (type B) software requires new ways of experimental evaluation, because high enough fidelity of modeling is impractical due to complexity. Also, traditional software engineering practices are insufficient: software as well hardware components must be integrated, and experience in the application domain is also necessary. This paper outlines the problem but does not offer specific solutions. Rather, it intends to call the attention of the software engineering community to spend more effort in this area of research.

1 Discussion

Since software engineering is relatively immature, its terms are rarely defined. In order to be better understood, this paper starts with *defining* the terms 'experimentation' and 'measurement' in software. Borrowing from traditional engineering, *experimentation* is exercising and observing an artifact, or its representative model, in order to find out whether it satisfies expectations. Experiments are also the source of learning, for instance how to fix the problem when results are unsatisfactory. Obviously, if a model is under observation, it must have an explicit relationship to the real artifact. Also, we must specify our expectation in advance, in order for the experiment to reveal deviations. Sometimes the experimental results can be expressed quantitatively in terms of metrics, in which case our observations become *measurements*.

There seem to be two classes of experiments performed in software engineering. One involves the product (artifact) itself, the other the process to build and modify it. The former has been around for three decades, concentrating on performance indicators such as response time, throughput and reliability. For the last two decades, however, emphasis shifted to the software engineering process as the culprit for the high cost and low quality of the software product. In particular, the effectiveness of software tools and techniques became the subject of experimentation and occasional measurements. The product-process classification is not perfect: process effectiveness is sometimes observed indirectly by measuring product properties such as fault density.

About a decade ago this author tried very hard to establish an *experimental software engineering center* within IBM to exercise in a realistic environment the speculative tools and techniques which, while remaining untested, kept accumulating frighteningly fast. The idea was then to select and experimentally refine the best technology for software engineering. When the attempt to fund such a center in IBM failed, the only remaining institution large enough to invest long term was the US government. It was hoped that the, at that time new, Software Engineering Institute would become an experimental center. However, not much has happened since and one can only speculate about the reasons for, and suffer the consequences of, this unfortunate failure.

What did, however, happen was the emergence of *systems integration*,[1] causing a split of the engineering of software into two branches: that of components, and of application systems. Let us call them type A and type B[2]. The former is about the construction of familiar software products - from simple PC packages to full operating systems - which are relatively straightforward to specify and usually sold in large number of copies. Some of these software components are now developed using techniques of computer science based software engineering, such as formal verification and interchangeability under reuse. With type A, elaborate experimentation is rarely needed.

Type B, that is system integration *software*, is different: it *is the glue* which holds - and helps coordinate - the software and hardware components of an enterprise wide application system, a network linking existing and new programs into a loosely coupled distributed cooperation. Most importantly, each such system is unique to a given enterprise. It is therefore useful first to construct a large application within a given industry segment - a kind of experiment - then build others in the same segment based on experience accumulated while doing the first.

Software expertise does not seem to be enough to build these systems: a good deal of *hardware and application domain expertise* is indispensable. Accordingly, we must involve in our experimentation hardware engineers and those who know the application better than software people do. Furthermore, type B software is very difficult to model even if domain experts are also involved. This leads to the increased importance of instrumentation of production level type B software since the real thing becomes the only target of observation. Our approach to process measurement must also change: for instance we must focus on the productivity of the interdisciplinary team.

2 Conclusion

This author does not dream about a software engineering laboratory anymore. Rather, he believes that we must prepare for the ways type B software will have to be developed by (a) shifting to *interdisciplinary* education and practice, and (b) focusing our data gathering and evaluation studies on *actual systems integration* projects and products. Indeed, to establish a scientific basis, we must "organize our observations" (phrase derived from the two-word definition of science by Whitehead).

References[1]

(1) - Systems Integration, - National Academy Press, Wash. D.C., 1992

(2) - International J. of SEKE , - Vol. I Nr 1, World Scientific Press, 1991

1. The two references serve as source for the more elaborate oral version of this paper.

Software Engineering Still on the Way to an Engineering Discipline

Norbert Fuchs

Alcatel Austria-ELIN Research Centre
Ruthnergasse 1-7, A-1210 Wien

1 Introduction

The following position paper investigates the impact of experiments on the software engineering discipline. First, the concept of goals and experiments is transferred to software engineering as an engineering discipline. It is pointed out that this concept is well known in other engineering disciplines as a mean to prove hypotheses based on models of a development process.

In part four and five the impact of experimental software engineering on the most problematic areas within software engineering is investigated. On hand of two examples - management methods and technology transfer - it is discussed how experimental software engineering can be used to bring software engineering to an engineering discipline.

2 Goals in Software Engineering

It is generally agreed that the three main goals in software engineering are

- to improve the productivity of the engineers,

- to enhance the quality of the software product,

- to shorten the time to market.

Of course these are goals on the highest level of ambition. They aim in changing (improving) the development process. To reach such goals implies that we first have to know where we are. On a lower level we normally start with more describing goals like

- to understand the development process,

- to control the progress against the time schedule,

- to assess the actual level of maturity of the development environment,

- ...

The main problem in software engineering today is the question how to reach such goals and how to prove and assess the progress. People aim in objective, absolute assessment criteria (an example is the level of maturity assessment done by the SEI) but they also have to accept more and more relative assessments. This development towards relative measurement is supported by quality standards (DoD2167A,

ISO9000, Total Quality Management) which definitely ask for the assessment of the process improvement. This is a main part of the demonstration of the effectiveness of a quality system against certification institutes.

Concentrating for a while on the "lower level" goals we easily see that we need an underlying model of the actual development process. Based on this model we assume dependencies and interrelations which we have to test.

3 Experiments in Software Engineering

In other words we have to prove hypotheses about the development process (in terms of understand, evaluate, control, predict, assess, ...) based on a model. This concept is not new. We find it in many other disciplines like economic science or sociology. The way how to prove hypotheses is the same everywhere: doing experiments of the form:

- make a model about the underlying process

- formulate goals (hypotheses) based on this model

- test this goals.

Such goals are

- economic science: to understand the influence of a new road toll on highways,

- sociology: to understand the impact of gentechnology,

- software engineering: to understand the actual development process.

The results of such experiments normally will change the model and / or the underlying process. To ensure that such changes are of benefit (increasing the income of government, less deformities by people, improve productivity) at the end of an experiment we have to add a feedback loop, make a new model, define new hypotheses, and so on.

In terms of software engineering the experiment can now be defined in more detail by the following four steps:

- definition (assessment, characterizing, motivating)

- planning (goals, subgoals, metrics)

- operation (execute, analyse, data collection)

- feedback loop (interpretation, data analyses, validation of metrics).

We can find these four steps with different wordings in

- the Deming wheel (evaluate - plan - do - measure)

- the Quality Improvement Paradigm (Basili) (characterize - planning - analysis - learning)

- AMI Handbook (Application of Metrics in Industry) [2]
  (assess - identifyand analyse problems, metrics - metrication - improvement)

4 Problems in Software Engineering

Taking this general concept of experiments with the need for measurements as accepted the next question is how to derive benefits from this concept within the special framework of software engineering. What is the nature of the software discipline? What are the problems? What is the main cause of the problems and what are the effects?

The nature of software development is various. We all know all these typical problem areas we normally are confronted with: development is out of budget, SW will be delivered late, SW has poor quality, SW doesn't fit the purpose, the productivity is to low, the maintenance costs are to high,...

Let us look from a slightly different perspective at this problems and asking for the reasons why all this goes wrong. Is the main reason technical limitations, usage of the wrong tools or languages? No, analysing projects which failed the answer you get more and more often is: "the main reason are missing software management methods". A survey done by Watts S. Humphrey in 1989 on 200 software organisations (all contractors of the Department Of Defence) showed that 80% of them adopt an ad hoc approach to software development [1].

For the experimental paradigm this means that different to the past where product metrics have been the main point of interest for most of researchers and practicioners we have to shift activities to process metrics and their impact on the development process. This means that easily management can be involved in software measurement activities. The assessment, the definition of hypotheses and the measure - improvement loop are activities well known by management. They are used to think in quantifiable goals. The experimental paradigm helps management to understand the problems in software engineering. It helps to overbridge the gap between management and software engineers.

5 Technology Transfer

Another main problem of the last years in software engineering was the problem of technology transfer. A lot of good ideas and methods have been developed from academics but the industry was not able to take over this developments. What is the reason for that? How can experimental software engineering change this?

In the last years languages (Pascal, Prolog, C, C++) and tools (CASE, IPSE) have been developed rapidly. Most of these tools concentrated on helping software engineers, but some also aimed in supporting management (at least up to the level of project managers). People got used in accepting new technologies as a panacea, later they even got used in accepting that these technologies don't solve their problems. Surprisingly people didn't get tired in moving to new tools and languages, it seems they really have a mania for doing it.

What happened in the last years is that the software engineering community suddenly started to speak about the development process (spiral model, evolutionary approach, prototyping, ...), about methods behind languages and tools (object orientation, rule based, ...) and about software engineering management methods (risk management, quantitative software management, ...). The same people who propagated new languages and tools in the last decade nowadays recommend that before speaking about languages and tools we have to think about processes and methods as a base for the development of software products. This classical development terminology also influenced the transfer of quality standards from more classical disciplines - like car manufacturing - towards software development (ISO9000-3).

For software engineers and managers this seems to be a step back. The base of their work is under discussion.

The implication for software engineering is that it is on the way to become an "engineering discipline". For a manager it is not sufficient any longer to say: "My people know how to write software." or "The quality of the software is not too bad.". For being an engineering discipline software engineering need to have a defined process with activities and relations between them.

How can experimental software engineering help here? From our experience as a research and technology transfer organization within a big telecom company we developed a model how we introduce new technologies:

- First we use a new technology in a cooperation where developers and researchers work together within a project. (Technology transfer through the transfer of people).

- After this cooperation we use the new technology within a pilot project. This means that the researchers play the role of a consultant, but are not directly involved in the project.

Concrete results achieved by using this approach can be read in [4].

Of course each of these phases has to be defined, planned, executed and interpreted. This is what experimental software engineering requires. We have a series of experiments and each experiment is influenced by the result of the former one.

The experimental paradigm can be seen as a global approach which also can be used for overcoming the problem of technology transfer.

References

1. W.S. Humphrey: Managing the Software Process. Addison Wesely (1989)

2. AMI - a quantitative approach to software management, ESPRIT 5494

3. V.R. Basili, R.W. Selby, D.H. Hutchens:Experimentation in Software Engineering. IEEE Transactions on Software Engineering Vol 12, No 7 (1986)

4. C. Debou, L. Pescoller, N. Fuchs: Softare Measurements on Telecom Systems - Success Stories?. Third European Conference on Software Quality Assurance, Madrid (1992)

Problems in Modeling the Software Development Process as an Adventure Game

Jochen Ludewig

Institut für Informatik, Universität Stuttgart

Summary

SESAM (Software Engineering Simulation by Animated Models) is a simulator for practicing the role of a software project manager. Its long term goal is to provide a tool for training CS students. As a research project, SESAM calls for an integrated model of the software development process, reflecting and quantifying many phenomena observed in real software projects.

We are currently using the second prototype, which can already demonstrate some rational behaviour. More important, however, were our observations in the process of constructing SESAM. They shed light on the current state of software engineering, and on the applicability of metrics.

SESAM is being developed in an evolutionary style by the Software Engineering Department (Lehrstuhl) at Stuttgart University; it is implemented in Smalltalk-80 on Unix-Workstations.

This paper concentrates on the fundamental questions raised by the work on SESAM. A more complete description of our work has been published before (Ludewig et al., 1992).

1 Software Process Modeling, and the Concept of SESAM

In the field of software process modeling, two very fundamental questions are still open:

1 How do the relevant factors (like staffing, skill, quality assurance, style of management, etc.) influence the results?

2 Which set of metrics is necessary and sufficient to describe the process, and the emerging product?

It seems that neither of these questions can be answered without the other one, so we try to combine them, and test various answers in an experimental, iterative way. That is the essence of SESAM. We try to build a simulator for education purposes, which can be described as a mixture of "Dungeon", or "Dark Castle", and a flight simulator, as used by future airline pilots. While we do not expect to finish a really useful simulator very soon, our work will continuously contribute to the solution of the problems stated above.

Our goal is to provide a tool which can be used as follows:

A player (let's call her Angela) opens the SESAM-system, and is prompted for a number of project-parameters. Then she starts the simulation. The project proceeds like a normal project, with all kinds of difficulties. But Angela will receive only little information about the actual state of her project as long as she remains passive. She may, however, decide to participate actively, e.g. she may see her employees and order them to do some particular task. Such activities consume her (simulated) time, so she cannot do everything she might like to do.

When the simulated project has been finished, her score is displayed, describing her relative success or failure by several indicators. She can run the project again, with all the (previously hidden) state variables displayed, which will help her to recognize her mistakes. She may also take over control again at some point, in order to try a different path.

Within a few hours, she has had an experience which would take months in reality, not to mention the costs, but would even then not allow for analysis, and a second try.

2 Problems in developing SESAM

After the idea of SESAM was born three years ago (Ludewig, 1989), there was a long period of confusion and irritation. The most difficult points are discussed below.

2.1 The Illusion of Detecting Natural Laws

Scientists, in particular physicists, have managed to reduce their theories to a comparatively small basic set of axioms. In software engineering, we have nothing but a large, and often inconsistent and inhomogenous collection of observations. We must be well aware of the fact that we cannot find any "natural laws of software engineering". Our very ambitious goal is to develop theories which can be used to predict observable phenomena.

2.2 The Lack of Quantitative Relationships

We are still far from being able to describe the software development process by, say, a set of differential equations. There is a number of less or (usually) more vague rules of thumb, of rumours, and of modern proverbs, which may explain certain phenomena. (And in most cases, there are others which explain the opposite.)

Assumed that Brook's law "adding manpower to a late project makes it even later" is correct, what does it say? It does not define a "late project," nor does it indicate to which extent the schedule is prolonged when people are added. It is nothing but the qualitative description of a relationship, very interesting (and fifteen years ago even surprising), but not sufficient for simulating the process, or predicting its success, or failure.

An interesting implication is that there are only very few proper theories in software engineering. COCOMO is one of the rare examples.

24

2.3 Choosing the Granularity

As we are building a model, the scale is critical. Which level is appropriate for simulating the process? Should we care about single persons, or regard groups as the acting units? Do we handle procedures, modules, or programs? By which factor should we shrink the time scale for simulation? Which granularity of time is required?

For our model, a day is chosen as the basic time unit. No effort is taken to care for precise synchronisation of people (e.g. in case of a meeting). Single persons are the only active units, though many "laws" (like Brook's law, e.g.) refer to groups, or projects. But many other relationships are obviously based on persons (like the cost of salaries, the responsibility for a certain task, or the possibility of intended or unintended changes in the project). If we had a mixed mode simulation, we must anyway convert all state variables to every level. Therefore, our first rule is: The whole is exactly the sum of its parts (including their relationships).

2.4 Hypotheses

As stated in the begin, most of the relationships on which our simulation is based are far from proven truths; they are just hypotheses which may, or may not make our simulator behave sensible. Therefore, we call such relationships hypotheses. While they define the very basic mechanisms of SESAM, they should be integrated in a way which makes it easy to modify, or to replace them.

We use graphs to describe the actual structure of the project; the graph may change when certain events take place, e.g. when a person is given a new task. Hypotheses are described by a graph grammar. Whenever a hypothesis may become applicable, the graph (and the state variables) is scanned for its target pattern. If it is found, the hypothesis docks into the target (like a virus), thus influencing the state transitions.

2.5 What is a Person?

When we simulate a person, we have to determine to which degree the personality should be mapped onto the model. Quite obviously, we have to record every person's abilities for each possible task (analysis, specification, etc.), and also for activities required in each task (like the abilities to communicate, or to take decisions). Other parameters certainly exist, e.g. a person's motivation has a strong influence on his or her productivity. We also have to describe how fast a person can learn, and how fast the person will forget.

But there is no line which separates the personal parameters relevant to the software project from those of purely private character. Every property may influence a person's performance, the distinction of a "public personality" from a "private personality" is fictitious.

3 A few Observations

1. Every system of metrics has to be based on exactly one basic unit in each dimension (e.g. hour, module, person or group or project).

2. When a metric is proposed, a new term is required. Terms which are widely used (e.g. "complexity") should not be used to identify a new function.

3. Even the most recent books on software engineering contain very little information which can be used to construct a project simulator, i.e. they contain very little falsifiable statements, but lots of noise. Boehm's whole work (starting from Boehm, 1973) is a notable exception.

4. If the player wants a single one-dimensional score, we have to map several ratings into one: adherence to deadlines, various aspects of quality, etc. In real projects, such a mapping is missing, though everybody has one in his or her mind. We believe it would be useful to agree upon the mapping in the very begin of every project, as part of the requirements definition.

References

Boehm, B.W. (1973):
  Software and its impact: a quantitative assessment. DATAMATION, 19, No.5, 48–59.

Ludewig, J. (1989):
  Modelle der Software-Entwicklung: Abbilder oder Vorbilder? (in German) Softwaretechnik–Trends, 9, 3 (Okt. 1989), 1–12.

Ludewig, J., Th. Bassler, M. Deininger, K. Schneider, J. Schwille (1992):
  SESAM — Simulating software projects.Proc. of the 4th Intern. Conf. on Software Engineering and Knowledge Engineering. IEEE Comp. Soc. Press Order No. 2830, pp.608–615.

QUALITATIVE TECHNIQUES AND TOOLS FOR MEASURING, ANALYZING, AND SIMULATING SOFTWARE PROCESSES

Walt Scacchi

Decision Systems Dept.
University of Southern California
Los Angeles, CA 90089-1421 USA
(213) 740-4782, (213) 740-8494 (fax)
(Scacchi@pollux.usc.edu)

October 1992

Much of the current effort directed at empirical assessments of software production processes and their associated artifacts focuses on the use of quantitative measures or metrics as a basis for understanding. I believe that empirical studies of software engineering processes can benefit in a fundamental way through the use of qualitative research methods and tools.

Quantitative metrics are fundamentally limited to the measurement of the values, frequency, and distribution of data or events in ways that can then be subjected to descriptive or inferential statistical analysis. When examining software processes, this means that one can measure the occurence of product characterists, process states or events, but it becomes very difficult to infer what the process and how it affected the product characteristics unless the process was previously known. Surveys, questionnaires, and online performance measures are not well-suited instruments for building process models.

Qualitative methods and tools for data coding and analysis can be used to address the problem of how to empirically determine the nature, composition, and the present and historical context of software processes within an organizational setting. Qualitative methods are complimentary to quantitative methods, rather than a competing alternative. For example, qualitative methods can be used to empirically observe and construct the descriptive form and content of software processes as they are practiced within a given organization, while quantitative metrics can then be used to measure the frequency, distribution, and statistical patterns of process states and events when the process is repeated.

Qualitative methods rely upon observational case studies, ethnographies, field studies and comparative case/field studies as part of their experimental designs [15, 14]. Clearly, qualitative methods are best suited for building a deep, knowledge-intensive understanding of processes occurring within or across selected organizational settings. Hence, the scope of the analytical findings one can derive from qualitative methods is bounded. But it is possible to construct qualitative research designs that employ comparative studies utilizing multiple levels of analysis in order to increase the scope and generalizability of the results [14]. On the other hand, while quantitative metrics are problematic to use when constructing models of software processes, they are most useful when validating or improving models of software processes, through descriptive statistical means. Thus, it is possible to construct controlled comparison, factorial, and quasi-factorial experimental designs for empirically studying selected software process phenomena. As such, it is possible to construct robust and evolutionary research designs--called "triangulation studies" [4, 6]--that combine qualitative and quantitative methods in ways that draw upon the respective strength of each kind of method, while counterbalancing their respective weaknesses.

Computational tools supporting qualitative research methods are now becoming more widely available. Since qualitative methods tend to be best for acquiring knowledge about the who, what, where, when, why, and how of software processes, then it should be of no surprise that knowledge-based modeling, analysis, and simulation environments are well-suited to serve as the logical counterpart of statistical packages for analyzing quantitative data. In fact, at the USC System Factory Project, we have incorporated a statistical data analysis package within our knowledge-based process modeling environment [10] so that we can support triangulation research designs for studying selected software processes occurring within the industrial firms that support our research effort. Accordingly, our strategy for employing these qualitative methods, together with the tools for analyzing qualitative data appear elsewhere [10, 13, 9, 11, 12]. However, we now have a growing base of experience in using them to study more than 20 real-world software processes of varying size and scope in different industrial settings, and the results from these studies are also beginning to appear [5, 2, 8], as have our earlier studies which employ qualitative methods [7, 3, 1].

REFERENCES

1. Bendifallah, S. and W. Scacchi. Work Structures and Shifts: An Empirical Analysis of Software Specification Teamwork. Proc. 11th. Intern. Conf. Software Engineering, ACM, 1989, pp. 260-270.

2. Bendifallah, S. Understanding Software Specification Teamwork: An Empirical Analysis and Model. unpublished dissertation, Computer Science Dept., USC, Los Angeles, CA, 1991.

3. Bendifallah, S. and W. Scacchi. "Understanding Software Maintenance Work". IEEE Trans. Software Engineering 13, 3 (1987), 311-323.

4. Denzin, N.K. The Research Act, 2nd. ed. McGraw-Hill, New York, 1978.

5. Jazzar, A. Understanding the Production and Consumption of Software Documentation: An Empirical Analysis. unpublished dissertation, Computer Science Dept., USC, Los Angeles, CA, 1988.

6. Jick, T.J. "Mixing Qualitative and Quantative Methods Triangulation in Action". Administrative Sciences Quart. 24, 4 (1979), 602-611.

7. Kling, R. and W. Scacchi. "The Web of Computing: Computer Technology as Social Organization". Advances in Computers 21 (1982), 1-90. Academic Press, New York.

8. Mi, P. Modeling and Analyzing the Software Process and Process Breakdowns. unpublished dissertation, Computer Science Dept., USC, Los Angeles, CA, 1992.

9. Mi, P. and W. Scacchi. Modeling Articulation Work in Software Engineering Processes. Proc. First Intern. Conf. Soft. Process, IEEE Computer Society, 1991, pp. 188-201.

10. Mi, P. and W. Scacchi. "A Knowledge Base Environment for Modeling and Simulating Software Engineering Processes". IEEE Trans. Knowledge and Data Engineering 2, 3 (1990), 283-294.

11. Mi, P. and W. Scacchi. "Process Integration for CASE Environments". IEEE Software 9, 2 (March 1992), 45-53.

12. Mi, P. and W. Scacchi. "A Unified Model of Software Systems, Agents, Tools, and Processes". (submitted for publication) June, (1992), .

13. Scacchi, W. "A Software Infrastructure for a Distributed System Factory". Software Engineering Journal 6, 5 (September 1991), 355-369.

14. Strauss, A. and J. Corbin. Basics of Qualitative Research: Grounded Theory Procedures and Techniques. SAGE Publications, Newbury Park, CA, 1990.

15. Yin, R.K. Case Study Research: Design and Methods. SAGE Publications, Newbury Park, CA, 1984.

On Experimental Computer Science

Walter F. Tichy

University of Karlsruhe

The experimental branch of Computer Science appears to be underdeveloped. Few quantitative, experimentally verified results are published, depriving the field of answers to questions where theory cannot reach.

A classification of papers in three systems-oriented journals yielded alarming statistics. Articles in ACM TOPLAS, IEEE Transactions on Software Engineering, and Comm. of the ACM are classified according to theory, design, quantitative evaluation, and hypothesis testing. Papers classified as theory typically contain mathematical models, theorems, proofs, or algorithms, but include no empirical evaluation. Design papers describe systems or languages. Although these papers may contain some qualitative evaluation, they contain neither theorems nor quantitative results. If a paper includes non-trivial, quantitative evaluation (at least two pages), it is counted in the third category. The fourth category, hypothesis testing, covers papers that state hypotheses and specify experiments in sufficient detail so they could be repeated by others.

The results of the classification appear in table 1. TOPLAS published a total of 89 papers in the four years beginning with 1988. Theory papers accounted for 61% and design papers for 24%. Only 13 papers (15%) had a non-trivial, quantitative evaluation. There was no paper on hypothesis testing.

IEEE Transactions on Software Engineering published 92 full-length papers between June 1991 and June 1992. There were about 35 papers on theory and 40 on design (including case studies). Only 17 (18%) included quantitative evaluation. Again, no papers on hypothesis testing were published.

During the same period, Comm. of the ACM published 38 full-length, technical papers in its "Special Section". All papers were on designs. None presented quantitative results or discussed experiments. (Theory papers were excluded by the editorial guidelines.)

While these data points are far from representative, they permit two interpretations:

1. Computer scientists may produce too many designs and not enough quantitative results. While designs of systems are important, science and engineering also need hard, empirically verified results.

Publication and period	theory	design	quantitative evaluation	hypothesis testing	total
TOPLAS Jan 88 to Oct 91	55 (61%)	21 (24%)	13 (15%)	0 (0%)	89 (100%)
IEEE TR SE June 91 to June 92	35 (38%)	40 (43%)	17 (18%)	0 (0%)	92 (100%)
CACM Special Section June 91 to June 92	0 (0%)	38 (100%)	0 (0%)	0 (0%)	38 (100%)

Table 1: Classification of papers

The design papers in the surveyed publications should have included sufficient quantitative analysis to be one column to the right; some of the papers that are now in that column might have been improved significantly by stating a hypothesis and performing more careful testing. Even though not every non-theory paper needs to report on hypothesis testing, having none at all in the surveyed time periods points to a serious weakness of the science.

2. The balance between theory and experiment in Computer Science seems skewed. There may be too few researchers performing experiments and too few students being trained in experimentation. The result will be that students going into academic and industrial careers will be biased against experimentation. They will not have the skills required to build large systems or experiment with them. We will possess few empirically verified facts. In the long run, such deficits will weaken Computer Science and industry.

Why is there so little experimentation, even though there are plenty of important questions to be tackled? Part of the problem is that there is no agreement on what constitutes valid, experimental work in Computer Science. In traditional sciences, experimentation consists of stating a hypothesis, constructing an apparatus to test the hypothesis, collecting data, and analyzing the results. In experimental Computer Science, unfortunately, the emphasis so far has been on apparatus building. Researchers have been intent on showing that certain problems can be solved by computers *in principle*. If a solution is demonstrated for the first time, then comparison is not possible and experimentation not always necessary. While we should continue to look for such "firsts," most of the research in Computer Science is making incremental improvements to already existing solutions. In this case, quantitative comparisons are indispensable.

Applying the traditional experimental paradigm will change the character of much research in Computer Science. First, a hypothesis and the results must be stated concisely and must be objectively testable. Second, the apparatus is less important than the results, even though building the apparatus may represent most of the work. This view is in stark contrast to the declared method of some research laboratories today, where the systems being built are supposed to be used by the researchers themselves in daily work. Though this approach leads to usable designs, the results are often inconclusive and the costs too high. Third, researchers must perhaps state more modest, but verifiable claims. For example, the popular claims about expert systems, object orientation, and neural nets, to name a few, may well be unverifiable.

Unfortunately, there are few examples of experimental designs to draw on in Computer Science. Some areas, such as hardware design, operating systems, compiler construction, and speech recognition are doing acceptably well, because there are metrics and benchmarks to measure performance and quality. Programming languages and software engineering are examples where few solid, experimentally verified and useful results are available. Consequently, researchers may address the wrong problems and never find out. Also, industry takes on enormous risks when adopting, say, a formal specification language, an object-oriented programming language, or a new set of software development tools. Laboratory experiments testing the claimed properties of languages and tools would be vastly cheaper than the large-scale, uncontrolled experiments that software companies are now forced to perform instead. Of course, it is more fun (and arguably better for a computer scientist's career) to publish many claims supported by poor evidence than to carefully validate a few. It is also clear that some properties cannot be measured and should not be measured. But in those cases we should also refrain from stating claims that would require measurement for validation.

As scientists, we need to take evaluation of our work seriously. To make evaluation possible in the first place, we must define the problem being addressed, specify the assumptions, and clearly state hypotheses. We must learn to decide when qualitative comparisons are sufficient, when quantitative results are required, and when quantitative measurement is hopeless. We must especially increase our efforts in devising benchmarks and carrying out experiments that yield quantifiable and reproducible results. Establishing and evolving reliable experimental methods in the various subdisciplines of Computer Science, and applying them conscientiously, is of utmost importance for progress.

To change the carless attitude towards evaluation and experimentation, computer scientists will have to start with themselves, their PhD students, and colleagues. Building yet another system without any plans for evaluation should no longer constitute acceptable research. Instead, scientists must formulate hypotheses and design experiments to test them. An important function of industry will be to help with stating useful hypotheses and to provide the data for benchmarking and experimentation. Finally, the peer review system must not only give experimental work a chance, but actually encourage it. As we accumulate experimentally verified results, education should improve as well by emphasizing knowledge of solid, verified facts and by teaching how to obtain and apply them.

Session 1 Summary
The Experimental Paradigm in Software Engineering

William W. Agresti

In session 1, the keynote presentation and position papers explored various aspects of the experimental paradigm in software engineering. Following the papers was the kind of wide ranging discussion that may be expected in an opening session that is addressing the subject of the workshop in its full breadth.

The session opened with an enumeration of questions and issues for discussion. Several of the specific questions for session 1 were intended to lead into more complete treatment in later sessions, so the discussion of those questions is likewise deferred to the appropriate other sessions. Three questions were not identified as leading into later sessions:

- Why are measurement and experimentation important?

- What is the nature of software development?

- What are -- based on the nature of the software discipline -- ramifications for measurement and experimentation in software engineering?

Of these three remaining questions, the first question was covered in session 2. The second and third questions were indeed addressed in session 1. In the remainder of this section we review the workshop participants' discussion of these two questions, followed by a summary that addresses themes emerging from both the open discussion and the position papers.

What is the Nature of Software Development?

Discussion relating to the underlying nature of software development centered on the the notion of a theory or theories in this subject. One view was that such consideration was premature; that we lack universal agreement on essential terms, such as software, software engineering, experimentation, and validity. Other comments drew on analogies with more established disciplines and considered any such theory to be composed of various distinguishable elements or micro-theories. In this sense, software engineering was seen as an empirical science involving the application of principles arising from other disciplines, including mathematics and psychology.

Theories were claimed to be relatively well known in physics, yet in software engineering we make no distinction between experiments based on theories and those conducted without a theoretical basis. When there is no theory, we obtain the knowledge necessary for experimental design from observation, requiring being present where software is created in organizational settings.

It was observed that we really should be seeking a theory of software, not of software engineering. A theory of software is the basis for software engineering. Also, perhaps what we are discussing as theory is more appropriately disaggregated into theories, laws, and beliefs. In this sense, a theory of software engineering includes a collection of elements such as principles, models, and guidelines: some of which have a mathematical basis, while others more closely resemble theories in the social sciences. We should not expect the whole package to reduce to a set of equations, but its elements should be supportable by experimentation, empirical studies, and a great deal of observation and understanding. If this collection of elements were characterized now, it would be dominated by heuristics; we want to shift toward more and stronger empirical support.

Some of the participants contended that we have the beginnings of theory in software engineering, but it is scattered across the various specialized subjects in our field; others felt that, in any case, the elements of theories are too immature. An expressed interest was to pursue micro-theories of software. The micro-theories can be distinguished based on the strength of their supporting evidence and the extent to which they derive from mathematical, engineering, or social science considerations. For example, compiler engineering is relatively well understood; and reliability modeling is a specialty area with a strong mathematical basis. It was mentioned that, with regard to structured programming -- broadly advocated as a desirable practice -- a recent survey found the supporting evidence to be equivocal. The implication is that an approach to theory in software engineering is first to get our micro-theories in order before we move forward.

What are -- based on the nature of the software discipline -- ramifications for measurement and experimentation in software engineering?

Several viewpoints were expressed on the ramifications for experimentation, given the discussion on the notion of a theory of software engineering:

- We can use theory to predict something; if it doesn't predict correctly, we can invalidate the theory

- We don't give any indication that we believe in falsification; if the theory is not upheld by an experiment, then we consider the experiment to be flawed

- We cannot prove things with experiments, we can only falsify things

- The term "experimental research" is too restrictive; we should not rule out observational research

The feasibility and scalability of laboratory-style experiments were viewed as persistent concerns, because we are not interested in toy problems. If we do conduct laboratory-style experiments, we should clearly state our hypotheses, assumptions, and axioms. Of particular importance, the hypotheses should be testable.

Interpretive studies were cited as a means of treating a problem in detail across organizations. In one case, an attendee at the workshop investigated a problem by studying four organizations. At each organization, the researcher spent approximately three months and interviewed approximately 30 people.

Given that both laboratory experiments and field experiments have a place in empirical software engineering, one participant pointed out the need to recognize that control is not a Boolean variable; there are degrees of control. While the measure of control may be lower in the field than in the laboratory, nevertheless there exists some level of control in the field.

A practical consideration in experimental software engineering is understanding the range of technical papers published under this rubric in leading professional journals. It was observed that such papers were predominantly reporting on the design of a tool, rather than the conduct of an experiment or other empirical analysis. While we want to see high quality papers on empirical studies, we must be careful not to discourage discovery, in general, and worthwhile papers on software designs, in particular. There was encouragement for papers reporting on empirical analyses, but such papers should state testable hypotheses and reflect proper use of experimental design, statistics, analysis, and interpretation. Validation and replication studies were especially encouraged.

The most widely practiced paradigm in software engineering begins with observation to understand a process, product, or setting. Observations lead to data collection and model building to establish useful relationships for explaining behavior and predicting outcomes. It is essential that the aim not be to collect massive amounts of data, but rather to understand the data we collect and the reason we collect them.

An example of an organization pursuing the observation/model-building paradigm was cited in the discussion: the Software Engineering Laboratory (SEL) at the National Aeronautics and Space Administration (NASA)/Goddard Space Flight Center (GSFC). As an example, the SEL, through observation and data collection, has established simple models to estimate the eventual size and cost of a system in terms of factors available earlier in the development process. The estimates are very rough initially, becoming more accurate as more is known about the design of the system. These estimating relationships, from one environment, are very simple examples of models that can emerge from a process of observation, data collection, and model building. Such examples suggest what is possible for an organization to accomplish over time through a systematic approach to measurement for understanding and improvement.

In the sense of software engineering as an emerging empirical science, it was seen as natural that observation was playing such a prominent role. Science in general was characterized by a workshop participant as beginning with observation of phenomena -- that is, keeping our eyes and minds open to look for invariants. With observation comes the first opportunity to pose experiments, hypotheses, and theories. In fact, it was suggested that a potentially fruitful focus may be on the origins of hypotheses.

One line of discussion focused on the significant human role in our software processes. The software in which we are interested is created by many people working together. Given this reality, it makes sense to look to models from the social sciences and economics. One view was that the need for models comes from management, so we should also look to models of organizations. If we do so, we find that the notion of a contingency framework, from organization theory, may be a reasonable way to view software engineering.

Another approach to considering the human element focuses on the behavior of the system as a whole, claiming that something akin to statistical normality will arise from the decisions made by a large number of people. Pursuing this view points toward a software engineering theory helping with nominal system behavior rather than activity of individual elements comprising the system. The appeal here is to physics in which we cannot predict the actions of individual atoms, but we can discuss the behavior of the entire system.

Summary

Several of the noticeable themes of the position papers and open discussions, related to the topic of the first session, are briefly summarized.

Observation and analysis of software projects should be accompanied by an understanding of the environment or context in which the development is taking place. In this sense, any results of a study may be seen as setting-specific; that is, having relevance in context but requiring substantiation and calibration for use in other environments.

Also significant as an influence on software development are the individuals and teams working on the projects. Case studies and field studies of software development and evolution have a role to play in contributing to our understanding in this area. The influential human element further suggests that, as we envision a route to a more mature base of knowledge in experimental software engineering, we perhaps should look to the evolution of theories in social sciences.

The influences of setting and personnel on project outcomes affect the relative use of different paradigms for studying software projects. Controlled experiments are desirable as a way of establishing convincing results. However, such experiments using multiple industrial projects and teams are frequently impractical because of their cost. A more accessible paradigm is an approach of observation, for purposes of understanding, leading to the creation of hypotheses about relationships and patterns among software processes, products, and settings. The utility of these hypotheses is explored through measurement and analysis on additional projects. Through feedback and refinement, improved hypotheses can be the basis for models that can be used in the particular setting to support decisions such as those for prediction and planning.

The predominance of the observation/model-building approach led to a suggested characterization of the subject of the workshop as empirical (rather than experimental) software engineering. Empirical software engineering encompasses software-related experimentation as well as qualitative methods, for example, to characterize our processes. It includes models, like those in reliability theory, that have a mathematical basis and those based on persistent relationships deduced through observation in a particular setting. The unifying features of empirical software engineering are

- the aim of establishing a sound basis for the practice of software development, evolution, and management through the appropriate use of measures and models
- the development of measures and models that capture relationships among processes, products, and settings
- the use of experimentation, observation, quantitative and qualitative measurement, data collection, analysis, and interpretation

Session 2:

Objectives and Context of Measurement/Experimentation

Session Chair:	Norman E. Fenton
Keynote:	Michael Cusumano
Position Papers:	Norman E. Fenton
	Günther R. Koch
	Nazim Madhavji et al.
	Karl-Heinrich Möller
	Adam A. Porter

Objectives and Context of Software Measurement, Analysis and Control

Michael A. Cusumano

Sloan School of Management
Massachusetts Institute of Technology
Cambridge, Massachusetts USA 02142

Abstract This paper focuses on the *what* and *why* of measurement in software development, and the impact of the *context* of the development organization or of specific projects on approaches to measurement, analysis, and control. It also presents observations on contextual issues based on studies of the major Japanese software producers.

1 Introduction

This paper focuses on the *what* and *why* of measurement in software development, and the impact of the *context* of the development organization or of specific projects on approaches to measurement, analysis, and control. It begins by discussing three basic questions: (1) Why do we measure? (2) What is it we want to know? And (3) how does the context affect the ability to measure? The second section presents observations on contextual issues based on my ongoing study of the Japanese [3]. This paper also relies heavily on extensive interviews conducted at Hitachi, Fujitsu, NEC, and Toshiba during May, August, and September 1992.

2 Basic Questions

Why we measure aspects of the software development process and conduct analytical exercises or experiments, as well as what we try to do with this information, depends very much on who is doing or requesting the measuring and analysis. There already exists a broad literature on technical aspects software measurement and the relationship to process management, which will not be reviewed here [1, 2, 5, 6]. In general, firms as well as academic researchers measure software activities and outputs across the development life-cycle to facilitate the following: (1) development planning and control, for particular projects; (2) learning and improvement, about products, the development process, planning and control methods, customer preferences, or to validate what is measured; and (3) bench-marking, consisting of comparisons of products, projects, or organizational performance. Managers generally use bench-marks to establish baselines for control or improvement, or for competitive analysis.

These categories of planning and control, learning, and bench-marking may seem obviously essential to every organization. Yet most industrial software projects operate under severe delivery time and budget constraints, suffer from shortages of good technical or managerial personnel, or have to cope with top managers or customers who do not fully understand the problems inherent in software development. For example, all but the very simplest planning, measurement, analysis, experimentation, and feedback activities require specific allocations of time and people. These allocations will not happen spontaneously within firms because they drain resources from current projects and primarily provide benefits only over the course of multiple projects. It is useful, then, to think about what we measure in software development in terms of who is measuring and what functions these groups normally perform. There are at least five relevant functions to consider:

(1)   top management control and resource allocation;
(2)   project management and internal project QA;
(3)   independent inspection and QA;
(4)   marketing and customer QA;
(5)   process R&D.

2.1 Top Management Control and Resource Allocation

Top management in a firm -- that is, management above the project level, such as division-level managers or senior executives -- usually requests a set of relatively coarse data that indicate the status of major projects and how company divisions are allocating resources. These kinds of measures are too coarse to be useful for direct learning about processes or products, and do not help very much in managing projects more effectively.

Nonetheless, managers request such data for a variety of reasons. These include high-level purposes of control (such as management of multiple projects), performance comparisons (projects with other projects, divisions with other divisions, yourself with industry standards or competitors), or identification of major trends (such as increases in system size or changes in the mix of products). This information is useful, therefore, for creating a high-level picture of how an organization is utilizing its resources, and how resource needs are evolving. Top managers then need to adjust to changes or make policies and major resource-allocation decisions that could eventually affect software planning and control as well as learning activities.

2.2 Project Management and Internal Project QA

Project managers, including sub-project leaders or managers in software organizations organized by product departments and functions rather than by projects only, measure the development process primarily to know how long it takes to build, review, and test particular kinds of systems with teams of given skill levels. More specifically, project managers need enough information to formulate estimations, make plans, and then monitor current projects. They need to be able to recognize problems before projects are finished, and need sufficient information to make adjustments in the project team, in tools or processes, in product requirements, or in the schedule and budget, or they may want to alert senior management (and sometimes customers) in extreme cases of problems.

The kinds of data collected at organizations with good reputations for process and quality control can be quite simple. Table 1 presents an example of data items from NEC, this time from the Basic Software Division. The items listed are comparable to what Hitachi, Fujitsu, and Toshiba collect in their better development divisions [3], as well as to what the Software Engineering Institute [5] recommends (which is based heavily on IBM practices in its better divisions). Some companies, particularly for applications projects, add items such as percentage of design structures or lines of code reused (including minor changes). Hitachi also includes more data on personnel backgrounds and skill levels.

Table 2 contains another example of more detailed process data that relates to progress and comparisons of the quality assurance process, and shows how these data are used in NEC's Switching Systems Division. Of particular note is that NEC tries to measure quality as well as the progress of reviews quantitatively even in a phase (specifications) where progress is difficult to quantify. Management also has used historical data on comparable projects to establish baseline or "model values" for the various quality indicators as well as for "control boundaries." If actual values fall below or beyond the model values, this requires a specific manager to authorize or take a specific action.

2.3 Independent Inspection and QA

Why and to what degree independent inspection departments (including QA or software-engineering departments responsible for quality control and process issues) measure characteristics of the software development process or of software products depends on the scope of their responsibilities and their authority relative to project managers. Many software organizations have no independent inspection or third-party reviews, no independent QA or

Table 1: Process-Control Data Items in NEC Basic Software Division

1. Requirements Analysis/Definition Process
-- estimated date of completion of each process phase
-- estimated program size
-- estimated man power
-- person in charge of development and years of experience
-- language in use
-- development form (new development/modification/division transplant)
-- difficulty level of development [type of program]

2. Functional Design Process
-- completion date
-- actual man power used and break-down by persons in charge
-- difference between the standard times and the man power used
-- quantity of functional specifications and revision history
-- scale of design review (number of workers/time) and the number of corrections

3. Detailed Design Process
-- completion date
-- actual man power used and break-down by persons in charge
-- difference between the standard times and the man power used
-- quantity of design specifications and revision history
-- scale of logic inspection (number of workers/time) and the number of corrections

4. Coding Process
-- completion date
-- actual man power used and break-down by persons in charge
-- difference between the standard times and the man power used
-- the development size
-- detailed information for each program to realize functions
-- scale of code inspection (number of workers/times) and the number of corrections

5. Unit Test/Function Test Process
-- number of test cases to be executed
-- target bugs to be detected
-- required man power
-- number of test cases executed previously in a certain period of time
-- number of bugs detected previously in a certain period of time
-- man power used in the past

6. System Test Process
-- number of test cases to be executed
-- target bugs to be detected
-- required man power
-- number of test cases executed previously in a certain period of time
-- number of bugs detected previously in a certain period of time
-- man power used in the past

Source: [3] p. 304, taken from [8] pp. 3-9

Table 2: Design Quality Indicators Model in NEC Switching Systems Division

<u>Specifications Phase</u>

Indicator	Specifications Volume	Review Coverage Rate
	(# of Spec Sheets/ Total Est. LOC)	(# of Pages Reviewed/ # of Spec. Sheets)
Model Value	15 pp/KL	90%
Control Boundaries	- 40%	- 20%
Control Method/Tool	Spec Sheets	Review Record Chart
Action Items	Intensive review of described items, gaps, content check	Continue review of uncovered portion
Decision Level	section manager	group leader
Indicator	Review Manpower Rate	Bug Count
	(Review Work-Hours/ # of Spec. Work-Hours	(# of Serious Items in Review Comments/# of pages reviewed)
Model Value	15%	0.3/page
Control Boundaries	+/- 30%	+/- 40%
Control Method/Tool	Review Record Chart Man-Hours Total	Review Record Chart Bug Estimate Curve
Action Items	If +30%, then reviews are inefficient; correct method, more review items focus	If +30%, then analyze comments & recheck specs.
	If -30%, reviews are insufficient; check bug count, and review again if too few	If -40%, check review points, and revise review check list
Decision Level	group leader	group leader

44

Table 2 continued

Summary of Other Phase Indicators, Model Values, and Control Boundaries

Quality Indicator	Model Value	Control Boundary
Design Phase		
Design Sheets Volume (# of Design Sheets/Total estimated LOC)	50pp/KL	-30%
Review Coverage Rate (# of pages reviewed/Total # of design sheets)	70%	-20%
Review Manpower Rate (Review Work-Hours/# of Design Work-Hours)	10%	+/- 30%
Bug Count (# of serious comments in review items/ # of pages reviewed)	0.4/page	+/- 40%
Coding Phase		
Review Coverage (# of source lines reviewed/total est. LOC)	30%	-20%
Review Manpower Rate (Review Work-Hours/Coding Work Hours)	10%	+/- 20%
Bug Count (Detected bugs/total est. LOC)	7/KL	+/- 40%
Unit Test Phase		
Test Items Selection Rate (Test items/total est. LOC)	30/KL	+/- 30%
Trace Comprehensiveness Rate (Items Traced in Desk-Top Debugging/ Estimated items to be found)	100%	-20%
Review Manpower Rate (Review Work Hours/Unit Test work hours)	10%	+/- 20%
Bug Count (# of detected bugs/total est. LOC)	8/KL	+/- 40%

Integration Test

Test Items Selection Rate	8/KL	+/- 50%
(Test items/total est. LOC)		
Bug Count	4/KL	+/- 30%
(Bugs detected/total est. LOC)		

System Test

Test Items Selection Rate	30	-30%
(# of test items)		
Bug count	1/KL	+/- 30%
(detected bugs/total est. LOC)		

Source: [7]

engineering departments; project members (alone or with customers) make all decisions on methods and tools, and conduct, if there is time, their own final reviews, final testing, and other QA activities. In other organizations, QA, inspection, or engineering staff departments exist to help or make sure projects do what they are supposed to do, but even they exist in a spectrum from "weak" to "strong."

There are ways to measure how centralized are independent inspection or QA activities, or, alternatively, how time-consuming are process-control and QA activities. Possible measures include (1) percentage of project manpower or time planned for project management as well as for quality-assurance activities (the latter may include reviews, configuration management, test management, post-release quality assurance, or problem-solving meetings); (2) to what extent independent personnel from a QA, inspection, or engineering department actually become involved in monitoring and improving the quality of the development process, and (3) to what extent an independent QA or inspection department can and does hold up the shipment of major projects if the manager of this department feels the quality of the final product is inadequate.

In organizations with little process-control or QA activities, there usually are only a few staff hours dedicated to outside reviews and independent inspection or QA tasks. Inspection and QA personnel may also not be software experts or even engineers. Their primary role is to collect numbers, such as numbers of defects found in testing or reported by customers, or review documents, to give project management and upper management no more than a coarse indication of how the development organization is doing and how projects are proceeding. If top management instructs project managers to devise tactics and policies to improve quality on the dimensions measured, QA or engineering departments might get involved in planning quality-improvement activities. Weak QA or inspection departments, however, generally do not have the technical expertise, respect from development personnel, or the data to become important mechanisms for learning and then transferring knowledge about quality and process improvement within or across projects.

Japanese organizations with "strong" centralized process-control and QA functions include the basic software divisions of Hitachi, Fujitsu, and NEC, and the applications divisions of Hitachi and Toshiba. These companies generally devote from 3% to 10% of project manpower to QA and inspection activities, depending on the type of system and the project characteristics. Independent staff for inspection or QA, or QA sections within software engineering departments, are thus relatively large. They also have broad responsibilities, extending from monitoring the quality of the development process, to validation of metrics, to evaluating the quality of the final product and reserving the rights of final approval for shipment.

Managers of large QA or inspection departments and their staff are a combination of experienced engineers and specialists in testing, process management, and quality assurance. In Hitachi, for example, personnel in these strong departments may become integral parts of projects and participate actively in reviews, perform checks throughout the development process, classify problems, help project members with examples from other projects, become heavily involved in training personnel to spread expertise and process knowledge, and even take charge of final testing for some kinds of systems or do product testing to mimic customer situations. The Hitachi QA departments are also responsible for interfacing with customers and assuring follow-up solutions to quality problems ranging from major faults that cause system crashes to more subtle design issues such as those affecting ease of use or man-machine interfaces (Table 3). These broad responsibilities obviously require various kinds of data on the development process and on the software products themselves. In the Japanese firms, these data again usually take the form of numerous simple but quantified and complementary metrics, as in Tables 1 and 2. The Japanese also use subjective or "soft" data, such as comments in review meetings.

Major questions that need to be answered are how necessary and cost-effective are independent QA, inspection, or testing activities. When, and to what extent, can project members manage themselves and "build-in" quality from the very beginning of the development process, with no one looking over their shoulders or checking their work independently? There is another way to look at these kinds of measures: Are large, strong QA departments or large percentages of time devoted to QA activities signs of a good process or a poorly controlled or perhaps an immature process? The software industry needs more data as well as more organizational case studies to answer these questions.

2.4 Marketing and Customer QA

Some marketing departments in companies, and independent market research organizations, including industry organizations and trade publications, collect detailed data about items such as prices or, more usefully, customer

Table 3: Activities of a "Strong" Independent QA Department

-- Managed by Respected Software Development, Testing & QA Experts

-- Responsible for Collecting & Analyzing Quality Data from Multiple Projects & Customers

-- Active Participation in Reviews Through Checklist Analysis & Discussion of Problems in Other Projects

-- Independent Testing of Final Products

-- Formal Approval Over Shipment

-- Participation in Defining Methods, Tools, Procedures

-- Participation in Training

-- Responsible for Meeting with Customers on Quality Problems to Ensure Follow-Up

-- Classification of Problems From All Phases of Development

-- Dissemination of this Knowledge Through Reports, Training, Review Checklists & Discussions, Project Procedures, New Tools & Methods, etc.

Sources:　　Interviews with managers in Hitachi's QA Departments for Basic Software and Business Application Systems reactions to software products and to company performance in various aspects of the software development process. Table 4 contains an example of such data collected by *Nikkei Computer*, Japan's leading computer-industry journal.

The immediate purpose of this data-gathering for company marketing departments is internal bench-marking, which provides a source of information to improve products and operations. Public compilations of these kinds of data are also for bench-marking, but for comparing performance across multiple firms or products, and usually for the benefit of consumers, who then have more information that they can use to choose among vendors. Whatever the source of the data, analyses of customer satisfaction can provide important information to marketing and QA departments, top management, and development departments on whether the company is doing well compared to competitors and meeting the needs of customers, as opposed to performing well or not on more technical dimensions of the software-development process, such as project progress and estimation accuracy, bug detection and correction, testing coverage, and the like (which may and often are related to customer satisfaction). For these data to be most useful, they should relate characteristics of the software products or services to the development or systems engineering process, although few firms have yet to do such sophisticated analyses.

2.5 Process R&D

Increasing numbers of software organizations now have process analysis or auditing activities as well as a process R&D function. The latter consists of a group of people who do not have project responsibilities but whose primary job is to learn and transfer knowledge, if possible. They analyze project performance and needs, develop and evaluate new metrics, tools, and methods, they may help introduce these technologies into projects, or study recurring process or quality problems and try to propose solutions, which may take the form of particular metrics, tools, or techniques. These groups may also be involved in validation exercises as well as comparative bench-marking.

Process analysis and R&D activities of this sort can take place within large projects or systems engineering departments through special assignments, or they may take place within functional departments such as for software engineering methods and tools, production management, quality assurance, common technology development, or R&D. Outside consultants can also undertake process analysis and R&D functions for clients. The major distinction with project activities, however, is that process R&D groups are not concerned with planning and controlling the development process or outcomes of particular projects. Process analysis and R&D groups within firms are generally interested in more fundamental questions that come close to what academic researchers in universities study, though with usually with more of an applied focus that combines concerns for quality, costs, and practicality.

3 The Development Context

It is relatively easy for researchers and industry experts, quality-assurance specialists, or project managers to define a set of ideal measurements that they believe would be useful for planning, control, and learning. Even if these measurements can be satisfactorily validated as being effective for management and process feedback, the *context* of the project and the development organization very much affect what kinds of measurements firms or projects actually use, and what they do with the information that results. Since contextual issues themselves constitute a very broad topic, this section focuses on some examples taken from Japanese software development organizations, and discusses what appear to be particularly important contextual parameters:

(1)   optimal process for the product;
(2)   business characteristics of the project;
(3)   development-organization culture.

3.1 Optimal Process for the Product

In *Japan's Software Factories*, I argued that it was possible to identify a spectrum of software product or system

49

Table 4: Nikkei Computer Customer Satisfaction Survey Questions

Sampling of Questions asked by *Nikkei Computer* during 1988-89 in National Surveys, with ratings on a 1 (dissatisfied) to 10 (satisfied) scale.

Systems Systems-Engineering Service
1. Explanation of new products
2. Systems software version-up support.
3. New system configuration support
4. Proposals for solving problems related to improving system efficiency
5. Technical support for software development
6. Technical support for machine security
7. Promptness in responding to requests to fix defects
8. Technical support in communications areas
9. Offering of broad information from a neutral standpoint
10. Businessman-engineer morality
11. Total satisfaction.

Applications Systems-Engineering Service
1. Proposals for system planning and design
2. Understanding of business strategy
3. Knowledge regarding the application
4. Knowledge of industry trends
5. Ease of understanding product documentation
6. Communication ability
7. Application-system development methodology
8. Technical support in communication areas
9. Businessman-engineer morality
10. Total satisfaction

Factors Influencing System Selection
1. Price-Performance
2. Upward compatibility
3. Reliability and fault tolerance
4. Available software
5. Company policy and business contacts
6. Systems engineering support
7. Same industry operating results
8. Maintenance service
9. Technology excellence
10. Salesman enthusiasm
11. Installation conditions
12. Reputation
13. Other

Source: [3] pp. 58, 462-463

characteristics for any type of application as well as a corresponding set of process options. These options range from a craft or job-shop approach, such as a unique, complex system that developers must fully customize or invent for a single customer; to an application-oriented project for a broad set of general users, as in a personal-computer applications package; to a more "factory-like" approach. What I have described as a software-factory approach in many ways overlaps with the concept of a structured, well-defined software-development process, where project managers, developers, quality-assurance staff, and process R&D staff utilize quantitative measurements and qualitative information, including a store of historical data for baselines as well as current project data, for planning, control, reuse-promotion, and learning. A problem with this factory-like approach, however, is that it requires historical data and applies best in cases where current projects are more-or-less similar to past projects, i.e. where the problem domain and development personnel are relatively stable, and where projects are not trying to write the equivalent of the first version of a best-selling book.

For systems on the high-end of the spectrum ("high" in the sense of relative system cost and innovative or inventive technical requirements), historical data, like reusable components, are scant or do not exist, because the requirements or architectures are almost completely new. In these jobs, managers may decide to measure various aspects of the process to begin creating historical data for future project control or process improvement. But unless measurement is highly automated, then the resources required to collect data only make sense if management expects to build similar systems in the future. Since most organizations do build series of similar systems (estimates of redundancies in system development in Japan and the United States range from 60% to 90%), measurement usually makes sense as an investment for the future, even if there are no historical baselines. Yet, as will be discussed below, many company managers and project managers under schedule, budget, and manpower constraints often do not have or, at least, they often do not allocate resources to tasks such as measurement that represent an investment which pays off only in the future.

On the bottom end of the spectrum shown in Table 5 managers of application-oriented projects aimed at producing best-seller packages might also not want to impose a strict measured process on their developers. If the task is to invent for a broad range of users, and the system can be electronically replicated for thousands or millions of users, then the development costs are trivial, and it may not be possible or advisable to attempt to plan and control the cost of development. On the other hand, measurements that affect defects or other forms of quality are critical, since they affect sales of the system and other products of the same company, and it is costly to replace products for such a large user base.

Data from various firms indicate that the middle of this spectrum might account for the majority of all systems built, as well as subsequent versions of full-custom systems or low-end packages. For development organizations building multiple versions or generations of similar systems, a development process emphasizing measurement, historical baselines, feedback mechanisms for control and learning, or systematic reusability, make the most sense technically and economically.

Another implication of this framework is that large systems cannot be built, or cannot be built very well, in an ad hoc manner, because these require some division, coordination, and then integration of work. Division of work, as well as coordination and integration, require some degree of standardization in interfaces and probably in design methods, tools, management practices, and other areas. Thus even producers of high-end custom systems or of large packages may find that they have to move toward a more standardized process simply to survive, and this requires measurement and control; and the more continuity or redundancy there is in the tasks they undertake, the more logic there is in pursuing a measured, controlled, and continually improved process.

These different process options can also exist within a single organization. For example, Hitachi, Fujitsu, NEC, and Toshiba have "elite" in-house development organizations that build large and complex, but relatively routine, systems, in a factory-like process, with extensive subcontracting of detailed design, coding, and unit-test work to subsidiaries and subcontractors for the more routine applications. They also use special projects, laboratories, or specialized subsidiaries for unique or one-of-a-kind systems, and employ software houses for routine work or small-scale projects that are not economical to do in-house.

It is also important to realize that software and hardware technology are still dynamic. Firms may evolve from a craft-like approach to a factory-like approach for many of their systems, but then find that technical changes force them back to a partial craft-like or invention mode at least in the sense that reuse of existing designs or of historical baseline data is no longer helpful. For example, Hitachi has an historical database of 150 projects from the mid-1980s that managers use to estimate defects in large-scale basic software and applications systems that run on Hitachi mainframes. The database, estimation algorithms, and procedures are called the Software Quality Estimation Systems (SQE) ([3] pp. 188-191). For basic software and for many large-scale applications systems,

Table 5: Product-Process Strategies for Software Development

Product Type	Process Strategy	Organization Type
HIGH END:		
Unique Designs (Full Custom, "Invention")	Meet Customer Requirements & Functionality	
High-Priced Premium Products	Hire Skilled Workers To Design, Build Needed Tools & Methods	**CRAFT-ORIENTED** **JOB SHOP**
Small To Medium-Size Systems	No Organizational Skills To Perform A Series Of Similar Jobs Or Do Large Jobs Systematically	
MIDDLE:		
Partly Unique Designs (Semi-Custom)	Balance Customer Needs & Functionality With Production Cost, Quality	
Medium-Priced Products	Skilled Workers Mainly In Design, Standard Development Process	**SOFTWARE** **FACTORY**
Small To Large-Sized Systems	Organizational Skills Cultivated To Build Large Systems And Reuse Parts, Methods, Tools, And People Systematically	
LOW END:		
Unique, Mass-Replicated Designs (Scale Economies)	Maximize Application Functionality For Average User Needs	
Low-Priced Products (Packages)	Hire Highly-Skilled Workers Knowledgeable In Application	**APPLICATION-ORIENTED** **PROJECT**
Small to Medium-Sized Systems	No Organizational Skills To Develop Large Products Or A Series Of Similar Products Systematically	

Source: [3] p. 15

52

an independent quality assurance department needs to give its approval for shipment, and this is far from automatic. The QA Department's decisions are driven primarily by historical data: whether or not the number of detected defects in testing equals the projected number, which is based on historical data and quality objectives for the system being built (Figure 1).   However, Hitachi customers are gradually demanding more basic software and applications for distributed networks of work stations and smaller computers. While many functional requirements remain the same, the architectures of the small-scale distributed systems are sufficiently different that Hitachi management has decided not to use the SQE system for these projects until they accumulate a sufficient store of projects to generate new baseline estimates. For project management (cost, schedule, and manpower estimation), Hitachi has also had to accumulate separate sets of data and create a version of its project management system for work-station software. In addition, reusable components that made it relatively simple to build "semi-customized" versions of systems that run on mainframes are also not completely transferable to distributed work-station-based systems, hence, estimates of productivity and quality affected in the past by high reuse rates are no longer accurate for these new systems. Fujitsu, NEC, IBM, and other mainframe software producers around the world have undergone similar transitions, although it is primarily a matter of time before they update their historical databases.

3.2 Business Characteristics of the Project

Table 5 refers to management decisions to adopt variations in process standardization, control, reusability, divisions of work, and other process elements because of basic product characteristics. In practice, however, for economic and contractual reasons, not all of the projects where measurement and control through historical baselines are technically possible will be measured and controlled with the same degree of intensity. In other words, even the elite Japanese programming organizations will select, for business reasons, which projects receive the "best-practice" process and which do not. Part of the rationale for such variations is that, at least in Japanese organizations, much of the data-collection and analysis process is not automated, and thus requires considerable work-hours. In addition, management requires the best-practice projects to devote considerable time to reviews, testing, problem-solving, and other quality-assurance activities; for economic, technical, or scheduling reasons, certain types of projects may curtail these activities and the measurement or analysis work they require.

For example, in applications development, Hitachi managers identify two types of projects: One type are customer in-house or "private" applications, used internally only by the customer, such as systems for inventory management or hospital information management. A second type are "public" applications where there might be one customer but the system has many end-users or a high possibility of affecting many end users. These include systems such as for stock exchanges, on-line banking, and reservations (Table 6).

Hitachi managers apply a higher level of control for public systems. Members of the QA Department join these projects from the beginning, and work closely with project members to assure quality of the development process through reviews and the quality of the end product by reviewing test plans and performing some independent tests. Hitachi manages these high-priority public systems in the same way as basic software, and allows the QA Department to take on some of the responsibility for quality assurance. The goal is essentially to deliver systems with zero defects, and management chooses to organize and invest in an independent QA or inspection department to assist projects.

The private, internal-use systems require a lower level of inspection because they do not need to be zero-defect. These are projects where the impact of a software failure is minimal on the customer or on society, and where there is only a small number of users. Hitachi will curtail some control and inspection activities to reduce short-term development costs, while also believing that, in the long term, the small number of users will mean relatively few bugs will be found in the future. Hitachi will deliver a system to the quality (reliability) specifications required by the customer, which is usually decided along with the cost of the total system, since testing time is a major component of reducing defects. For customers without specific quality requirements from the customer, Hitachi delivers a level of quality that the project manager, with the agreement of the QA Department, feels is appropriate given the price the customer has agreed to pay for a system. The QA Department monitors negotiations between project managers and customers on price and quality issues, although project managers have de facto control over these kinds of projects. Part of the reason for this behavior is that, in contrast to basic software or public systems, for the private in-house systems, ownership rights rest with the customer, and customers generally fix their own bugs after a set period.

NEC, Fujitsu, and Toshiba make similar kinds of distinctions in their applications projects, and vary accordingly what they measure and how closely they attempt to review and control the development process and the quality of final products. For example, Toshiba's Fuchu Works, which builds a variety of process-control systems, classifies its projects into three categories -- A, B, and C -- depending on several contextual factors, as quoted in Table 8. The "A-category" systems are comparable to Hitachi's public systems, which have many end-users, like an on-line banking system, or where a major failure in a software control system (such as in a nuclear power plant or chemical plant) can have disastrous social consequences.

There are other examples of areas where Hitachi makes different decisions depending on the project categorization. Again, Toshiba, as well as NEC and Fujitsu, make similar kinds of decisions.

One area is the extent of independent system testing. The QA Department in Hitachi's applications development division operates its own testing facility called the SST (System Simulation Test) Center. This has a staff of approximately 100 engineers, which develop and conduct tests and build testing tools. The facility is used by Basic Software Division also in that they test operating systems with applications programs on Hitachi hardware. While the SST is a special phase of testing that comes after system test done by project systems engineers, Hitachi puts only about 10% of the applications systems it develops through the SST Center, because this is expensive. The QA Department selects which 10% of systems to put through SST. The 10% are usually totally "new" software products, such as new packages or new private/internal software, or public systems with high reliability requirements.

Another area is the extent of total QA activities. Hitachi allocates from 3% to 10% of project manpower to QA activities, which includes the cost of QA Department staff working with particular projects (development plan audits, reviews, quality audits, customer service, and special testing) as well as the quality activities of project personnel such as participation in reviews. These percentages do not include system and integration test work done by the systems engineers. This does include SST work. In basic software, the common figure for QA activity allocations is 10% of project manpower, including more extensive product testing done by the QA Department. In applications, the 10% allocation occurs mainly for the large-scale public systems, and 3% for the internal-use systems. Percentages are affected by the number (and position) of people who attend reviews and the amount of time they spend, as well as the amount of time spent by the QA Department in their regular activities of test planning, special testing, problem analysis, and customer support.

A third example is the extent of independent QA or inspection department authority. For internal/private as well as public systems, Hitachi project managers have access to and are required to use data from past projects for scheduling as well as for quality targets, although quality targets are adjusted to customer specifications and prices. The QA Department is aware of the customer requirements and contract price for the system, and is supposed to take these factors into consideration, rather than seek absolute quality levels such as zero defects for these kinds of systems.

In basic software, the QA Department has final authority on determining shipment of a product. There are few disagreements with project managers in the cases of systems where there is extensive historical data, primarily number of bugs detected and fixed in system test versus projected and targeted numbers. For new systems or systems with many new features, the historical projections may be inaccurate, and the quality targets require considerable negotiation among division management, project management, and the QA department.

In applications projects, formally, the QA Department has the authority to stop shipment on all systems, and does occasionally do this even for in-house private systems if QA people are not satisfied with the quality of the system. If QA people are not satisfied but the project manager argues that a system has met the customer requirements and the customer wants it, the QA manager will check directly with customers that this is the case before approving shipment. For all but the newest systems, the QA Department has historical data that allows it to estimate how many bugs remain in a system (see Figure 1). If the customer accepts this situation, then the department will agree to ship. The contract will determine who pays for fixing bugs over what period of time.

In the case of public systems, as in basic software, quality targets are driven by historical data and experience. The QA Department collects data that comprise the guidelines, and project managers make the actual decisions on targets at particular stages, as with in-house/private systems. However, the guidelines are relatively clear, and project managers cannot set goals far from the guidelines. Their plans are also closely checked by the QA Department. If QA people feel a project manager has set quality objectives that are too low and the project manager does not want to change them, the QA manager will go to the department manager or the factory manager. The QA Department also has much clearer and absolute authority on shipment for the public systems.

There appear to be few cases where project managers conflict seriously with the QA Department on public systems, where goals are pretty much data driven. There is more opportunity for disagreements with the

Figure 1: Hitachi Quality Target Management

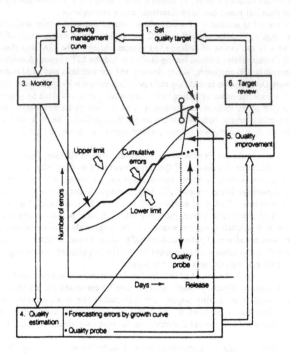

Table 6: Hitachi Applications Categorization

(1)   Customer in-house ("private") applications, used internally only by the customer.

   Comments: Software failures are not critical for the customer or for
                society, and the small user base means few errors are likely to
                be found in the future, so less intensive reviews, testing, and
                independent inspection is needed.

   Examples: inventory management, hospital information systems.

(2)   Customer with many end-user ("public") applications or used by the customer
       to service end users.

   Comments: Software failures are potentially critical for the customer or
                for society, and the large user base means many errors are
                likely to be found in the future, so intensive reviews, testing,
                and independent inspection is needed.

   Examples: stock exchange, on-line banking, reservations systems.

Source: Personal interviews at Hitachi Information Systems Development Center, 4 August 1992,
         with Yasuo Yoshida, Dept. Mgr., Quality Assurance and Inspection Dept.; Katsuyuki
         Yasuda, Dept. Mgr., Software Engineering Department; and Takamasa Nara, Deputy
         Dept. Mgr., Quality Assurance and Inspection Dept.

Table 7: Toshiba Applications Categorization

1)   The level of the system's influence on society, our customers, and on our own
       business;

2)   The level of risk involved, depending on:
   a)   our technical experience in the system to be developed;
   b)   the number of new items that must be developed;
   c)   the amount of modification to the existing system that is to be
          renovated;
   d)   the size and complexity of the system;
   e)   the urgency of the product's delivery date and system acceptance date;
   f)   the tightness of available project funding.

       In the beginning of each project, we assign a management-level ranking that has been
determined using the above criteria. There are three ranks: A, B, and C. Compulsory
attendance by each level of managers and specialists at design reviews and internal acceptance tests
are defined based on this rank classification.

Source: [9] p. 383

internal/private systems, where project managers are given more authority, and QA plays more of a role of setting guidelines. However, QA people recognize that public systems have different reliability requirements than private systems or non-critical systems, and that business decisions have to be made sometimes that are compromises with quality, but only for one-user, non-critical internal/private systems.

3.3 Development-Organization Culture

In addition to the product, process, and project characteristics described above, there is a hierarchy of cultural influences that affect to what extent companies attempt to use measurement for planning, control, and learning:

(1)   national culture (weak influence);
(2)   company culture (strong influence);
(3)   product division culture (stronger influence).

Discussions of Japanese software development practices might indicate to some people that characteristics of the Japanese people, including how they are educated in general, or how they expect managers, workers, and customers to behave, make it easier to introduce and utilize measurements or even a factory-like process in software development. This may be true. Japanese customers demand highly reliable products; in response, companies have developed elaborate mechanisms to root out errors and causes of errors, using quantitative and qualitative methods. Even Japanese high schools teach basic statistics, and even blue-collar workers in most manufacturing industries are required to record, analyze, and monitor performance, and then take corrective action if necessary and as indicated by simple statistical data. It also appears that the culture of software programming in Japan is somewhat different than in the United States or Europe, with many managers and engineers viewing this more as a production activity, rather than as an art or craft.

Yet there are as variations among Japanese managers, engineers, and firms, especially when comparing the large computer manufacturers, who also develop most of the basic software and large amounts of applications programs in Japan, to smaller software houses that may have no defined process of their own. In addition, there are many non-Japanese firms that measure intensively and use quantitative data for management control as well as for process improvement. This suggests that company culture, as well as the cultures of particular product divisions, play an even more important role in determining the context of the project than the national culture.

Variations within firms sometimes exist as the result of a rational selection process, such as technical differences in reliability requirements, system complexity, or customer contracts. Other times, however, variations may be the result simply of chance, history, timing -- such as different stages of maturity -- or bad management. For example, Hitachi and Toshiba have long histories as electrical equipment and heavy machinery manufacturers, and they brought into their software development operations in the 1960s and 1970s managers with hardware backgrounds or backgrounds in inspection who believed firmly in process and product measurement as well as the collection of historical data and active use of this data. Fujitsu and NEC followed the lead of Hitachi as well as IBM, attempted to meet rigorous quality standards set by NTT for switching systems, and, under the influence of insightful managers, introduced rigorous standards into their basic software operations, which then influenced gradually how other parts of the company developed software.

But while Hitachi more-or-less applied the same practices started in basic software to applications (both areas were managed within the same software factory organization from 1969 until 1985), NEC and Fujitsu exhibit more variations. Applications in general are controlled less than basic software, and neither company utilizes an independent quality assurance or inspection department to determine product shipment. Both companies have independent QA or inspection departments that collect data and make this available to project managers for reference, but managers in Fujitsu and NEC both complain that the performance of their applications projects in terms of cost, schedule, or quality management is not as predictable and thus not as well controlled as in Hitachi. The NEC and Fujitsu approaches may be lower in cost during the short run but higher in cost over the long run or for unusually complex projects.

4 Conclusions

The discussion above reflects an unfortunate reality. It is naive to expect a consensus to emerge easily within even a single organization, let alone within an entire industry or among a set of different actors or observers, regarding what to measure and control in software development. The perspective of senior managers, project managers, QA or inspection personnel, marketing and customer service groups, and researchers from companies or academics can be very different. Different types of systems and customers, as well as different company and division cultures, also may have an enormous impact on how projects use data for planning, control, and learning.

Top management, for example, may not have the foresight to act for the long term and may react to high software costs by pressuring project managers even more on current projects; this, in turn, makes it more difficult for project managers to escape the pressures of short-term schedules and budgets. Top management may also not allocate the resources needed for effective metrics, QA, or process R&D programs. Within projects, engineers may not want to be measured or to collect data that is needed for effective planning, control, and improvement, or for bench-marking. Hitachi, for example, tests its programmers and records their scores for project planning and estimation purposes. But many software personnel do not like to be treated in this manner, even in Japan, and academic researchers as well as company researchers may not be interested in metrics or technologies that project managers and engineers see as practical or immediately beneficial at a reasonable cost.   Improved tools, techniques, and metrics, and more automated or unobtrusive data collection and analysis, will solve some of these difficulties in time. But it is also important to try to create a culture of measurement where projects collect, analyze, and use data primarily to improve quality and overall efficiency. This will require identifying and assisting weak project members or weak projects, which will provoke some resistance; and there is only a subtle distinction between using measurement for improvement and using it for control. But companies need to make these distinctions because there is a larger danger: that managers and engineers can become paralyzed by these debates on resource allocations or the search for "perfect" metrics to the point where projects measure inconsistently or measure nothing at all. Either option makes it almost impossible to learn because companies must establish a quantitative baseline from which to improve.

Part of the resistance to measurement relates to an old quality-management debate that centers around the issue of whether a company can "build-in" rather than "inspect-in" quality. In industries such as automobiles, Japanese managers in the 1950s and 1960s made all production workers serve as inspectors of the previous person's work, and taught workers how to use simplified statistical control techniques. Companies thereby were able to eliminate large inspection or QA departments, eliminate large amounts of rework, and improve productivity as well as quality. Japanese firms also extended the concept of quality circles and quality-improvement activities to engineering departments, research departments, and all other white-collar jobs [4]. But, in software development, to what extent can we build-in quality while eliminating or drastically reducing time spent in outside reviews, independent testing, and other forms of inspection? Can software developers measure and control themselves, or is software development a different kind of activity from what we see in other industries? Or is this combination technical and business decision, reflecting the nature of the system, the specific user requirements, the developer's general process, the likely amount of profit from the project, and other factors?

The Japanese, who are innovators and experts in quality management, seem to be playing it both ways technically and to let business as well as technical decisions determine what they actually do in a given project. Companies allocate many hours to personnel training in common development methods, to problem-solving meetings and reports, to reviews, and other activities that project personnel plan and do to assurance a high level of quality in their work. But Hitachi and Toshiba, in both basic software and applications, as well as NEC and Fujitsu at least for basic software, also believe that short-term pressures of schedules and budgets make it difficult for project managers and developers to take adequate care in designing, testing, documenting, reviewing, and doing other tasks not directly related to building and delivering code. Therefore, managers in these companies, for their most critical projects -- basic software and large "public" systems -- insist on having independent departments measure as well as monitor the quality of the development process and the quality of the final product. For less critical projects, they will vary how carefully they manage. The ideal approach is not to have to manage very much and to build-in quality every time, but no one has yet reached this ideal. In the interim, projects must continue to measure, control, inspect, and test to the extent that this is economically and technically practical, as well as important to the user. At the same time, and with the help of process researchers, companies must strive to reduce the amount of time and effort they spend in measurement and control activities.

References

1.   J. Arthur: Measuring Programmer Productivity and Software Quality. New York: Wiley 1985

2.   S.D. Conte, H.E. Dunsmore, and V.Y. Shen: Software Engineering Metrics and Models. Menlo Park, CA: Benjamin/Cummings 1986

3.   M.A. Cusumano: Japan's Software Factories: A Challenge to U.S. Management. New York: Oxford University Press 1991

4.   M.A. Cusumano: The Japanese Automobile Industry: Technology and Management at Nissan and Toyota. Cambridge, MA: Harvard University Press 1985

5.   W.S. Humphrey: Managing the Software Process. Reading, MA: Addison-Wesley 1989

6.   C. Jones: Applied Software Measurement: Assuring Productivity and Quality. New York: McGraw-Hill 1991

7.   NEC Corporation: Discussion on the Switching Software Development Process. Switching Software Engineering Division, Abiko Works, 31 August 1992

8.   NEC Corporation: QA System in NEC: Scientific Control of Production and Quality in NEC -- Basic Software. Unpublished internal document, September 8, 1987

9.   K. Yamashita and O. Sasaki: Computer Application Systems Engineering Center -- A Software Factory. Fuchu Works, Toshiba Corporation 1992

10.   K. Yasuda: "Software Quality Assurance Activities in Japan," in Y. Matumoto and Y. Ohno, ed., Japanese Perspectives in Software Engineering. Reading, MA: Addison-Wesley 1989

Position Paper

Norman Fenton

City University

Experimental Methods: One of the most important challenges in software engineering is the objective assessment of methods. Excellent examples like the Scanlan experiment [1] show that we cannot continue to put our faith in anecdotal evidence or the opinions of 'experts' who often have a self- interest in promoting a particular method. However, we have to accept that formal, controlled, experiments are almost invariably impractical. The way forward is via carefully executed case studies where the data collection activities are clearly specified to meet some specific measurement objectives. Our approach (currently being used to assess the efficacy of software engineering standards [2]) is to measure: 1) the quality (normally reliability) of the output products, 2) the extent to which the method (standard) has been applied, and 3) the cost of applying it.

Organizational forms for experimental research: In the case study approach used in the SMARTIE project the industrial partner (British Rail) invited the academic partner (CSR) to provide significant input to the selection of measures for data collection. They saw this as enhancing their existing serious committment to a measurement programme, and CSR saw it as the only real means of assessing the efficacy of standards and methods. Compared to other industrial/academic case studies (where the academic partner is expected to make some sensible interpretation from whatever data happens to be provided) this approach is working well.

Model Building: The use of some of the basics of the theory of measurement has a unifying and positive effect in software measurement [3], much of which has been adversely affected by the use of 'metrics' which do not actually measure what they are claimed to measure. Making clear the following distinctions are all crucial but are ignored so often that the message needs to be drummed home: measurement in the assessment sense and measurement in the predictive sense; attributes of products, processes and resources; internal and external attributes.

Teaching curricula: We are currently teaching software measurement on final year undergraduate and Masters degrees. The problem is that we are having to spend time teaching foundational material like: principles of measurement, probability and statistics. All of these basic 'quantitative methods' should be taught to all first year computing/software engineering students. The METKIT project (which did extensive surveys) came to the same conclusion.

Other topics I would like to see discussed:

Standards: The SMARTIE project has concluded that software engineering 'standards' are not standards in any engineering sense because it is generally impossible to measure conformance to any of the requirements. Moreover, none of them specify measurable properties of products.

ISO 9126 Standard: This standard is devoted to assessing software products. It is very poor and should be discussed at Dagstuhl because it could set software measurement back several years.

Assessing safety critical systems: We are interested in how you combine diverse types of information in order to determine how safe a system is.

References

[1] Scanlan DA, 'Structured flowcharts outperform pseudocode: an experimental comparison', IEEE Software, Sep 1989, 28-36

[2] Fenton NE, Littlewood B, 'Evaluating software engineering standards' Eurometrics 91

[3] Fenton NE, 'Software Metrics: A Rigorous Approach', Chapman & Hall, 1991

Software Engineering as an Organisational Challenge

(Or: Egomanic Programming Considered Harmful)

Günter R. Koch

2i Industrial Informatics GmbH, Haierweg 20e,
7800 Freiburg

Abstract. This position paper argues along two lines. First, Software Engineering today is much more a challenge of organisational and methodogical improvement than a technological one. Second, the growth and direct and indirect importance of software industry needs a much higher level of professionality in running SW development processes.

Modelling and measuring such processes in industry is one focus of institutions like the SEI, analysing strengths and weaknesses in software engineering. This paper refers to a similar European exercise, the BOOTSTRAP project, and lists the advantages of organisational assessments for improving the competitiveness of software industry.

One of the most recognized institutions for Software Engineering Improvement Programme, the Carnegie Mellon's Software Engineering Institute (SEI) was created when the software crisis was discovered not to be an intellectual crisis only. Barry Boehm [1] being one of the early path finders towards the managerial approach to software engineering, created a discipline of "Software Engineering Economics" already in the 70's. However, most of his arguments reflected the old paradigm that managing software complexity is an affair in which talented heros have to attack the dragon. In the short history of software engineering this sounds to us like the fable of St. George.

We have to award SEI, and there in particular Bill Curtis [2] for having shifted our concern towards the organisational dimension of the problem: Software engineering is no longer a matter of a closed community of highly talented inventors of program code, it is much more a question of managing the processes of creating informational systems and carrying about the methods to do so.

Favouring the organisational approach is by no reason a vote against the humanistic understanding of software development which recently starts to be developed by a community of constructionistic philosophers. (The author considers the compendium titled "Software Development and Reality Construction" [5] to be a most important starting point for a modern epistemological foundation of Computer Science and in specific Software Engineering)

This fundamental change from individualistic to organisational software development has led us to the hypothesis that managing the so-called software crisis is
- firstly a problem of *organisation,* i.e. organizing and managing software engineers for cooperation and intellectual communication
- secondly a matter of engineering and finding *methods* well understood and applied in creating systems as constructional entities,
- thirdly and lastly an activity which has to be supported by an up-to -date technical *infrastructure* including CASE-tools, easing and automating the engineer's ndividual and collective work.

Here, we hypothize that high productivity and high quality in software engineering in the first place will be achieved by changing organisational conditions.
(Expectations in productivity gain by purely organisational measures as high as to 30%)

It is a simple but elucidating exercise to forcast the fundamental and yet under-estimated importance of the software industry for our future economy. IT & Com Industry at the end of this century will by all figures published have overpassed the today's lead industry which is the car manufacturing industry. The proportion of software in IT products in terms of value share will fastly grow from today's average of about 40% to a maximum of 80%. The conclusion is that software will become the oil of the next century and as professionals it is our duty to provide all means to keep the process of its construction and maintenance manageable.
Process has become the magic keyword in our community. Modelling and optimizing (organisational) processes in SW Engineering indeed is the key strategic challenge besides the reuse of software constructions.

One of the most stringent scientists of the age of elucidation, Lord Kelvin stated "What you can't measure you can't understand" and we think that gaining understanding of the essence of our discipline is the permanent motivation. As Vic Basili teaches us in his contribution to this book, measuring means adding the quantitative dimension to the structural modelling dimension thereby helping us to understanding the weights and sizes of issues in the SW engineering process structures which we are interested in.

Is process modelling and process measurement just a new, fashionable "l'art pour l'art " exercise of an extravagant computer sicentist community? Indeed not: it is one of the clearest consequences of the challenges arising from the evolution of competition of the economies in the so called triade of US-Japan-Europe [7]

If software is a key entity for our economies, so is competitiveness in software engineering the driving force and the identification of a "lean" software development must be one subject of our future work.

The terms "software crisis", "paradigm shift to organisational SWE", "process modelling", "process transparency" and "software economy competition" span the space in which the author in 1990 founded a project funded under ESPRIT called BOOTSTRAP [3]. It focusses on strengths and weaknesses analysis Software Producing Units (SPUs). The goals of this project are:

- to motivate SPUs to improve their organisational, methodogical and technical strength towards a self -optimizing quality organisation,
- to raise motivation for introducing modern software engineering methodology and technology,
- to analyse the inherent and implicit organisational model of an SPU thereby making its process model transparent
- to characterise by an attribute profile strengths and weaknesses of SPUs in absolute and relative measures. Relative means that any SPU is compared to a collection of reference SPUs.
- to provide data enabling us to compare the state of European software industry to SW industrie in USA and Japan. Eventually these results may help to reorientate the European efforts in R&D in SW Engineering methodology and technology.

The detailed results of the BOOTSTRAP project are reported elsewhere [4]. The two figures in the sequel give a condensed survey on the achievements. The chart represents a typical strengths and weaknesses profile which was derived from an SEI-type maturity assessment by scaling and differentiated the measured profile from the "average profile" of all SPUs analysed so far.

In the table we present a comparison of data collected by SEI as well as by BOOTSTRAP thus giving a tentative(!) picture on SW engineering status in USA, Europe and Japan.

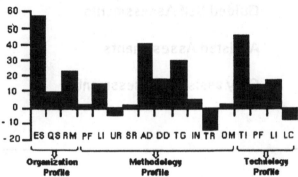

Organization		Methodology	
ES	Embedded & Structure	PF	Process Functions
QS	Quality Systems	LI	Life Cycle Independent
RM	Resource Management	UR	User Requirements
		SR	Software Requirements
Technology		AD	Architectural Design
TI	Technology Introductions	DD	Detailed Design
PF	Process Functions	TG	Testing
LI	Life Cycle Independent	IN	Integration
LC	Life Cycle	TR	Transfer
		OM	Operation and Maintenance

Fig. : Typical strengths and weaknesses profile of an SPU

Assessing Institution	Data Points	Distribution of maturity				
		1	2	3	4	5
SEI (1) in USA	113	85%	14%	1%	-	-
SEI (2) in USA	55	74%	22%	4%	-	-
SEI (1) in Japan	196	95%	3%	1%	-	1%
BOOTSTRAP in Europe	20	50%	45%	5%	-	-

SEI (1)   :   Guided Self-Assessments

SEI (2)   :   Assisted Assessments

BOOTSTRAP :   Only assisted Assessments

Table: Comparative data of SEI-type maturity ranking

Although the author wishes to be extremely careful in drawing conclusions from the data collected from about 30 SPUs and 60 projects so far, it looks that European software engineering (*not* software technology invention and *not* marketing of software!) on average seems to be considerably stronger in Europe than in the US. Following SEI's SW Capabilities Maturity Classification [6], maturity in European SPUs shows about 50% to be above the basic "level one" compared to about 25% in the US, i.e. twice as many SPUs in Europe are already on the path towards high quality (and hopefully high productivity) SW engineering organisations.

References

1. Boehm, B.W.: Software Engineering Economics. Prentice-Hall, Englewood Cliffs, N.J., 1981
2. Curtis, B.; Krasner, H.; Iscoe, N: A Field Study of the Software Design Process for Large Systems.
   CACM, Nov. 1988, Vol. 31, No. 11
3. BOOTSTRAP Phase I Interim Report. Composite Deliverable, July , 1991
   Obtainable through project coordinator: 2i Industrial Informatics GmbH,
   Haierweg 20e, D-7800 Freiburg i. Br..
4. BOOTSTRAP Consortium (Eds): Lean Software Development:
   ESPRIT Conference Procedings, Stuttgart, October 1992. To be
   ordered from Steinbeis-Zentrum für Europäischen
   Technologietransfer, P.O.B. 10 43 62, D-7000 Stuttgart 10
5. Floyd, Chr.; Züllighoven, H.; Budde, R.; Keil-Slawik, R. (Eds): Software
   Development and Reality Construction. Springer-Verlag, Berlin/Heidelberg, 1991
6. Humphrey, W.: Managing the Software Process. Addison-Wesley 1989.
7. Seitz, K: Die japanisch-amerikanische Herausforderung. Verlag
   Bonn-Aktuell, Stuttgart, 1990

Quantitative Measurements based on Process and Context Models *

Nazim H. Madhavji[†]
John Botsford[‡]
Tilmann F. W. Bruckhaus[†]
Khaled El Emam[†]

[†]School of Computer Science - McGill University,

3480 University Street, Montréal, Québec, Canada H3A 2A7,

madhavji@opus.cs.mcgill.ca

[‡]IBM Canada Ltd. Laboratory, Centre for Advanced Studies,

895 Don Mills Rd., North York, Ontario, Canada M3C 1W3

Abstract

Measurement of a software development process is an important way to understand and improve processes. In this paper we propose that measurement programs should be based on a solid understanding of the process and the process context. One way to achieve this type of understanding is to first build formal process and context models. It is pointed out that process and context models can be used to systematically adapt, improve, reuse and standardise measurement programs. We conclude by describing briefly the currently conducted case studies that led to the views expressed in this position statement.

1 Introduction

Measurement of a software development process is an important way to understand and improve processes [1]. However, there is overwhelming evidence that measurements, where carried out at all, are predominantly applied to entities of informally defined or undefined software processes and process contexts. In-process measurements are often captured from processes that are described, if at all, in natural language. Omissions, errors,

---

*This research was in part supported by NSERC, IBM, and CRIM.

and inconsistencies in processes are difficult to detect in natural-language documents. For example, definitions of entry and exit criteria, specific roles, and inputs and outputs may be described for some activity but left out for others. Similarly, the process context is rarely documented. For example, information such as the type of the product to be developed, project constraints, and the organisational environment remain implicit. As a consequence of the absence of process and context models, the understanding of the process and the effect of the process context on both the process and on the measurement program is often inadequate [5].

Common problems resulting from this lack of understanding include:

- *Control:* difficulty in controlling the process, in identifying critical situations throughout the development life cycle, and in identifying the activities causing variability in the product quality.

- *Assessment and Improvement:* difficulty in causal analysis of detected process failures and software defects.

- *Estimation and Prediction:* difficulty in estimating schedule, budget, and product quality, and in predicting process characteristics and trends.

In order to overcome these problems, we propose that project-specific measurement programs be based on process and process context models.

2 Measurements based on Process and Context Models

2.1 Measurement Objectives

Measurements can be gathered and interpreted for retrospective and prospective purposes. Retrospectively, measurements can be used to assess the appropriateness and quality of decisions made in past software development efforts or activities. Prospectively, packaged historical data can be used to determine those decisions that are likely to guide on-going or future projects to attain project goals within the given project constraints.

When measurements are used for retrospective purposes, the aim is to determine whether time, budget, and quality considerations were optimal in order to meet business constraints. Example questions posed are: Did the project manager arrange for a sufficient number of design reviews? How much did the complexity of the requirements document increase between two given releases? Were the members of the design team in a specific project sufficiently well educated in the design method that was employed?

When measurements are used for prospective purposes, the aim is to determine how the time, budget and quality considerations would meet business constraints. Example questions posed are: Should a thorough but costly review process be applied, or should a review process be used that consumes less time and/or budget? Should an error-prone component be re-written, or should time and budget be spent on writing new components? Which one of two design teams or which one of two individual designers is more appropriate for developing a future product design?

2.2   Assumptions about Process and Process Context

Where measurements in current development environments have been perceived as successful, they are often based on certain implicit assumptions about the process and process context, such as: existence of experienced personnel; stability of the software process; and the availability of specific resources. Such assumptions are often a result of individual knowledge, experience or bias.

Basing a measurement program on invalid process and process context assumptions may lead to inaccuracy in collected data, invalid measurement interpretations, and difficulties in determining reasons for inconsistencies in gathered measurements. This, in turn, will affect adversely the attainment of measurement objectives.

There are at least two factors that can invalidate assumptions about the process and the process context: (a) changes in process and process context over time in one project and (b) differences in process and process context across projects. Example factors invalidating such assumptions include: staff turnover; change in the team organisation; change of the product characteristics; and changes in the tools employed for development.

Therefore, the ability of the measurement program to convey the necessary information depends on the continuous validity of the assumptions as the process and its context evolve.

2.3 Adaptation and Reuse of a Measurement Program

Changes in the process and the process context affect what measurements should be taken, how the data is gathered and how the measurements are interpreted. For example a change in the corporate policies, such as the requirement of continued training to junior staff, may necessitate new measurements in certain parts of the development process to assess how much the junior staff's understanding has improved. Similarly, when certain activities in the process are eliminated due to automation, the measurements associated with deleted activities (and all related elements – measurement process, measurement tools, measurement roles, budget, etc.) also need to be deleted.

The adaptation of a measurement program to a changing process and process context, and the reuse of measurement programs across projects (or case studies), can thus be facilitated by creating and evolving models of the process and the process context [4].

The benefits of this approach are manifold:

- When the process or the process context has changed, and the models have updated accordingly (descriptive changes), then the models can be used to *reactively adapt* the measurements program;

- When the process needs to be improved, and the process model has been modified to reflect the future improvement (prescriptive changes), then the process model can be used to *pro-actively adapt* the measurement program;

- When the measurement program needs to be improved in the current process and process context, then the models can be used to *improve* the measurement program; and

- When a measurement program that is successful in one project needs to be applied in multiple projects, then the models can be used to *reuse* the measurement program, or to *standardise* the measurement program across multiple projects.

In essence the process and process context models form a solid base from which changes to the measurement program can be planned. On the one hand, if activities in the process are removed, changed, or added it will often be necessary to delete, change, or add specific measurement points in the measurement program. On the other hand, changes in the process context also influence the measurement program. For example, if the business objectives change from delivery within schedule to delivery of near-zero-defects software, the measurement program may need to be strengthened to emphasise defect prevention.

In the following section an outline of the empirical work being conducted to investigate the above concepts is presented.

3 Empirical Work

We are currently conducting two case studies in collaboration with our industrial partners. In one case study the objective is to improve the requirements engineering process for a particular on-going project. The second case study's objective is to design a process to improve a generic process model [3]. In both cases the existing process (requirements engineering or generic model improvement respectively) must be elicited [6], defined, measured, analysed and an improved one prescribed.

Measurement is not an end in itself. Instead, it is part of a larger process. In the case studies, this is a process to improve existing processes. Therefore, in addition to the benefits cited earlier from a measurement viewpoint, the elicitation and definition of the process context would facilitate:

- Duplication of the case studies either at the same companies but for other projects or at other companies with similar contexts. This could be achieved through either enaction of the described elicitation, definition, measurement and analysis processes, or reuse of the case study results.

- The adaptation of the case study results to either other projects within the same companies or to other companies with differing process contexts. By defining the new process contexts, comparing these with the case study contexts, identifying the differing context characteristics and determining how these affected the case study results, then the results can subsequently be modified for adaptation.

- The formulation of a set of specifications for a computer aided process engineering environment [2]. By taking into consideration all the factors that have significantly effected the case study processes, we expect to learn more about how processes should be designed and how these can be supported through automation.

From our experiences thus far, however, it has become evident that process context is very much tied to the business objectives and the peculiarities of a company. Therefore, the applicability of one company's process context to another company needs to be evaluated, and the impact of each process context characteristic on both the measurement process and the overall improvement process must be determined.

References

[1] V. R. Basili and H. D. Rombach. The tame project: Towards improvement oriented software environments. *IEEE Trans. on Soft. Eng.*, SE-14(6), June 1988.

[2] Tilmann F. W. Bruckhaus. Towards a computer-aided process engineering environment. In *(to appear) Proceedings of the 1992 CAS Conference*, Toronto, ON, November 1992.

[3] K. El Emam, N. Madhavji, and K. Toubache. Empirically driven improvements of generic process models. Technical Report SE-92.7, School Of Computer Science, McGill University, October 1992.

[4] N. H. Madhavji. Environment evolution: The prism model of changes. *IEEE Transactions on Software Engineering*, 18(5):380–392, May 1992.

[5] N. H. Madhavji. The process cycle. *IEE/BCS Software Engineering Journal*, 6(5), September 1991.

[6] N. H. Madhavji, W. K. Hong, T. F. Bruckhaus, and J. E. Botsford. Elicit: A meta process and supporting tool for eliciting software process models. Technical Report SE-92.4, September 1992.

Selecting, Implementing, and Measuring
Methods to Improve the Software Development Process

Karl-Heinrich Möller

Siemens AG

Munich, Germany

Abstract. In time the availability of similar competitive application software packages increases, and the users may become dissatisfied. They begin to demand higher quality and to consider more the price of competitive products. It has been shown that the quality practices and awareness of the software developers are important factors influencing the quality of the product development, the product cost, and the development schedule.

1 General remarks

Many software engineering organizations today have the desire to improve their software development process as a way of improving product quality and development team productivity and reducing product development cycle time to support the business goals of increased competitiveness and profitability. Although many organizations are motivated to improve, very few organizations know how to best improve their development process. There are a wide assortment of available methods such as TQM, QFD, FPA, DPP, SWQA, CM, etc. which often create confusion for software engineering managers with respect to which methods should be introduced at which point within their process evolution.

There is a need for industrial software engineering experimentation for measuring the impact of process improvement methods. The approach to improve a software development process is initiated by an assessment of the current practices and maturity. A number of improvement methods are then recommended and implemented. Experimentation is necessary to measure the impact of these methods within the industrial environment. The selection and successful implementation of the optimal improvement methods are dependent on many variables such as the current process maturity, skills base, organization, and business issues such as cost, risk, implementation speed, etc. Measuring the impact and predicting the success of a specific improvement method are difficult. This is often due to environmental variables external to the method such as staff skills, acceptance, training effectiveness, and implementation efficiency. Once the improvement method is in place, there is also the question of what to do next. It is necessary to determine whether the method was implemented successfully, is the process mature enough to consider implementing additional methods, or is the selected method appropriate for use within the current process maturity level and environment.

2   Relationships between goals, improvement methods and measurement

Once faults are identified as a primary contributor to quality costs, one must ask how these costs can be reduced. The best strategy is simply to prevent faults from occurring, and reduce the number of faults that are introduced into the development process. However, today's software systems are developed by people, and people do make mistakes. Through increased staff experience gained over time, perhaps the number of introduced faults can be decreased by about 5% per year. This can be further improved using methods such as a software defect prevention process.

As faults are found later in the development process, the cost to detect and correct the fault increases, which can be seen in Figure 1. Most of the faults are introduced during design (40%) and implementation (50%). It was measured that 10% of the total number of faults were introduced during the requirements definition phase. The costs associated with finding and correcting these faults significantly increase for later phases of the development process.

In the example given there are six opportunities for finding and correcting introduced faults. These opportunities span faults found during requirements reviews to those found by users in the field. The percentages given indicate how many faults of the total number of faults found were found during the specific product

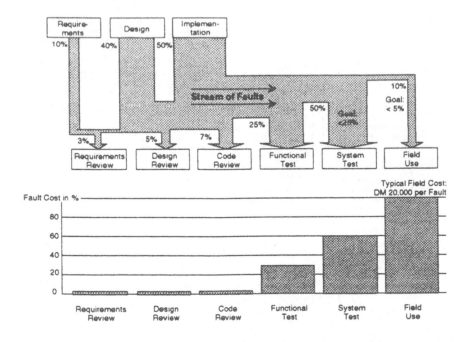

Figure 1. Fault Streams and Costs

74

development phase. For this example most of the faults have been introduced into the product by the end of coding. The only faults added later than the end of coding are due to bad fixes or side effects resulting when code added to fix a bug creates a new bug. However, by the end of the code reviews only 15% of the introduced faults had been found.

In the lower part of Figure 1, the costs associated with finding and correcting faults during each development phase are indicated. Faults found in the field by customers each cost about DM 20,000 to find and fix in this example with more than fifty system field installations. Faults found in system test cost about DM 10-15K or about 60% of what a fault found in the field cost. During reviews, the cost of finding and fixing faults is substantially lower than during test and field use.

When faults are detected and corrected earlier in the development process, there is the potential to reduce the development costs by 20% or more. The goal should be to find as many of the faults as possible during reviews and functional testing. A realistic goal would be for less than 15% of the faults to be found in product and system test and less than 5% during field use. To achieve this goal many Siemens development organizations are putting a strong emphasis on methods and training for conducting better reviews.

The evolution of fault distribution over time can be seen in Figure 2. As the

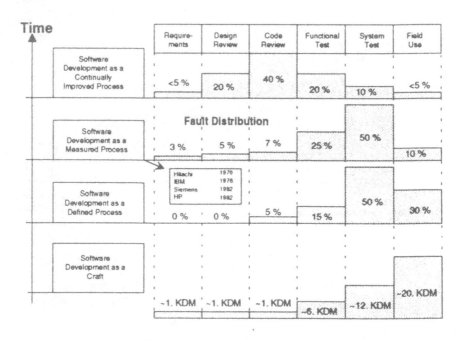

Figure 2. Fault Distribution Costs

75

software development process evolves from initially a craft to eventually a controlled process that is measured and continually improved, a higher percentage of faults are discovered in the earlier phases of software development. This in time reduces the costs associated with software product development. Also indicated are the dates when some major companies began integrating measurement or the use of software metrics into their development process. As can be seen from that example the relationship between the goals and the improvement methods is not obvious.

3   Proposal

It is proposed that this issue be explored within the context of the SEI Software Process Maturity Model. Specifically, it is proposed that three theses be discussed.

1. A specific process improvement method can often be applied at all five levels of the Process Maturity Model depending on the degree of sophistication during the implementation of the method. For example, the use of the method "Testing" can be applied at Level 1 where an individual only occasionally spends time testing their code, Level 3 where test procedures are documented and controlled, and Levels 4-5 where the testing process is measured and optimized.

2. A software organization may perform at a high maturity level within certain aspects of their process and at a lower level within certain other aspects. For example, an organization may optimize within certain phases of their development process but not in all phases depending on the improvement methods that have been selected (e.g. CASE Tools purchased for design). Therefore it is not always possible to characterize an organization's total performance with a definitive maturity level.

3. Which measures to choose with a particular method for improving from one maturity level to the next higher maturity level are not clearly understood. For example, if an organization were to implement a Metrics Program, it is not clear that they would predictably progress from say Level 3 to Level 4.

If these theses can be discussed within the context of which methods should be chosen to progress from one maturity level to the next higher level, insights may occur for what experiments could be devised for measuring the impact of process improvement methods within an industrial software development organization.

Rethinking Measurement to Support Incremental Process Improvement

Adam A. Porter [1]
Department of Computer Science
University of Maryland
College Park, MD 20742
Internet: aporter@cs.umd.edu

1 Introduction

Software engineering research has failed to provide a detailed mechanism for systematic, incremental process improvement. There are a variety of explanations for this situation. For example, we lack the knowledge necessary to select the right processes, methods and tools to combat specific problems. Also, we have not developed models that illuminate the link between local actions and global process goals. In the absence of such information and improvement models, we cannot reason about the tradeoffs associated with alternative processes, risking arbitrary side-effects.

This article briefly describes requirements for a formal process improvement model and discusses the obligations that it imposes on measurement.

Modeling Incremental Process Improvement: Currently available assessment frameworks have limited their focus to determining how individual methods (subprocesses) affect individual goals. (e.g. how many defects are discovered by a new testing method.) From the perspective of process improvement this information is incomplete. Process improvement not only requires an assessment of the local effects of candidate methods; it also requires a process-wide perspective that considers: the interplay between multiple methods and defect types; the applicability of methods to different stages of the software development process; and the influence of methods on project-specific goals, such as cost, schedule and quality.

We are developing a formal model of process improvement to compare alternative processes. The goal of such a model is to quantify the value of candidate process improvements with respect to project-specific goals and constraints.

Although there are many strategies for process improvement, we are concentrating on incremental improvement (i.e. fine grain redesign of an existing process). We emphasize incremental improvement because there is a growing recognition that sustained excellence will more likely be achieved through evolutionary rather than revolutionary improvement.

---

[1] This work has been developed jointly with GianLuigi Caldiera and Sandro Morasca

Requirements for a Process Improvement Model: Significant research energy has been devoted to project estimation. Numerous models have been constructed to estimate quantities such as cost, schedule, staffing, reliability, and expected fault density. Typically, these variables are modeled as functions of project and system characteristics. Unfortunately, these models do not support improvement because the development process is not a model parameter. Clearly, process modification has no influence on models that do not consider its effect.

Ultimately, we need to understand the effects of candidate improvements in the context of a specific software development process. Therefore, proposed improvements must be evaluated in a context that closely mirrors their execution environment. The following section draws some observations about process improvement. We then propose a preliminary set of requirements, based on these observations, that should be incorporated into the design of a process improvement model.

Reflections on Software Process Improvement: This section draws a number of observations about incremental process improvement. They are:

Ob1 Software processes have multiple, often conflicting goals and constraints. For example, a desire to shorten time-to-market is likely to conflict with the desire to minimize long term maintenance costs. Consequently, improvement must be viewed from several perspectives.

Ob2 Preferences among goals are project-specific. Different processes will emphasize different goals. This situation can be seen in large scale systems that undergo continuous enhancement or where independent validation and verification is subcontracted. In these cases managers may emphasize schedule conformance to cost reduction.

Ob3 Process modifications can have far-reaching implication due to interdependencies. Although the distinction is somewhat arbitrary, process improvement can have both local and global consequences.

   Ob3.1 Local effects. Processes that implement similar tasks may interact. If, for instance, we determine that two verification processes detect a similar class of faults, it may not be necessary to apply them both.

   Ob3.2 Global effects. Processes that implement dissimilar tasks also interact. Suppose a new requirements analysis technique is employed. It may lessen the need to test for missing functionality during design.

Ob4 Software processes exhibit considerable variability. Describing process effectiveness through a single-valued measure is often not desirable.

Ob5 New processes involve uncertainty. Although we may have observed a subprocess in a similar context, it is new to the process being improved. Consequently, its performance may not be fully predictable.

Desirable Properties of a Process Improvement Model: Based on the preceding observations, we have developed a preliminary set of requirements for a process improvement model. Any formal process improvement model should:

R1 [Satisfies Ob1, Ob2] Address multiple goals and constraints via a single modeling scheme.

R2 [Satisfies Ob2] Allow users to specify preferences between conflicting goals.

R3 [Satisfies Ob2, Ob3] Reflect the structure of the actual process.

R4 [Satisfies Ob3, Ob4] Integrate empirical - possibly uncertain - information about process performance.

R5 [Satisfies Ob3, Ob4] Be applicable at many levels of detail.

R6 [Satisfies Ob1-Ob5] Be formal and analyzable.

2 Prototype Framework

We view the software development process as a network of tasks (subprocesses) whose execution results in the creation, delivery and servicing of software systems. Modifying this network changes the performance of overall development process. We are developing a prototype process improvement model to assess the improvement expected from using the modified process. To satisfy these requirements, our approach merges process modeling with empirical performance information. The model has four major components. They are:

Goal Specification: The set of goals and constraints that must be achieved by the process. Using the GQM approach [BCC92], we create a vector of state variables that quantifies the goals and constraints of interest.

Process Model: A formal model is used to represent the development process and to identify areas of change during process improvement. Our representation formalism is based on hierarchical Petri-nets because they provide a simple, state-based representation that naturally supports analysis.

Performance Model: To evaluate the improvement expected from a process modification, the process model is augmented by a stochastic performance model. It relates the many changes caused by individual subprocesses to changes in the state of the overall development process.

Technology Assessment: Technology assessment involves quantifying the effect of a process on the state vector. One important implication of process improvement is that it may produce previously unseen process organizations. In these situations, we must introduce an estimate of the effectiveness of the modified subprocess. This estimate can be determined through experimentation, prototyping or subjective estimation.

3 Obligations for Measurement

Our process improvement model depends on the availability of information that characterizes a specific environment and quantifies the effect of applying subprocesses. These functions may be supported by an experience factory[BR88]. We have identified a number of obligations that the process improvement model places upon the provider of this performance data. In particular we note that considerable attention must be paid to evaluating the performance of subprocesses.

- Measurement goals: Measurements of subprocess performance should consider the effect of subprocesses on both local and global goals.

- Measurement should capture changes to process state: To make performance measures independent we need to understand the condition of the system before and after a subprocess is applied.

- Recognize that subprocesses may be applied with different intensities: A subprocess may be applied in different doses or may be introduced gradually into the development process.

- Measurements should be given with associated distributions to capture uncertainty: In process improvement we are interested in the effect of a subprocess that has never been used in the current process. Consequently, the effectiveness should be given in terms of a distribution of values.

- Measurements should not change their meaning when the process changes: For example, measures that are normalized by lines of code may be misleading if a new subprocess greatly reduces the amount of new code produced.

- Fine grained measurement, performed accurately, will provide increased opportunities for improvement: By better understanding the specific strengths of subprocesses we can better match them with likely problem areas.

4 Summary

In this article we have described a prototype process improvement model. Such a model is essential to sustained, incremental process improvement. It provides a formal mechanism that when supported by data aids decision making for process improvement, helps to identify tradeoffs in different processes and highlights important measurement considerations for supporting sustained, incremental process improvement. In particular, we notice that considerable attention must be paid to evaluating the performance of subprocesses.

References

[BCC92] V. R. Basili, G. Caldiera, and G. Cantone. A reference architecture for the component factory. *ACM Transactions on Software Engineering and Methodology*, 1(1):53–80, January 1992.

[BR88] V. R. Basili and H. D. Rombach. The TAME project: Towards improvement-oriented software environments. *IEEE Transactions on Software Engineering*, SE-14(6):758–773, June 1988.

Session 2 Summary
Objectives and Context of Measurement/Experimentation

Norman Fenton

The main question which this session addressed was 'why do we measure?'. Two other questions originally proposed, namely 'what is it we want to know?' and 'how does the context affect the ability to measure?' were felt to be subsidiary; this is because knowing why we want to measure determines both what it is we want to know and the context for measurement.

Cusumano felt that there were three general reasons for doing software measurement (which covered companies as well as academics) and that these were:

- development planning and control
- learning and improvement
- benchmarking

However, we wanted to look beneath the general objectives. Thus, in focussing on the question 'why do we measure?' the session objective was to try to determine a set of specific measurement objectives, expressed as experimental hypotheses, which were felt to be important.

The remainder of this article is a summary of the session findings.

Lessons learnt in the last ten years

There was no concensus on the single most important reason, or objective, for measurement. However, there was broad agreement on each of the following points which relate to objectives for measurement.

Measurement must have clear goals or objectives

Individual software measurement programmes are unlikely to be successful unless they address clear goals or objectives. This is because the objectives determine the kind of measurements which have to be made [BR88, Fen91]. Michael Cusumano suggested that this does not mean that measurement without clearly stated prior objectives is never useful. However, collecting data simply in the hope that you might discover something useful was insufficient reason in itself to start a measurement programme. Companies which had amassed large amounts of software measurement data, simply because this was felt to be a good thing, were now the ones most sceptical of metrics programmes.

Having clear objectives also leads to greater co-operation and motivation for personnel who need to be involved in the measurement programme (as long as the objective is not to assess *them* as individuals). The lack of such co-operation has been an often cited reason for the failure of measurement programmes.

Process/product relationships

The last ten years have seen the widespread acceptance of the idea that to improve software product quality you have to improve the whole software development process. Consequently process measurement has been seen as increasingly important. This is the major point of the presentations by Koch, Madjahvi and Porter, and is the underlying principle of the SEI process maturity programme [Hum89]. In addition, Madhavji proposed formally defined process models [MS91] as a basis for identifying, controlling and changing what is to be measured, where, when, how, and by whom. Möller's paper also adresses this issue, but focuses on the empirical evidence which describes the significant difference in cost of fixing faults at different phases in the software life-cycle; for example, the typical cost of fixing a fault found during operation is DM 20,000 compared with less than DM 1000 if the fault was found during code review.

We have learnt something about the process/product relationship from the Japanese: they have demonstrated that product quality can be improved by using process quality control and assurance techniques (which include careful measurement), which feed back to *incremental* changes to the process.

Relationships between process and product attributes are always *stochastic* rather than deterministic. Unfortunately there are very few specific relationships which are known. Assertions such as 'the use of formal specification languages generally lead to more reliable code' are currently based on purely anecdotal evidence. Even where widely held beliefs have been supported by empirical work, the latter have often been subsequently disputed or discredited altogether. Thus, for example: Vessey and Weber [VW84] concluded that the empirical evidence to support the assertion that 'the use of structured programming generally leads to improved quality code' was *equivocal*; Scanlan [Sca89] demonstrated that previous experiments which had supposedly shown that structured flowcharts were inferior to pseudocode as a means of documentation were flawed, and that exactly the converse was true.

Assessing product quality

It has become increasingly important to assess the quality of software products. The only effective way to do this is by measurement. Reliability, that is the likelihood of failure-free operation in a given environment in a given period of time, is widely accepted as a key component of software quality. There are now techniques available which allow accurate measurement of software reliability providing we have information on inter-failure times [BCL90].

Key points of dissent

The right level of abstraction

While people inevitably had widely varying views about which specific measurement objectives were important, this was not the most serious point of dissent about objectives. More serious was the widely varying view about whether 'macro' or 'micro' objectives had to be tackled first. For example, some people felt that the macro issue 'understand the whole software development process' (this was cited by at least three participants from both industry and academia) took precedence over micro issues like 'understand the effects of a particular testing technique on defect discovery'. A number of participants (including the author) felt that the micro issues had to be tackled first.

This point of dissent raises a very important issue for the GQM approach [BR88]: What is a sensible level of abstraction for our initial goal? If the level of abstraction is too high then the framework does not really help develop a measurement programme to meet the goal; on the other hand, choosing a level of abstraction which is too low may turn out to be irrelevant for the goal you *really* want to achieve.

Kitchenham made an important point about the radically different implications for experimentation between macro and micro type objectives. Many of the macro objectives amount to process improvement goals (for example, 'decrease maintenance costs'), for which experimentation does not provide obvious help. This contrasts starkly with a micro goal like 'determine if documentation method X leads to decreased maintenance costs' which can only be achieved experimentally.

Measuring people and the Hawthorne effect

There seemed to be genuine dissent about whether measuring *people* should ever be an objective. Many were against the idea of ever assessing people's individual performance. However, assessing productivity is a very common measurement objective, and there is no escaping the fact that people are the subject of such measurement.

It was surprising to discover that there was also dissent about the effect on people's performance of introducing a measurement programme. Scacchi asserted that the Hawthorne effect was likely to be present (a point which seemed intuitively reasonable to me), but this was strongly disputed by McGarry, who cited 16 years of measurement experience to back up his view.

Key issues for the next five years

In this section we review the more general or commonly occurring measurement objectives which were cited. Most of the specific objectives can be seen as a special case of identifying process/product relationships as discussed above.

Evaluate validity of SEI process maturity scheme

There appears to be a very urgent desire to assess the validity of the SEI process maturity rating scheme. This specifically amounts to determining whether the five-level 'scale' really is an ordinal scale of company maturity; i.e. do companies on level($n+1$) generally produce more reliable software than level(n) companies?

Evaluate efficacy of specific development methods and tools

Excellent examples like the Scanlan experiment [Sca89] show that we cannot continue to put our faith in anecdotal evidence or the opinions of 'experts' who often have a self-interest in promoting a particular method. However, we have to accept that formal, controlled, experiments are almost invariably impractical. The way forward is via carefully executed case studies where the data collection activities are clearly specified to meet some specific measurement objectives. This normally involves determining how the use of the method or tool affects the quality of the final product, and at what price.

Move from process to product certification

If we want to know the likelihood of a software product being fit for purpose then it would be nice to know that the product itself has been certified using measurement. Although this is normal in other engineering disciplines, this is very rare in software engineering, where benchmarking and reliability assessments are restricted to a tiny class of products. Where certification is performed at all it is likely to be process-based. This means that the company which produced the software has conformed to certain process requirements; this is true of both the SEI approach and certification schemes based on standards such as ISO9001 and BS5750. In the absence of many established relationships between process and product it seems reasonable to seek genuine independent product-based certification.

Specific measurement studies

Leaving out objectives which are so general that they are not really interesting (such as 'improve the organization'), the specific measurement objectives (not already mentioned) proposed by participants were:

1. To identify variability in processes.

2. To get better effort/schedule prediction.

3. To identify level of conformance to process models.

4. To identify optimal testing strategies with respect to fault removal during development.

5. To identify bottlenecks in the process.

6. To identify process breakdown points and idle time.

7. To assess the efficacy of specific testing techniques.

8. To assess the efficacy of formal methods.

9. To motivate personnel.

10. To assess the relationship between test coverage and faults found.

11. To assess the effects of conflict.

References

[BCLS90] Sarah Brocklehurst, P~Y Chan, Bev Littlewood, and John Snell. Recalibrating software reliability models. *IEEE Trans Software Eng*, 16(4):458-470, 1990.

[BR88]   Victor Basili and Dieter Rombach. The tame project: Towards improvement-orientated software environments. *IEEE Trans Software Eng*, 14(6):758-773, January 1988.

[Fen91] Norman E Fenton. *Software Metrics: a rigorous approach*. Chapman \& Hall, London, 1991.

[Hum89] W Humphreys. *Managing the Software Process*. Addison Wesley, 1989.

[MS91]   N H Madhavji and W. Schäfer. Prism - methodology and process-oriented environment. *IEEE Trans Software Eng*, 17(12):1270-1283, 1991.

[Sca89] D A Scanlan. Structured flowcharts outperform pseudocode: an experimental comparison. *IEEE Software*, pages 28-36, Sept 1989.

[VW84]   I. Vessey and R. Weber. Research on structured programming: an empiricist's evaluation. *IEEE Trans Software Eng*, 10:397-407, July 1984.

Session 3:

Procedures and Mechanisms for Measurement/Experimentation

Session Chair: Barbara Kitchenham

Keynote: Richard W. Selby

Position Papers: Warren Harrison
Ross Jeffery
Chris Kemerer
Barbara Kitchenham
Hausi A. Müller
Ed Sumner
Marvin Zelkowitz
Horst Zuse

Software Measurement and Experimentation Frameworks, Mechanisms, and Infrastructure

Richard W. Selby

Department of Information and Computer Science
University of California, Irvine, California 92717
U.S.A. e-mail Office +1-714-xx, FAX
selby@ics.uci.edu

Abstract

Software measurement and experimentation provide a cross-cutting foundation for software understanding, analysis, evaluation, and improvement. Effective measurement and experimentation requires a variety of issues to be addressed ranging from goal specification to metric definition to data interpretation. This paper focuses on a subset of the measurement and experimentation issues related to frameworks, mechanisms, and infrastructure. In particular, this paper highlights research results in these areas: frameworks for measurement and experimentation, defining measures, determining appropriate measures, data collection, experimental designs, and infrastructure for measurement.

1 Frameworks for Measurement and Experimentation

Many frameworks and organizational paradigms have been proposed to help define, compare, and evaluate software measurement and experimentation studies. These frameworks and paradigms and related work include the measurement framework [Bas86], growth dynamics approaches [BLV76], factor-criteria-metric paradigm [MRW77], measurement and experimentation foundations [CuR80], data collection and analysis methodology [BW84], goal question metric paradigm [BW84], quality improvement paradigm [Bas85], environment evaluation methodology [WPRK86], measurement and experimentation framework [Sel86], SEI capability maturity model levels four and five [Hum88], define-use-monitor-evaluate [DUME], and pan-do-check-act. There have also been several surveys of experimental methodology in empirical studies, e.g., [Bro80], [Fra81], and [MS83].

The following sections introduce three of these frameworks: factor-criteria-metric paradigm [MRW77], goal question metric paradigm [BW84], and measurement and experimentation framework [Sel86].

This work was supported in part by the Defense Advanced Research Projects Agency under grant MDA972-91-J-1010; National Science Foundation under grant CCR-9704714 with cooperation from the Defense Advanced Research Projects Agency under Arpa order 6108, program code 7T10; National Aeronautics and Space Administration under grant NSG-5123; National Science Foundation under grant CCR-1921936; University of California under the MICRO Program; Computer Science Corporation, and TRW.

Software Measurement and Experimentation Frameworks, Mechanisms, and Infrastructure

Richard W. Selby

Department of Information and Computer Science[*]
University of California, Irvine, California 92717
714-856-6326, Office; 714-856-4056, FAX
selby@ics.uci.edu

Abstract

Software measurement and experimentation provide a cross-cutting foundation for software understanding, analysis, evaluation, and improvement. Effective measurement and experimentation requires a variety of issues to be addressed ranging from goal specification to metric definition to data interpretation. This paper focuses on a subset of the measurement and experimentation issues related to frameworks, mechanisms, and infrastructure. In particular, the paper highlights research issues or results in these areas: frameworks for measurement and experimentation, existing measures, determining appropriate measures, data collection, experimental designs, and infrastructure for measurement.

1 Frameworks for Measurement and Experimentation

Many frameworks and organizational paradigms have been proposed to help define, compare, and evaluate software measurement and experimentation studies. These frameworks and paradigms and related work include the measurement foundations [Leh69], growth dynamics approaches [BL72], factor-criteria-metric paradigm [MRW77], measurement and experimentation foundations [Cur80], data collection and analysis methodology [BW84], goal-question-metric paradigm [BW84], quality improvement paradigm [Bas85], environment evaluation methodology [WHBK86], measurement and experimentation framework [BSH86], SEI capability maturity model levels four and five [Hum88], define-use-measure-evaluate (DUME), and plan-do-check-act. There have also been several surveys on experimental methodology in empirical studies, e.g., [Bro80], [She81], and [MS82].

The following sections introduce three of these frameworks: factor-criteria-metric paradigm [MRW77], goal-question-metric paradigm [BW84], and measurement and experimentation framework [BSH86].

---

*This work was supported in part by the Defense Advanced Research Projects Agency under grant MDA972-91-J-1010; National Science Foundation under grant CCR-8704311 with cooperation from the Defense Advanced Research Projects Agency under Arpa order 6108, program code 7T10; National Aeronautics and Space Administration under grant NSG-5123; National Science Foundation under grant DCR-8521398; University of California under the MICRO program; Computer Sciences Corporation; and TRW.

1.1 Factor-Criteria-Metric Paradigm

The factor-criteria-metric (FCM) paradigm was defined to assist in the definition of metrics and to help show their relationships with specific quality factors [MRW77]. Users enumerate particular quality factors that interest them (e.g., reliability, testability, interoperability) and then define their particular interpretations based on their circumstances in terms of specific criteria and metrics. The metrics provide an operational mechanism for measuring the particular interpretations of the quality factors. This framework is very useful and general and parts of it can be tool-assisted.

1.2 Goal-Question-Metric Paradigm

The goal-question-metric (GQM) paradigm was defined as part of a six-step data collection and analysis methodology for defining, collecting, and interpreting metrics [BW84]. Users define characterization, evaluation, improvement, and other types of goals (e.g., characterize errors) that reflect their particular needs. These goals may or may not correspond directly to quality factors, unlike the FCM paradigm where they do correspond directly to them. Users then elaborate the goals into a set of specific questions, and the information required to answer the questions is defined as a set of metrics. The process of goals → questions → metrics serves as a metric definition process, and the reverse process of metric data analysis → questions → goals serves as a data interpretation process. This framework is also very useful and general and parts of it can be tool-assisted. The GQM paradigm focuses on tailoring goals and metrics to specific needs, while the FCM paradigm focuses on defining specific quality factors and corresponding metrics.

1.3 Measurement and Experimentation Framework

An organizational framework that can be used to summarize and compare software measurement, experimentation, and empirical studies has been proposed by Basili, Selby, and Hutchens [BSH86]. The framework outlines the measurement and experimentation issues according to four areas: definition, planning, operation, and interpretation. The framework for experimentation is intended to help structure the experimental process and to provide a classification scheme for understanding and evaluating experimental studies.

1.3.1 Example Classification of Experiments and Studies

One application of the framework is to use it to classify software experiments and studies into four general scopes of examination. The four scopes are: single project (a study of one team on one project); multi-project (a study of one team across several projects); multi-team (a study of several teams each working on the same project); or multi-team, multi-project (a study of several teams each working across the same set of projects). The following citations are example studies from each of these categories.

- single project: [Bak72] [OW84] [BP84]

- multi-project: [Boe81] [AE92] [Cus92]

- multi-team: [Par72] [BGS84] [BAB87]

- multi-team, multi-project: [CSM79] [SE84] [BS87]

1.3.2 Example Experiment Definition Template

Another application of the measurement and experimentation framework is to define templates for definitions of studies and experiments [BR88]. One example study definition using a template is: (Motivation:) To improve the unit testing process, (purpose:) characterize and evaluate (object:) the processes of code reading and statement coverage (perspective:) from the perspective of the developer (domain - team:) as they are applied by experienced developers (domain - project:) to unit-sized software components (scope:) in a multi-team, multi-project study.

1.3.3 Experimentation Phases

This section summarizes the experimentation framework. The framework of experimentation consists of four categories corresponding to phases of the experimentation process: I) definition, II) planning, III) operation, and IV) interpretation. The following sections discuss each of these four phases.

Experiment Definition The first phase of the experimental process is the study definition phase. The study definition phase contains six parts: A) motivation, B) object, C) purpose, D) perspective, E) domain, and F) scope. There can be several motivations, objects, purposes, or perspectives in an experimental study. For example, the motivation of a study may be to understand, assess, or improve the effect of a certain technology. The "object of study" is the primary entity examined in a study. A study may examine the final software product, a development process (e.g., inspection process, change process), a model (e.g., software reliability model), etc. The purpose of a study may be to characterize the change in a system over time, to evaluate the effectiveness of testing processes, to predict system development cost by using a cost model, to motivate the validity of a theory by analyzing empirical evidence, etc. (For clarification, the usage of the word "motivate" as a study purpose is distinct from the study "motivation.") In experimental studies that examine "software quality," the interpretation usually includes correctness if it is from the perspective of a developer or reliability if it is from the perspective of a customer. Studies that examine metrics for a given project type from the perspective of the project manager may interest certain project managers, while corporate managers may only be interested if the metrics apply across several project types.

Two important domains that are considered in experimental studies of software are i) the individual programmers or programming teams (the "teams") and ii) the programs or projects (the "projects"). Teams are (possibly single-person) groups that work separately, and projects are separate programs or problems on which teams work. Teams may be characterized by experience, size, organization, etc., and projects may be characterized by size, complexity, application, etc. A general classification of the scopes of experimental studies can be obtained by examining the sizes of these two domains considered. Blocked subject-project studies examine one or more objects across a set of teams and a set of projects. Replicated project studies examine object(s) across a set of teams and a single project, while multi-project variation studies examine object(s) across a single team and a set of projects. Single project studies examine object(s) on a single team and a single project. As the representativeness of the samples examined and the scope of examination increase, the wider-reaching a study's conclusions become.

Experiment Planning The second phase of the experimental process is the study planning phase. The following sections discuss aspects of the experiment planning phase: A) design, B) criteria, and C) measurement.

The design of an experiment couples the study scope with analytical methods and indicates the domain samples to be examined. Fractional factorial or randomized block designs usually apply in blocked subject-project studies, while completely randomized or incomplete block designs usually apply in multi-project and replicated project studies. Multivariate analysis methods, including correlation, factor analysis, and regression generally may be used across all experimental scopes. Statistical models may be formulated and customized as appropriate. Non-parametric methods should be planned when only limited data may be available or distributional assumptions may not be met. Sampling techniques may be used to select representative programmers and programs/ projects to examine

Different motivations, objects, purposes, perspectives, domains, and scopes require the examination of different criteria. Criteria that tend to be direct reflections of cost/ quality include cost, errors/changes, reliability, and correctness. Criteria that tend to be indirect reflections of cost/quality include data coupling, information visibility, programmer understanding, execution coverage, and size/complexity.

The concrete manifestations of the cost/quality aspects examined in the experiment are captured through measurement. Paradigms assist in the metric definition process: the goal-question-metric paradigm and the factor-criteria-metric paradigm. Once appropriate metrics have been defined, they may be validated to show that they capture what is intended. The data collection process includes developing automated collection schemes and designing and testing data collection forms. The required data may include both objective and subjective data and differents levels of measurement: nominal (or classificatory), ordinal (or ranking), interval, or ratio.

Experiment Operation The third phase of the experimental process is the study operation phase. The operation of the experiment consists of A) preparation, B) execution, and C) analysis. Before conducting the actual experiment, preparation may include a pilot study to confirm the experimental scenario, help organize experimental factors (e.g., subject expertise), or inoculate the subjects. Experimenters collect and validate the defined data during the execution of the study. The analysis of the data may include a combination of quantitative and qualitative methods. The preliminary screening of the data, probably using plots and histograms, usually proceeds the formal data analysis. The process of analyzing the data requires the investigation of any underlying assumptions (e.g., distributional) before the application of the statistical models and tests.

Experiment Interpretation The fourth phase of the experimental process is the study interpretation phase. The interpretation of the experiment consists of A) interpretation context, B) extrapolation, and C) impact. The results of the data analysis from a study are interpreted in a broadening series of contexts. These contexts of interpretation are the statistical framework in which the result is derived, the purpose of the particular study, and the knowledge in the field of research. The representativeness of the sampling analyzed in a study qualifies the extrapolation of the results to other environments. Several follow-up activities contribute to the impact of a study: presenting/ publishing the results for feedback, replicating the experiment, and actually applying the results by modifying methods for software development, maintenance, management, and research.

2 Existing Measures

2.1 Metric Sets

Many metrics and metric sets currently exist. Example metric sets are: STEP metrics (U.S. Army software test and evaluation panel), NASA SEL metrics [BZM+77], SEI "core" metrics [Car92], etc. These metric sets have evolved in a hybrid manner benefiting from goal-driven definitions (i.e., top-down approaches) and practical and cost-effective concerns (i.e., bottom-up approaches). A central benefit in defining a metric set is the ability to analyze metric data across multiple projects. A concern that must balance this benefit is the need to tailor and customize metrics to the needs of particular projects and constraints. Several comparisons of metrics have been conducted using both axiomatic comparison methods [Fen92] [Zel92] [Zwe92] and empirical comparison methods [BSP83] [SYTP85] [Sch92].

2.2 Flexible Metric Definition

An enabling technology for the definition of metrics and metric sets is the development of techniques for flexible metric definition. Two examples of flexible metric definition techniques are the MAE metric definition schema [HMKD82] [Har92] and the a-star queries of program parse trees [ESS92].

2.3 Metric Vectors

Several efforts have been undertaken to delineate the multiple factors that constitute software quality and supporting metrics (e.g., [CM78] [MRW77]). Several efforts have modeled software development and maintenance processes using numerous underlying factors as quality and cost indicators (e.g., [Boe81] [BB81]). One approach for organizing metrics is the idea of a "metric vector" that was proposed to organize the various "dimensions" of software metrics [BK86] [BK83]. The purpose of the metric vector was to support the measurement of various software quality factors. The eight dimensions proposed for the vector were: (a) effort, (b) changes, (c) errors, (d) size, (e) data use, (f) execution, (g) schedule, and (h) environment.

An idea related to the metric vector is the "characteristic software metric set," which is a concise collection of metrics that relate to distinct software cost and quality factors [Els84] [BS85]. Whereas the above metric vector is intended to categorize all (or a great number) of metrics, a characteristic metric set is intended to provide metrics customized for a particular purpose. The two papers cited examine alternate approaches for calculating characteristic metric sets.

3 Determining Appropriate Measures

3.1 The Need for Multiple Metrics

As introduced in the previous section, numerous articles have described particular metrics that can be used to characterize, evaluate, or predict some aspect of software development or maintenance. For example, Boehm has outlined 10 commonly used metrics in large systems [Boe87], Musa has described user-oriented reliability metrics [Mus89], Humphrey has motivated developer-oriented metrics [Hum89], and Brettschneider has described metrics that assess system releasability [Bre89]. Software developers apply metric definition paradigms, such as the goal-question-metric and factor-criteria-metric paradigms described in Section 1, to define and tailor metrics to their particular needs.

Researchers and practitioners have realized that no single metric meets their needs in general. They apply different metrics for different purposes depending on their goals and circumstances. In order to capture the desired information, developers require multiple metrics and need mechanisms for integrating them effectively. The metric sets described in the previous section provide help in organizing metrics, but do not address the integration of multiple metrics.

Metric *integration frameworks* are mechanisms that enable the synergistic use of multiple metrics. These frameworks integrate both numeric and symbolic information, and they should be extensible in terms of allowing the incorporation of new metrics. Extensibility is important because people will continue to define new, unforeseen metrics in the future. In order to be scalable, the frameworks should be objective -- i.e., different people using the framework produce the same result -- and automated. The frameworks should also be able to support both discontinuous (e.g., low or high value ranges are problematic but moderate ranges are not) and continuous relationships as well as a general set of analysis goals.

3.2 A Spectrum of Metric Scales

All software measurement abstractions, by definition, fall into one of four scales (or types) [Cur80] [Zus90]. In order to qualify as an *extensible integration framework*, a mechanism must support all four of these measurement scales. They are: [a] Nominal (descriptive categories), Example metrics -- error type, implementation language, design methodology applied, developer name, host system type, target system type; [b] Ordinal (rank orderings), Example metrics -- failure severity, priority, arrival order, change frequency; [c] Interval (equivalent intervals; or "relative differences"), Example metrics -- date, relative progress; and [d] Ratio (equivalent intervals and absolute zero; or "absolute differences"), Example metrics -- design effort, number of errors, mean-time-between-failure, years of experience in an application area, team size, lines of code, pages of documentation, execution time. Note that different definitions of some metrics may cause them to fall into different scales, e.g., the metric "relative complexity" could be defined so that it would fall into ordinal, interval, or ratio. The four scales are defined precisely by the operations that may be applied to them: nominal $\{=,\neq\}$, ordinal $\{<,>\}$, interval $\{+,-\}$, and ratio $\{+\}$. The operations listed for each scale are also applicable to all scales listed after it. For example, the operation $<$ is applicable to ordinal, interval, and ratio scales but not nominal scales; the operation $=$ is applicable to all four scales. The four scales span two general categories of information: *symbolic* (nominal data) and *numeric* (ordinal, interval, and ratio data).

3.3 Example Integration Frameworks

The following example metric frameworks qualify as extensible integration frameworks (this list is not intended to be comprehensive). A brief introduction is given for each of them, including a simple example. These examples are in addition to the goal-question-metric (GQM) and factor-criteria-metric (FCM) paradigms described in Section 1. GQM and FCM also qualify as metric integration frameworks.

Multiple regression models Multiple regression techniques can be used to define metric-based models that relate a dependent variable to a linear combination of other variables. These techniques are focused on calculating interval and point estimates of the dependent variable and are objective, automated, and very useful. These techniques are well suited for ratio data, and they can accommodate data from the other scales by using techniques such as indicator variables. Regression techniques can be used for exploratory data analysis or for building specific models based on existing metric data. Some examples are: $E = 5.2*L^{0.91}$, where E = total effort in man-months, and L = thousands of lines of delivered source code [WF77]; $ER = -0.36*Meth + 0.006*Cmplx + 0.86$, where ER = the effort-ratio relative to a baseline, $Meth$ = a measure of methodology use, and $Cmplx$ = a measure of cumulative complexity [BB81].

Classification trees and networks Tree- and network-based classification techniques use metrics to classify software artifacts (e.g., components, processes) according to their likelihood of having user-specified properties such as high error-proneness or high effort [SP88] [MS90]. These frameworks primarily support classification-related analysis goals, and they are objective, automated, and very useful. The frameworks use multiple metrics to classify software artifacts. As a hypothetical example, a software component that has fan-in plus fan-out of 12, was inspected for 1 hour, and was originally designed for the current system (i.e., was not reused) may be classified as likely to have integration testing errors based on historical data; a component that has fan-in plus fan-out of 4 and 2 I/O parameters may be classified as unlikely to have integration testing errors. Actual classification trees are generated from existing data and use metrics that are selected automatically based on their ability to differentiate existing "+" components from "-" ones. For example classification trees generated from actual project data, see [SP88].

For other examples, see optimized set reduction [BBT92] and multi-metric graphs [Pfl91].

3.4 Extensible Integration Frameworks

All four of these examples are extensible integration frameworks, and each of them has been used in various validation studies. Each framework has its own advantages, and there are trade-offs between them. None of the frameworks has objective, automated support for general analysis goals. The factor-criteria-metric and goal-question-metric paradigms support general goals, but neither is objective and automated. Classification trees and networks and multiple regression models have objective, automated support for the subset of analysis goals related to classification and interval and point analysis, respectively. The frameworks can be applied by themselves, but it is important to realize that they are complementary and can be combined into hybrid approaches. For example, the goal-question-metric paradigm can be used for "front-end" definition of candidate metrics and classification trees can be used for "back-end" data analysis. These hybrid frameworks share the advantages of each approach.

Extensible integration frameworks enable researchers and practitioners to leverage numeric and symbolic metric information derived from software products, processes, and personnel. Such frameworks are essential because a significant portion of the problems they face requires the integrated application of a broad array of metrics. Among other advantages, these frameworks enable the use of nominal metrics and the analysis of discontinuous relationships, which are two areas that have been underutilized in the past. The benefits of using multiple metrics in appropriate integration frameworks outweigh those derived from using individual metrics, so future research should highlight effective techniques for using metrics together.

4 Data Collection

Several data collection, analysis and evaluation methodologies have been proposed, applied, and refined. Recently, the SEI capability maturity model has further emphasized the need for systematic data collection and measurement to enable process and product improvement [Hum88]. One example methodology is a six-step data collection and analysis methodology proposed in [BW84] and refined in [BS84]. The following sections give an overview of the data definition, collection, and analysis methodology and an explanation of the related metric vector concept. Measurement systems to support various data collection methodologies are described in Section 6.

4.1 Data Collection and Analysis Methodology

The *goal-question-metric paradigm* [BW84] [BS84] [Sel85] [Bas85] defines a methodology for data collection and analysis and results in a set of software product and process metrics, a "metric vector" [BK83], sensitive to the cost and quality goals for a particular environment. There are several steps in the methodology spanning software metric definition, collection, analysis, and interpretation. The data collection and analysis methodology consists of seven steps:

1. Define the goals of the data collection and analysis.

2. Refine the goals to determine a list of specific questions.

3. Establish appropriate metrics and data categories.

4. Plan the layout of the study and the statistical analysis methods.

5. Design and test the data collection scheme.

6. Perform the investigation concurrently with data collection and validation.

7. Analyze and interpret the data in terms of the goal-question framework.

The first three steps in the methodology express the purpose of an analysis, define the data that needs to be collected, and provide a context in which to interpret the data. The formulation of a set of goals constitutes the first step in a management or research process. The goals outline the purpose of the study in terms of software cost and quality aspects. Refinement of the goals occurs until they are manifested in a set of specific questions. The questions define the goals and provide the basis for pursuing the goals. The information required to answer the questions determines the development process and product metrics needed. The organization of the defined metrics results in a set of software metrics, referred to as a "metric vector."

The following four steps involve analysis planning and data collection, validation, analysis, and interpretation. Before collecting the data, the researchers outline the data analysis techniques. The appropriate analysis methods may require an alternate layout of the investigation or additional pieces of data to be collected. The investigators then design and test the data collection method; they determine the information that can be automatically monitored and customize the data collection scheme to the particular environment. The data collection plan usually includes a mixture of collection forms, automated measurement, and personnel interviews. The investigators then perform the data collection accompanied by suitable data validity checks. After preliminary analysis to screen the data, they apply the appropriate statistical and analytical methods. They organize the statistical results and interpret them with respect to the goal-question framework. The analysis of the collected data can sometimes lead to the expansion of the original sets of questions, possibly resulting in more goal areas. Once all seven methodology steps have been completed, researchers can apply another iteration of the methodology with a new set of goals.

4.2 Metric Vector

A set of metrics can be described in terms of a "metric vector" [BK83], consisting of several dimensions, for example: { effort, non-error changes, errors, size, data use, execution, environment }. In this example, the seven dimensions are defined as follows: (1) effort - the time expended in producing the software product; (2) non-error changes - the modifications made to the product; (3) errors - the mistakes made during development or maintenance that require correction; (4) size - the various aspects of the product bulk and complexity; (5) data use - the various aspects of the program's use of data; (6) execution - information about the execution of the program; and (7) environment - a quantitative description of the development and maintenance environment. Each of these dimensions has a variety of metrics associated with it. These metrics depend upon the specific goals and questions articulated for the project. Both a metric vector containing all metrics defined and a vector containing a minimal number of metrics to collect could be outlined for a study.

5 Experimental Designs

An experimental design can control numerous factors simultaneously and statistically quantify the contributions of individual factors and their interactions on a dependent variable such as a quality or cost measure. Experimental designs provide an empirical approach that bases software process or product evaluation on a representative sample of developers and projects. As mentioned in Section 1.3.3, fractional factorial or randomized block designs usually apply in blocked subject-project studies, while completely randomized or incomplete block designs usually apply in multi-project and replicated project studies.

A summary of an example factorial design applied in [BS87] is as follows. The experimental design distinguishes among three testing techniques, while allowing for variation in the ability of the particular individual testing or in the program being tested. For example, Subject S1 is in the advanced expertise level, and he structurally tested program P1, functionally tested program P2, and code read program P3. All of the subjects tested each of the three programs and used each of the three techniques. Of course, no one tests a given program more than once.

5.1 Independent and Dependent Variables

The experimental design has the three independent variables of testing technique, software type, and level of expertise. The three main effects have the following levels:

- (1) testing technique: code reading, functional testing, and structural testing

- (2) software type: (P1) text processing, (P2) numeric abstract data type, and (P3) database maintainer

- (3) level of expertise: advanced, intermediate, and junior

Every combination of these levels occurs in the design. That is, programmers in all three levels of expertise applied all three testing techniques on all programs. In addition to these three main effects, a factorial analysis of variance (Anova) model supports the analysis of interactions among each of these main effects [CC50] [BHH78]. Thus, the interaction effects of testing technique X software type, testing technique X expertise level, software type X expertise level, and the three-way interaction of testing technique X software type X expertise level are included in the model. There are several dependent variables examined in the study, including number of faults detected, percentage of faults detected, total fault detection time, and fault detection rate. Observations from the on-line methods of functional and structural testing also had as dependent variables number of computer runs, amount of cpu-time consumed, maximum statement coverage achieved, connect time used, number of faults that were observable from the test data, percentage of faults that were observable from the test data, and percentage of faults observable in the from the test data that were actually observed by the tester.

5.2 Analysis of Variance Model

The three main effects and all the two-way and three-way interactions effects are called fixed effects in this factorial analysis of variance model. The levels of these effects given above represent all levels of interest in this example investigation. For example, the effect of testing technique has as particular levels code reading, functional testing, and structural testing; these particular testing techniques are the only ones under comparison in the study. The effect of the particular subjects that participated in the study requires a little different interpretation. The subjects examined in the study were random samples of programmers from the large population of programmers at each of the levels of expertise. Thus, the effect of the subjects on the various dependent variables is a random variable, and this effect therefore is called a random effect. If the samples examined are truly representative of the population of subjects at each expertise level, the inferences from the analysis can then be generalized across the whole population of subjects at each expertise level, not just across the particular subjects in the sample chosen. Since the analysis of variance model contains both fixed and random effects, it is called a mixed model.

6 Infrastructure for Measurement

Measurement-driven analysis and feedback systems enable developers to define empirically guided processes for software development and maintenance. These systems enable developers to achieve SEI process maturity levels 4 and 5, "managed" and "optimizing" processes. A fundamental principle in these systems is to make measurement active by integrating measurement and process, which contrasts with the primarily passive use of measurement in the past. A second principle is that these systems should provide capabilities for user-specifiable interpretation of process events, object state changes, and calendar time abstractions in order to allow a representative basis for project analysis. Another principle is that these systems should provide an extensible integration framework that supports the addition of new techniques and integrates approaches for synergistic application.

These and other architectural principles have been embodied in various prototype systems. Several metric-based analysis systems have been proposed or are under development: *Amadeus* [SPSB91], *TAME* [BR88], *Ginger* [TKiMK89], *MAE* [HMKD82] [Har92], *SME* [DV89], *SMA* [SYTP85], and *AMS* [MRW77], among others. These systems support empirically based techniques for using measurements to describe, analyze, and control software systems and their development processes. These modeling techniques leverage past experience and have many desirable properties, including being scalable to large systems, integratable, and calibratable to new projects. The underlying capabilities of these systems facilitate the definition, collection, analysis, and feedback of empirical metric data -- software *metrics* are numeric and symbolic abstractions of software artifacts, e.g., components, processes, systems. There are also several general paradigms for empirically based software development and evaluation: Basili's improvement paradigm [BR88] [Bas85], Humphrey/SEI's process maturity levels 4 and 5 [Hum88], McCall/RADC's factor-criteria-metric paradigm [MRW77], Basili/Weiss' goal-question-metric (GQM) paradigm [BW84], Selby/ Porter's classification paradigm [SP88], and Weiderman/SEI's environment evaluation methodology [WHBK86], among others.

Amadeus is one example prototype system that is intended to demonstrate the feasibility and merit of these systems and the principles for designing them. The *Amadeus* system provides an interactive script language that encapsulates environment mechanisms for static and dynamic interpretation of process events, object state changes, and calendar time abstractions. These three event types can be combined to form compound events, e.g., object changes and time abstractions can be combined in an event defined as "every time an object changes but no more frequently than daily." The system is composed of software environment architecture components, such as event monitors, data integration frameworks, and a language interpreter, as well as capabilities for specifying empirical analyses, collecting the underlying data, and feeding the results back into development processes. The *Amadeus* system embodies:

- scalable, calibratable, empirically based evaluation and analysis,

- triggering based on events from process model or program executions, object state changes, or calendar time abstractions,

- static or dynamic event interpretation,

- separation of event and agent specification,

- transparent, concurrent data collection, and

- low entry barrier through script reuse.

The *Amadeus* system can provide services to several different types of users. Software developers may use the system to localize components likely to be error-prone or to identify components likely to be reusable. Project managers may use the system to monitor human resource expenditure or system progress. Analysts and experimenters may use the system to compare the effectiveness of different processes or tools or to generate error frequency profiles. Validation studies showed that the Amadeus empirical guidance features correctly categorized 89.6 percent of the software components on the average, according to whether or not they were within a particular target class (such as having high errors or high development effort) [MS90]. The guidance had 79.5 percent consistency and 69.1 percent completeness on the average, which are measures of the intersection between the set of components predicted to be within the target class and those actually within it.

7 Concluding Remarks

Effective software measurement and experimentation requires a wide spectrum of issues to be addressed. This paper highlights selected current and future research issues and directions in several areas: frameworks for measurement and experimentation, existing measures, determining appropriate measures, data collection, experimental designs, and infrastructure for measurement. Some example issues for future discussion are the following. What formalisms are appropriate for expressing measurement goals? What degree of automation can be achieved in goal definition, metric selection, data collection, feedback, etc.? What should measurement infrastructure provide in order to enable the merging of large-scale projects with large-scale empirical studies? How can measurement researchers and practitioners cooperate to define a common set of abstract interfaces to enable interoperability of the numerous measurement tools and systems? How could we create, manage, and share a common metric data repository that would enable meaningful comparative analyses?

References

[AE92]   W. W. Agresti and W. Evanco. Projecting software defects from analyzing ada designs. *IEEE Transactions on Software Engineering*, SE-18(11), November 1992.

[BAB87]   C. E. Brophy, W. W. Agresti, and V. R. Basili. Lessons learned in use of Ada-oriented design methods. In *Proceedings of the Fifth National Conference on Ada Technology*, Arlington, VA, March 1987.

[Bak72]   F. T. Baker. Chief programmer team management of production programming. *IBM Systems Journal*, 11(1):131-149, 1972.

[Bas85]   Victor R. Basili. Quantitative evaluation of software methodology. In *Proceedings of the First Pan Pacific Computer Conference*, Melbourne, Australia, September 1985.

[BB81]   J. W. Bailey and V. R. Basili. A meta-model for software development resource expenditures. In *Proceedings of the Fifth International Conference on Software Engineering*, pages 107-116, San Diego, CA, 1981.

[BBT92]   L. Briand, V. Basili, and M. Thomas. A pattern recognition approach for software engineering data analysis. *IEEE Transactions on Software Engineering*, SE-18(11), November 1992.

[BGS84]   B. W. Boehm, T. E. Gray, and T. Seewaldt. Prototyping versus specifying: A multiproject experiment. *IEEE Transactions on Software Engineering*, SE-10(3):290-303, May 1984.

[BHH78]   G. E. P. Box, W. G. Hunter, and J. S. Hunter. *Statistics for Experimenters*. John Wiley & Sons, New York, 1978.

[BK83]   V. R. Basili and E. E. Katz. Metrics of interest in an Ada development. In *IEEE Workshop on Software Engineering Technology Transfer*, pages 22-29, Miami, FL, April 1983.

[BK86]   V. R. Basili and E. E. Katz. A formalization and categorization of software metrics. Technical report, Department of Computer Science, University of Maryland, College Park, 1986. (working paper).

[BL72]   Les Belady and Manny Lehman. An introduction to growth dynamics. In W. Freiberger, editor, *Proc. Conference on Statistical Computer Performance Evaluation*, pages 503-511, Academic Press, 1972.

[Boe81]   B. W. Boehm. *Software Engineering Economics*. Prentice-Hall, Inc., Englewood Cliffs, NJ, 1981.

[Boe87]   Barry Boehm. Industrial software metrics top 10 list. *IEEE Software*, 4(5):84-85, September 1987.

[BP84]   V. R. Basili and B. T. Perricone. Software errors and complexity: An empirical investigation. *Communications of the ACM*, 27(1):42-52, January 1984.

[BR88]   V. R. Basili and H. D. Rombach. The TAME project: Towards improvement-oriented software environments. *IEEE Transactions on Software Engineering*, SE-14(6):758-773, June 1988.

[Bre89]   Ralph Brettschneider. Is your software ready for release? *IEEE Software*, 6(4):100,102,108, July 1989.

[Bro80]   R. E. Brooks. Studying programmer behavior: the problem of proper methodology. *Communications of the ACM*, 23(4):207-213, 1980.

[BS84]   Victor R. Basili and Richard W. Selby. Data collection and analysis in software research and management. In *Proceedings of the American Statistical Association and Biometric Society Joint Statistical Meetings*, Philadelphia, PA, August 1984.

[BS85]   Victor R. Basili and Richard W. Selby. Calculation and use of an environment's characteristic software metric set. In *Proceedings of the Eighth International Conference on Software Engineering*, London, August 1985.

[BS87]   Victor R. Basili and Richard W. Selby. Computing the effectiveness of software testing strategies. *IEEE Transactions on Software Engineering*, SE-13(12):1278-1296, December 1987.

[BSH86]   Victor R. Basili, Richard W. Selby, and David H. Hutchens. Experimentation in software engineering. *IEEE Transactions on Software Engineering*, SE-12(7):733-743, July 1986.

[BSP83]   Victor R. Basili, Richard W. Selby, and Tsai Y. Phillips. Metric analysis and data validation across Fortran projects. *IEEE Transactions on Software Engineering*, SE-9(6):652-663, November 1983.

[BW84]   V.R. Basili and D. M. Weiss. A methodology for collecting valid software engineering data. *IEEE Transactions on Software Engineering*, SE-10(6):728-738, November 1984.

[BZM+77]   V.R. Basili, M. V. Zelkowitz, F. E. McGarry, Jr. R. W. Reiter, W. F. Truszkowski, and D. L. Weiss. The software engineering laboratory. Technical Report SEL-77-001, Software Engineering Laboratory, NASA/Goddard Space Flight Center, Greenbelt, MD, May 1977.

[Car92]   Anita Carleton. Software engineering institute software metrics initiative. In *Proceedings of STARS 92 conference*, Washington, D. C., December 1992.

[CC50]   W. G. Cochran and G. M. Cox. *Experimental Design*. John Wiley & Sons, New York, 1950.

[CM78]   J P. Cavano and J. A. McCall. A framework for the measurement of sofwtare quality. In *Proc. Software Quality and Assurance Workshop*, pages 133-139, San Diego, CA, November 1978.

[CSM79]   B. Curtis, S. B. Sheppard, and P. M. Milliman. Third time charm: Stronger replication of the ability of software complexity metrics to predict programmer performance. *Proceedings of the Fourth International Conference on Software Engineering*, pages 356-360, September 1979.

[Cur80]   Bill Curtis. Measurement and experimentation in software engineering. *Proceedings of the IEEE*, 68(9):1144-1157, September 1980. Also in [Cur81].

[Cur81]   Bill Curits. Overviews. In *Tutorial: Human Factors in Software Development*, pages 1-6, 7-8, 79-80, 279-280, 381-382, 483-484, 531-532, 589. IEEE Computer Society Press, 1981.

[Cus92]   Michael Cusumano. *Japan Software Factories: A Challenge for U.S. Management*. 1992.

[DV89]   W. Decker and J. Valett. Software management environment (SME) concepts and architecture. Technical Report SEL-89-003, NASA Goddard, Greenbelt, Maryland, August 1989.

[Els84]   J. L. Elshoff. Characteristic program complexity metrics. In *Proceedings of the Seventh International Conference on Software Engineering.*, pages 288-293, Orlando, FL, 1984.

[ESS92]   S. Eick, E. Steffen, and E. Sumner. Seesoft - A tool for visualizing software. *IEEE Transactions on Sofwtare Engineering*, SE-18(11), November 1992.

[Fen92]   Norm Fenton. Software measurment. In *Proceedings of the Dagstuhl Software Measurement Workshop*, Germany, September 1992.

[Har92]   Warren Harrison. Software measurement representation and analysis. In *Proceedings of the Dagstuhl Software Measurement Workshop*, Germany, September 1992.

[HMKD82]   Warren Harrison, Keneth Magel, Raymond Kluczny, and Arlan DeKock. Applying software complexity metrics to program maintenance. *IEEE Computer*, 15(9),:65-79, Septmeber 1982. Also appeared in the IEEE Computer Society *Tutorial on Software Restructuring*, order number 680.

[Hum88]   W. S. Humphrey. Characterizing the software process: A maturity framework. *IEEE Software*, 5(2):73-79, March 1988.

[Hum89]   Watts Humphrey. Quality form both developer and user viewpoints. *IEEE Software*, 6(5):84,100, September 1989.

[Leh69]   Manny Lehman. The programming process. Technical Report RC2722, IBM Research Report, December 1969.

[MRW77]   J. A. McCall, P. Richards, and G. Walters. Factors in software quality. Technical Report RADC-TR-77-369, Rome Air Development Center, Griffiss Air Force Base, NY, November 1977.

[MS82]   T. Moher and G. M. Schneider. Methodology and experimental research in software engineering. *International Journal of Man-Machine Studies*, 16(1):65-87, 1982.

[MS90]   R. Kent Madsen and Richard W. Selby. Metric-driven classification networks for identifying high-risk software components. In *Proceedings of the International Conference on Applications of Software Measurement*, San Diego, CA, November 1990.

[Mus89]   John Musa. Faults, failures, and a metrics revolution. *IEEE Software*, 6(2):85,91, March 1989.

[OW84]   T. J. Ostrand and E. J. Weyuker. Collecting and categorizing software error data in an industrial environment. *Journal of Systems and Software*, 4:289-300, 1984.

[Par72]   D. L. Parnas. Some conclusions from an experiment in software engineering techniques. *AFIPS Proceedings from the 1972 Fall Joint Computer Conference*, 41:325-329, 1972.

[Pfl91]   Shari Lawrence Pfleeger. Multiple metric graphs. In *Proceedings the Software Quality Workshop*, Alexandria Bay, NY, AUgust 1991.

[Sch92]   Norm Schneidewind. Software metric validations. In *Proceedings of the Dagstuhl Software Measurement Workshop*, Germany, September 1992.

[SE84]   E. Soloway and K. Ehrlich. Empirical Studies of programming knowledge. *IEEE Transactions on Software Engineering*, SE-10(5):595-609, September 1984.

[Sel85]   Richard W. Selby. Evaluations of software technologies: Testing, cleanroom, and metrics. Technical Report TR-1500, Department of Computer Science, University of Maryland, College Park, 1985. Ph.D. Dissertation.

[She81]   B. A. Sheil. The psychological study of programming. *ACM Computing Surveys.*, 13:101-120, March 1981.

[SP88]   Richard W. Selby and Adam A. Porter. Learning from Examples: Generation and evaluation of decision tress for software resource analysis. *IEEE Transactions on Software Engineering*, SE-14(12):1743-1757, December 1988.

[SPSB91]   Richard W. Selby, Adam A. Porter, Doug C. Schmidt, and James Berney. Metric driven analysis and fedback systems for enabling empirically guided software development. In *Proceedings of the Tirteenth International Conference on Software Engineering*, Austria, TX, May 1991.

[SYTP85]   V. Y. Shen, T. J. Yu, S. M. Thebaut, and L. R. Paulsen. Identifying error-prone software - an emperical study. *IEEE Transactions on Software Engineering*, SE-11(4):317-324, April 1985.

[TKiMK89]   Koji Torii, Tohuro Kikuno, Ken ichi Matsumoto, and Shinji Kusumoto. A data collection and analysis system Ginger to improve programmer productivity on software development. Technical Report, Osaka University, Osaka, Japan, 1989.

[WF77]   C. E. Walston and C. P. Felix. A method of programming measurement and estimation. *IBM Systems Journal*, 16(1):54-73, 1977.

[WHBK86]   N. H. Weiderman, A. N. Habermann, M. W. Borger, and M. H. Klein. A methodology for evaluating environments. In *Proceedings of the First ACM SIGSOFT/SIGPLAN Software Engineering Symposium on Practical Software Development Environments*, pages 199 - 207, Palo Alto, California, December 1986.

[Zel92]   Marv Zelkowitz. Axiomatic analyses of software measurement. In *Proceedings of the Dagstuhl Software Measurement Workshop*, Germany, September 1992.

[Zus90]   Horst Zuse. *Software Complexity Metrics*. 1990.

[Zwe92]   Stu Zweben. Axiomatic analyses of software metrics. In *Proceedings of the Dagstuhl Software Measurement Workshop*, Germany, September 1992.

Towards Well-Defined, Shareable Product Data

Warren Harrison

PSU Center for Software Quality Research
Portland State University
Portland, OR 97207-0751

1 Introduction

A major problem in experimental software engineering is the collection, maintenance and use of data. Data, especially industrial data, is painfully hard to find. Even when it is available, both its reliability and its consistency is in question. Furthermore, comparability across different data sets is hopeless - different conventions and formats are almost always used.

It seems clear that in order for experimental software engineering to advance, these issues must be addressed - after all, an experimental science is based on collecting and analyzing data. However, without readily available, consistent and reliable data we will never be able to draw meaningful conclusions. Two types of data are of interest to researchers: product data and process data. Product data refers to the measurement of the product (typically the software itself) while process data refers to the measurement of the process (eg, time to develop, number of code errors, etc.). This paper focuses on the problem of collecting, maintaining and sharing product data. While not necessarily any more important than process data, the ability to realistically automate the collection of product data suggests this as the more practical avenue of effort.

2 Problems With the Current State of the Practice

Perhaps the most visible symptom of the problems with the current state of software product measurement is the inconsistency of conclusions. A case in point is Software Complexity Metrics. Since the early 1970's, countless experimental studies have been published, some in support of various Complexity Metrics, others showing various Complexity Metrics are virtually worthless. There are at least two foundational problems which contribute to this symptom.

2.1 Inability to Use Prior Data Sets

First and foremost, virtually every study published is based on a different data set. In some cases, this is desirable. For instance, if one is trying to validate a metric which has been previously proposed and evaluated using empirical data, bringing additional data to bear on the problem can add to our understanding of the metric. On the other hand, if a new metric, or some modification of an existing metric is proposed, one should be able to see how the new metric or modification fares when applied to prior data sets before we even start looking for new data sets. Unfortunately, such a scenario is currently out of the question. With a few notable exceptions, such as the SEL and DACS collections, data is almost never shared among unrelated researchers. Thus, we will often see a new metric or modification that performs much better than an existing metric on a new data set, but will be unable to assess its performance on data from prior studies. Thus, we start from scratch each time a new metric is proposed. The net result is that we may have to reject years of accumulated data analysis on the basis of one or two new studies. Rather than "standing on the shoulders of giants" we end up stepping on each other's toes.

In fairness, of course, we must recognize that in the case of industrial product data, a researcher is fortunate indeed to simply be able to collect and retain the metrics. It is virtually unheard of for a researcher to be allowed to also keep the source code. Thus, even if researchers may be inclined to share their data, future analysis will be limited to whatever metrics happened to be collected during the original field work.

2.2 Inconsistent Counting Rules

Often a study purports to be a validation (or invalidation, as the case may be) of an existing metric, when in reality, due to subtle differences in counting rules it is actually a modification of the metric. Often such a situation is noticed when the results of studies appear strangely inconsistent. For instance, in a hypothetical example, one study may report on the superior performance of Software Science measures computed on a file-by-file basis in identifying error prone modules. Subsequently, a later study in which Software Science measures are computed on a function-by-function basis may report poor performance at exactly the same task.

When researchers go out of their way to replicate the counting rules of prior studies the descriptions of the counting rules used are usually incomplete. For instance, in the case of the C programming language, how are ifdef's counted? The code in the ifdefs? Are define'd constants that represent operators (eg, #define BEGIN {) treated as operators or operands? The only adequate description of the counting rules used is the source code of the analyzer that extracts the measures.

3 Well-Defined, Shareable Product Representations

No tool, proposal of data collection methodologies or other technical innovation can change the willingness of a researcher to share their data. This can only be addressed by the reward system within which most of us work. Proposing ways to encourage the sharing of data is outside the scope of this proposal. We will limit our discussion to those problems which have a "technical solution".

It is clear that any technical solution must address two points: (1) data must be available in a form that allows researchers in the future to explore different measures or counting rules than the ones originally used so prior data can be used to support new metrics, while at the same time ensuring that the original source code cannot be regenerated and (2) the data must support a way to completely and concisely articulate the counting rules that were originally used so new data can be added to the current collection rather than replacing it.

There is one general approach to collecting software product data that can address both points. This involves maintaining a database of specific characteristics of the software product from which the metrics can be extracted. This differs markedly from most current efforts which only store the metrics themselves. Likewise, if a standard database schema is published, the definition of a metric can be given as the query upon the schema necessary used to compute the metrics.

We have recently been experimenting with a PROLOG implementation of a schema first proposed in [1]. The schema (in PDC PROLOG) is presented for illustrative purposes only. Much work must still be done to arrive at a concensus before any standard can even be proposed.

```
code_line(line_id,line_type)
statement(stmt_id,stmt_type)
identifier(identifier_id,identifier_alias,identifier_type)
operator(operator_id,operator_item)
proc(proc_id,proc_name)
makes_up(line_id,proc_id)
appears(line_id,stmt_id)
executed_in(operator_id,stmt_id)
used_in(identifier_id,stmt_id)
assigned_in(identifier_id,stmt_id)
invokes(stmt_id,proc_id)
```

This schema provides the flexibility to support a variety of counting rules and metrics. In fact, this schema can support most code-level metrics and counting rules proposed over the last decade. As a consequence, prior data could be used to help validate metrics which were not known when the data was originally collected.

Besides sharing data, a standard metric repository schema could also yield more rigorous and replicable definitions of metrics and counting rules. For instance, the following example defines a "decision count" metric for a given procedure. Because such a definition is from the actual executable code used to make the computations, ambiguity is not possible.

```
do_dec_count(Proc):-
    findall(Stmt_ID,decision_in_proc(Stmt_ID,Proc),DecList),
    length_of(DecList,DecCount),
    write(DecCount).
```

```
decision_in_proc(Stmt_ID,Proc):-
    proc(Proc_ID,Proc),
    makes_up(Line_ID,Proc_ID),
    appears(Line_ID,Stmt_ID),
    executed_in(Operator_ID,Stmt_ID),
    operator(Operator_ID,OpItem),
    decision_ops(OpItem).
```

An added bonus of using PROLOG as the database language, is that "queries" can be phrased in a predicate calculus form, allowing the procedural aspects to be ignored. Likewise, such queries are usually concise enough to allow them to be published as part of a paper (or at least an appendix).

4 Future Steps

Before any such "universal schema" can be seriously proposed, much work must be done. Researchers must arrive at an agreement regarding:

1. which specific data objects which must be recorded in the database

2. which relationships among data objects should be preserved in the database.

In addition, a mechanism must be established by which data in this form can be made readily available to other researchers, while at the same time insuring the original collector of the data is appropriately credited for his/her effort.

Of course, we will not see the full impact of establishing a universal schema for product data until a similar set of conventions and formats can be established for process data as well.

References

1. W. Harrison: "MAE: A Syntactic Metric Analysis Environment", The Journal of Systems and Software, 1988.

A View on the Use of Three Research Philosophies to Address Empirically Determined Weaknesses of the Software Engineering Process

Ross Jeffery

University of New South Wales

1 Introduction

In a recently conducted interview survey of thirteen commercially oriented organizations and software companies (Jeffery 1992), it was found that the area of overwhelming concern about the software process in those organizations centred on requirements establishment and post implementation system evolution. The almost unanimous view was that the design, code, and test activities were in control. This is not to imply that these latter activities were at optimum, but rather that the other activities were presenting more obvious problems to the software managers. A summary of the managers concerns as expressed in this study is given in Table 1.

Process Issues

Level of Importance

Category	#1	#2	#3	#4	#5	Total
User requirement/ Specification	5	3	2			10
Project Management	2	1				3
Strategic Direction	2					2
System Enhancement	1	5			1	7
User relationships	1		1			2
Re-engineering	1		1			2
Hardware Platform	1			1		2
Time to produce		2				2
Defined Process Quality				2		2
Configuration Management			1			1
Reuse				2	2	4
Totals	13	11	5	5	3	37

Table 1: Process Issues

The category which had both the largest total number of responses as well as the largest "most important" response was that of specification difficulties. Managers reported the following.

> "Our software process works well if the requirements are well documented, understood, and signed off. When this is not the case the process is difficult to control."

> "The second most important issue we have is that of ensuring that we understand the users' requirements."

> "Our major concern is the provision of sufficient manpower to liaise with users in the field in order to understand their requirements."

> "Our (requirements) process is currently quite ad hoc. Problems are experienced in understanding user requirements."

> "Keeping up with rapidly changing business requirements is difficult."

> "User requirements are hard to define. The systems do not meet their needs."

The categories of strategic direction, user relationships, project management, and system enhancement also centred around difficulties with requirements. For example, "understanding the company strategy and managing the software process so that the systems meet this is the main issue" according to one manager. In the area of project management, the issue also came down to the difficulties of managing the process in an environment of evolving and changing user requirements. A similar underlying cause was evident in the category of system enhancement. As was stated:

> "Maintenance is not a problem of coding, but one of understanding the user needs. Maintenance issues are a function of user requirements."

> "The changing business requirement is hard to track. Maintenance is seen as a back room function, but that is not where the issue is."

If we combine the user requirements, user relationships, strategic direction, project management, and system enhancement categories which all derive from requirements issues, we see that they account for 22 of the 37 issues (59%) reported. Moreover, they account for 20 of the 24 top two responses (83%).

The other problem areas are either technical or process related issues. The technical issues concern (a) one organization in the process of moving to a distributed open system hardware/software environment, and (b) difficulties in effectively re-engineering applications and making the decision to rebuild or re-engineer. Other process issues were largely the result of recognized needed improvement in the software process of the organization. This was evidenced by difficulties in (a) configuration management, (b) system delivery rates, and (c) less than satisfactory process definition in the organization. These particular process problems were largely seen as solveable with the current knowledge, management, and technology, but were never-the-less major practical issues at this point in time in these organizations.

The opinion was stated by Brooks (1987) and picked up by Harel (1992) that the main problem we have today is in specifying, designing and testing the "conceptual construct" underlying the system. In this study we were interested to see if through the efforts, developments, and products of recent years, the software problems were now largely constrained to this "conceptual construct", or whether major issues remained in the design and construction of the software product.

Software engineering encompasses both technical and social components. Activities such as "obtaining requirements, discussing design options, performing walk-throughs, prototyping, and the like, are all intensely social in nature" (Hirschheim & Newman 1991). It is in these software lifecycle sub-processes, that encompass a higher degree of social components, that we see the relative lack of success as evidenced by Jeffery (1992).

The questions of importance to the software engineering researcher are:

1. What is it about our research and development that has led to this, and

2. What research techniques are appropriate to the resolution of these weaknesses?.

2 Research Approaches

There is little doubt that much of the current success in the technical domain has arisen as a result of the past computing research concentration on languages and techniques. The solution to our weaknesses lies perhaps in the alternative research philosophies which might be applied to software engineering. Chua (1986), classified research epistemologies into positivist, interpretive, and critical studies. Positivist research can be theory-test based or descriptive (Orlikowski & Baroudi, 1991).

The premise of theory-test based positivist research is a fixed relationship surmised on the basis of theory which is tested by some form of structured instrumentation. Thus there is a process of measurement aimed at hypothesis testing. The findings of this style of experimentation aim to increase our understanding of future events through evidence concerning the validity of the tested theory. An example of descriptive positivist research is case study research where, rather than pursuing hypothesis testing, the research aims to describe the research object, with a goal of deriving lessons applicable to other environments. Two criticisms which have been levelled at positivist research are (1) that the search for universal laws tends to lead to insufficient consideration of the context and history of the events under study, and (2) that the research is restricted to stimulus/response experimentation which may not be adequate to describe the social setting within which the ! phenomena of interest normally tak es place. Both of these criticisms could likely be applicable in some software engineering research.

Interpretive studies attempt to understand the phenomena without searching for determinism or universal laws. The interpretive aim is to generate an understanding of outcomes based on the context, the participants, and the resources. It is therefore deeper knowledge than is likely under positivist research. This type of research rejects the notion of "factual" description of events but attempts to understand the phenomena behind behaviour. Thus one study is not used to predict the outcome in other settings. Rather the study leads to an understanding of the phenomena behind the observed behaviour. It is also realized in interpretive research that the researcher may intervene in a research setting, because of prior knowledge and beliefs, and therefore in part create the reality being studied. Using interpretive research it s possible to (a) generate hypotheses for positivist research, and (b) triangulate between positivist and interpretive studies.

Critical studies aim to transform the status quo by taking an active stance toward the phenomenon under study and critical attitudes toward the status quo. It is assumed that social reality is historically constituted and therefore it is possible for the researcher to enact change.

One of the common problems in positivist research in social environments is that the interpretation of the findings will be based on incomplete information. For example the Jeffery & Lawrence (1985) study concluded, in part, that the higher programming delivery rates evidenced in programs where no time estimates were calculated before programming commenced, was likely the result of these tasks being at the small and/or simple end of the program set. De Marco (1987) interpreted the same results as being likely due to the improved motivation provided when tight control was absent in the professional work environment. Both conclusions are possible because of the absence of real data in the study on these variables. Other positivist research at University of New South Wales exhibits this limitation (Dean, 1991). In this study into the relationships between programming performance, resources and group processes it was found that understanding of group processes in the program! ming domain could be studied only in a limited way within the positivist theory-test framework.

Interpretive research at the University of New South Wales into productivity of lower CASE tools (Low & Jeffery, 1989) has provided, through detailed interviews (a) an understanding of elements of the software process from the participants perspective, and (b) triangulation and insight into the positivist findings of empirical research. In this work rather than coming to the study with a well-defined set of instruments and constructs, it was decided that better findings were likely if the constructs were derived from an understanding of the phenomena (i.e. CASE tool usage) derived from in-depth examination. It is unlikely that positivist research in this case would have been able to provide the insight available from detailed participant interviews in the field. These are examples of how a more complete understanding of the software process will require the use of both positivist and interpretive philosophies.

Another piece of the puzzle will be provided through the critical research philosophy. If we recognize weaknesses in the current process, then research which aims to change the status quo can provide an effective vehicle for process improvement. Both positivist and interpretive philosophies have weaknesses in identifying improvement strategies if these strategies are beyond the proficiency of the participants studied. The SEI CMM work has some of the characteristics of this research philosophy.

3 Conclusions

Returning to the study of software process issues, it is likely that empirical interpretive research will be a necessary form for those areas in which social activities make up a significant component of the process problem type. This would be the case for the identified areas of requirements specification, project management, strategic direction, system enhancement, and user relationships (the five most problemmatic areas). This is not to sya that critical research may not contribute to these and the other problem areas, but critical research gains are more difficult to predict because of their dependence on positive insights, usually from individuals. Other areas such as re-engineering decisions, probably lend themselves more to positivist research because of the relatively simple decision goals involved which have a high technical componentand lower social component.

References

F.P.Brooks, "No Silver Bullet: Essence and Accidents of Software Engineering," *Computer*, 20,4, 1987, pp.10-19.

Chua, W.F. (1986) "Radical Developments in Accounting Thought," *The Accounting Review*, 61, pp. 601-632.

Dean, R.G. 1990, The Relationship Between Group Cohesion, Group Resource and Group Performance - unpublished Masters Thesis, University of New South Wales.

De Marco, T & Lister T. (1987), *Peopleware: Productive Projects and Teams*, Dorset House, Publishing Co. Inc.

David Harel, "Biting the Silver Bullet," *Computer*, 25,1, 1992, IEEE Computer Society, pp.8-20.

Hirschheim, R & Newman, M (1991), "Symbolism and Information Systems Development: Myth, Metaphor and Magic", *Information Systems Research*, 2:1. The Institute of Management Sciences, pp. 29-62.

Jeffery, D.R. & Lawrence, M.J. (1985) "Managing Programming Productivity, *Journal of Systems and Software*, 5, 49-58.

Jeffery, D.R. (1992), "Process and Environment Problems and Solutions: A Practitioner View," *4th International Symposium on Future Software Environments*, Sydney, 1992.

Low, G & Jeffery, D.R. "Productivity Issues in the Use of Current Back-end CASE Tools", 3rd International Workshop on CASE, *Case 89*, IEEE & BCS, July 1989, London.

Orlikowski, W.J. & Baroudi, J.J. "Studying Information Technology in Organizations: Research Approaches and assumptions." *Information Systems Research*, 2:1, TIMS, pp. 1-28.

Bridging the Gap between Research and Practice in Software Engineering Management: Reflections on the Staffing Factors Paradox

Chris F. Kemerer

MIT Sloan School of Management

First, let me thank the organizers of this Dagstuhl Seminar on Experimental Software Engineering Issues for creating this unique opportunity for dialogue between researchers and practitioners in software engineering. As a former manager of software development and a current researcher in software engineering management, I feel keenly the need for greater communication between these two groups if we are to make progress on the issues on our shared agenda.

The gaps between our two communities are typically discussed in very general terms. Practitioners are seeking workable solutions to current problems. Researchers are concerned with performing research that is highly rigorous and sufficiently generalizable. Yet, we have as our common goal the eventual improvement of software engineering practice.

To illustrate the type of problems we face and the steps we might take to alleviate them, I will focus in this position statement on a single example, what will be referred to as the "Staffing Factors Paradox."

The Staffing Factors Paradox

If you were to give an experienced project manager a proposal and schedule for a software development project, but allow her to dictate one other factor, what would she choose? Most project managers that I know would want to select the staff members to be assigned to the project. This would be in preference to choosing a hardware platform, software tools, or even the identity of the user.[1] The conventional wisdom on this topic is that with a small team of highly capable performers almost anything is possible. This conventional wisdom is commonly expressed in several ways. For example, we are told of order of magnitude differences in individual productivity, usually documented with an anecdotal story of an entire system that was re-written by some hero over the weekend. Or, claims of success for new tools or techniques on pilot projects are discredited though the comment that "any tool would look great with that hand-picked team."[2]

Now, let us contrast that with the attitude adopted by researchers in the field of software engineering management. In developing models to support cost estimation, pro-

---

[1] Although this last item might be a close second!

[2] This line of reasoning was employed, for example, in the early 1970's to discredit IBM's experience with the chief programmer's team concept on the New York Times project.

ductivity evaluation, or other outcomes of interest we confine ourselves to the metric of "man-months", even though we know that all such man-months are not created equal. Sometimes we will use man-months, but add one or more independent variables to the model to attempt to account for the quality of the project team. These variables are generally highly subjective and poorly scaled, a combination that severely limits their predictive ability.

In fact, in one of those coincidences that arise from gatherings like this workshop, I have learned that the chair of this session, Barbara Kitchenham, and I both recently independently documented that the typical staffing variables added to cost estimation models provide no predictive value.[3] In Kitchenham's analysis of the MERMAID data-set and the COCOMO data-set no independent effect was found for either experience or ability. My review of other published work found similar results.

This differential belief in the value of staffing factors by researchers and practitioners thus presents us with a paradox. How can managers place such great stock in these ideas, yet researchers either ignore them, or are unable to validate these results when they try?

Let's start with those researchers who ignore these factors by not including them in their models. I doubt that this is due to a lack of belief in their importance. More likely is the fact that it is simply very difficult to collect these data in the field, given (1) the poor job done by most organizations at keeping project staffing records, and (2) managers' sensitivity about permitting access to any data deemed confidential.

While omitting important variables from models produces very poor results in any research, software engineering field research is especially vulnerable given our typically small sample sizes. Another problem with failing to include staffing variables in our models is that it severely limits our ability to investigate many phenomena of interest. For example, the empirical literature has generally been unable to document claims of improved productivity for new software engineering tools and techniques. One possible explanation for this is that there is a learning or investment phase that organizations must go through initially in order to reap benefits later. Unfortunately, documenting this phenomenon will require the collection of data concerning the project teams that used these tools, in particular, their degree of training, experience, and skill in using the tools, data that are not collected on a routine basis by any organization with which I am familiar.

From a practitioner's point of view there are other important deficiencies inherent in the simple man or work-month variable. For example, the salary cost of 100 work-months of senior staff is considerably more than 100 work-months of junior staff, yet cost (as opposed to effort) is rarely modeled. And much has already been written about

---

[3]See Kitchenham, B.A. "Empirical Studies of assumptions that underlie software cost-estimation models", *Information and Software Technology 34*, 4 (1992) pp. 211-218 and Kemerer, C.F. and M.W. Patrick. "Staffing Factors in Software Cost Estimation Models", in Keyes, J. ed., *The Handbook of Software Engineering Productivity*, McGraw-Hill, New York, NY, 1992.

the common failure even to document what we mean by a work-month as to whose hours are included and what project phases are considered.

Alternatively, when we do attempt to include staffing variables in our models, they are often poorly measured. For example, we still include the variable "years of experience", despite the fact that we strongly suspect that the effects of experience are non-linear. While great gains are made from year 0 to year 1, and gains likely continue into year 2, beyond this a decline in the rate of growth seems likely.[4] How great the decline probably relates to the individual's specific duties, i.e., whether five years of experience represent increasing responsibilities, or merely the same year of experience repeated five times. In particular, "years of experience" is likely to be an imperfect substitute for the real variable of interest, which is ability. For example, a person who has been "fast-tracked" to a senior programmer/analyst position is likely to have higher ability than a regular programmer/analyst with more years of experience.

A cooperative research experience

To illustrate how such limitations can be overcome, I will briefly describe a research project I was involved with at a large commercial bank.[5] The bank's IS managers were interested in identifying factors that affected the productivity of their maintenance projects.[6] In terms of the staffing variables we captured in our model, two bear mentioning here. Rather than letting industry experience stand in for the relevant variables, we used previously collected data from the bank's human resource group to match project hour data with staff members' yearly performance evaluation ratings, which were rated on a 1 (best) to 5 (worst) scale. As a variable in the model we used the percentage of the project's hours that were charged by the staff who were rated as above average (1s and 2s). This was designed to reflect the ability levels represented on the team. In addition, we collected data from the project team members about the number of months experience they had with the individual applications being maintained. The idea that differentiates this from other work is that while individuals may have many years of industry experience, they may have been assigned to a particular application only recently. For maintenance it is this specific experience that is likely to be the most relevant. This was modeled as a binary variable where "1" indicated that at least one member of the project team had 24 or more months experience with the application,

---

[4]Jeffery, D. R. and M. J. Lawrence, "Managing Programming Productivity", Journal of Systems and Software, 5, 49-58, (1985).

[5]Banker, R.D., S.M. Datar and C.F. Kemerer, "Factors Affecting Software Maintenance Productivity: An Exploratory Study", Proceedings of the 8th International Conference on Information Systems, (ICIS) (December 1987, Pittsburgh, Pennsylvania), pp. 160-175.

[6]As another example of the disconnection between research and practice, maintenance is a topic that has been generally under-researched relative to its practical importance. See, for example, Schneidewind, N. F., "The State of Software Maintenance", IEEE Transactions on Software Engineering, SE-13, (3): 303-310, (March 1987) and Bendifallah, S. and W. Scacchi, "Understanding Software Maintenance Work", IEEE Transactions on Software Engineering, SE-13, (3): 311-323, (March 1987).

under the assumption that such an individual's experience could be leveraged across the small project group of maintainers.

Both the ability variable and the application experience variable were statistically significant at the 95% confidence level in the expected directions. One beneficial effect of this was that it reassured managers that the model had surface validity. More importantly, the inclusion of the staffing variables allowed greater confidence in our interpretation of the other variables in the model. For example, the significant impact on productivity of the use of a particular technology could not be conveniently but inaccurately attributed to the chance assignment of staff to use it.

Recommendations and points for discussion

From this example, I think there are a number of general points that may be made about the Staffing Factors Paradox and about industry-researcher relationships. For researchers, I think more attention needs to be paid to practitioners' views on the important elements of research questions. In the case of staffing factors we need to expend greater effort to create better operationalizations of variables like ability, experience, and motivation. This is also an excellent opportunity for us to bridge the gap between field researchers and laboratory researchers who have done considerable work in these areas.[7] At a minimum, when inclusion is not possible, we need to note explicitly in our papers (and in the papers we influence, such as those we review and edit and those written by our students), when such variables have been omitted to raise the general level of consciousness and research standards around this issue.

For practitioners, the main message is that you need to collect detailed data on your projects if you expect your staff and/or outside researchers to be able to draw useful lessons from the experience.[8] More specifically, you need to develop mechanisms and disciplines within your organizations to deal with what are almost always considered very sensitive data. Data on training and experience need not be threatening, and can be collected in a skills inventory database, which also serves as a useful project planning aid. Data related to the ability of project team members are a more difficult issue. In some organizations, job titles, which are public, can serve as surrogates. In organizations where this is not the case, attempts need to be made to include salary or other confidential data in the models in order to weight the staffing variables appropriately. In order to protect individuals' legitimate rights to privacy, strict procedures must be followed to sufficiently aggregate or code the data so that no single individual's data can be extracted. One probable outcome of this procedure is that small projects will not be included in the database at all since it may prove impossible to safeguard such

---

[7]Curtis, B. "Fifteen Years of Psychology in Software Engineering: Individual Differences and Cognitive Science", in DeMarco T. and T. Lister ed., *Software State of the Art: Selected Papers*, Dorset House, New York, NY, 1990.

[8]Collecting better data is a commonly espoused theme, but one that is getting increased attention with the current emphasis on the SEI maturity model. See also Deutsch, M. S., "An Exploratory Analysis Relating the Software Project Management Process to Project Success", *IEEE Transactions on Engineering Management*, 38, (4): 365-375, (November 1991) for an example of the types of data that might be useful.

data. However, this is not too high a price to pay, especially given that most often our interest is in leveraging our knowledge against the large projects.

In summary, while the focus here has been on the Staffing Factors Paradox, this is meant merely as an illustration of the types of software engineering management problems that will require significant joint industry-researcher cooperation if we are to achieve our shared goals. An event such as this seminar provides us with a useful vehicle with which to start the process.

A methodology for evaluating
software engineering methods and tools

Barbara Kitchenham

National Computing Centre
Oxford Road
Manchester M1 7ED

Abstract. The DESMET project is attempting to develop a methodology for evaluating software engineering methods and tools. DESMET supports quantitative and qualitative assessments. It leads to organisation dependent comparisons using locally defined measurements.

1 Introduction

There are numerous methods and tools which the vendors/developers claim will improve software development. Managers in the IT industry need to be able to select methods/tools that are appropriate for their own organisations. Thus, the IT industry needs methods of evaluating the effects of methods and tools that assist initial selection of methods/tools, and the monitoring of the impact of any selection.

The DESMET project, which is collaborative project part-funded by the U.K. Department of Trade and Industry, aims to provide a methodology to support method/tool evaluation. DESMET views the issue as an example of *industrial experimentation* in which the manager has a *hypothesis* about the benefit of a method or tool and needs an unbiased means of *testing* his/her hypothesis.

After doing a review of current evaluation methods, we concluded that a complete evaluation methodology should:

i.   Address qualitative as well as quantitative evaluation techniques.

ii.   Give an evaluator guidance on which evaluation method was most appropriate given his/her specific requirements and constraints.

iii.   Provide clear guidelines for performing a specific evaluation exercise that would consider both technical concerns such as the problems of determining the controls and using surrogate measures, and managerial and sociological issues such as the motivation of the people taking part in an evaluation exercise and the "doctor effect".

iv.   Provide guidelines for software data collection, storage and analysis to support quantitative evaluations.

This paper discusses the basic approach taken by DESMET to experimentation and measurement.

2　Evaluation Framework

Disciplines such as medicine share with software engineering the problem that the *effect* of *treatments* (e.g. drugs in medicine, tools in software engineering) is affected by the individuals who use them. In medicine a variety of techniques are used to evaluate treatments: formal experiments, case studies, large scale trials, epidemiological studies etc. DESMET therefore attempted to identify a variety of basic experimental methods that would be appropriate in different circumstances. In particular we attempted to separate the *technical organisation* of an evaluation from the *results* of an evaluation.

We selected three technical organisation types: formal experiments, case studies, and surveys; and three result types: quantitative assessment, qualitative assessment, and a hybrid type, expert opinion which is a subjective assessment of quantitative effects.

We have developed a procedure for determining the most appropriate evaluation method given:

- the nature of the expected impact of the method/tool (quantitative/qualitative);
- the nature of the treatment (method/tool/generic method);
- the measurement capability of the organisation doing the evaluation;
- the scope of the treatment (e.g. whether it acts on the product as a whole or product components, whether it affects many phases or a single phase, or other projects);
- the maturity of the treatment (e.g. the extent to which the treatment is already used in the organisation or elsewhere);
- the learning time associated with the treatment.

3　Status of work

3.1　Basic approach

Our basic approach has been to develop a common terminology for evaluation based as far as possible on the terms used in formal experimental design. The most important concept is the experimental *hypothesis*. Evaluators must define what it is they want to know, in order to select the appropriate evaluation method and determine (for quantitative approaches) what needs to be measured. The concept of an hypothesis leads to the view of evaluation as a *comparison* of the status quo against some alternative.

3.2　Quantitative evaluation methods

We have identified the basic differences between the approaches in terms of the trade-off between the precision of experimental results, the representativeness of case study results, and the generality of survey results.

Our approach has been to use the common evaluation terminology to highlight the similarities and the differences between the evaluation methods. In particular, we have found it useful to consider the different ways that formal experiments, case studies and surveys use the concepts of *blocking* and *replication*. For example:

- *formal experiments* use blocking to control variability (we can identify factors such as staff experience and ensure that we select subjects at random from different experience groups);

- *case studies* use blocking to establish the extent of variability (we can identify the type of projects performed in an organisation and their frequency in order to select representative projects for case studies);

- *surveys* use blocking to partition the data and minimise extraneous variability during analysis.

Currently, we are developing guidelines for quantitative case studies, these cover the definition, design, implementation and analysis of an evaluation exercise. A particular area of concern, has been to identify appropriate *baselines* or controls against which the use of a new method/tool can be compared. We have identified three basic methods: cross project comparisons, within project comparisons, organisational baselines.

3.3   Measurement

The DESMET project has adopted a Data Collection and Storage tool, developed partly by the ESPRIT MERMAID project, as a means of collecting software engineering data. It permits the user to specify a *local data model*, including definitions of all the required measurements. The tool generates a data base to store the collected data and provides several mechanisms for collecting project data.

3.4   Evaluating the DESMET approach

In parallel with the development of the evaluation methods, the project has also been concerned with the evaluation of the DESMET methodology itself. The project plans to establish the appropriate evaluation method for its various elements and undertake appropriate industrial evaluations.

4   Conclusions

Within the context of industrial evaluations of method and tools, DESMET suggests the following answers to the questions raised in this seminar concerning procedures and mechanisms for measurement/experimentation.

Question: How should we perform measurement and experimentation?

Answer: Experimentation and measurement should be performed within a specific organisation. A variety of experimental methods are available and the selection should depend on the experimental goals and the specific circumstances of the experimenter.

Question: How should we specify objectives and context characteristics?

Answer: Objectives should be specified in terms of an experimental hypothesis. The context characteristics for a specific experiment are given in the six bullet points in section 2. In addition, the characteristics of a specific organisation should be modelled as state variables describing the types of projects undertaken and development constraints enforced.

Question: What models and measures exist?

Answer: Most quantitative evaluations are concerned with assessing improvements in quality and/or productivity. The means by which these attributes can be measured are context dependent, but there are more than enough suggestion in the literature. For experimentation, the types of models we require are: *process models* to decide at what point in the lifecycle measurements should be take, and *experimental designs* with their associated statistical models.

Question: How should we determine the appropriate measures for a given objective.

Answer: By correct formulation of the experimental hypothesis which should define what we expect to happen, to which software properties, at what point in the lifecycle.

Question: How should we design appropriate experiments?

Answer: Carefully. We should select the appropriate experimental method after reviewing the criteria presented in section 2. We should specify our hypothesis fully, in order to determine what to measure and what the basis of our comparisons will be.

Question: How should we collect and validate data (especially process data)?

Answer: We should ensure our metrics and our counting rules are consistent with the working practices of our own organisation. We should integrate data collection with software development and utilise existing data collection systems. We should not expect software data in industry to be as accurate as in an experimental laboratory. However, this is not a serious objection to industrial experiments because industry is only likely to be interested in effects large enough to show up even in noisy data.

Experimental Software Engineering Should Concentrate on Software Evolution

Hausi A. Müller

Department of Computer Science, University of Victoria
Victoria, British Columbia, Canada V8W 3P6

Abstract. For the future of software engineering it is critical that we devote sufficient energies to software evolution commensurate with its socio-economic implications. We propose that the area of experimental software engineering focus more on software analysis and understanding to reflect the needs of large, evolving software systems properly. Since the results of evolution experiments do not necessarily scale up, we argue that the experiments should be performed in situ using large systems such as telephone switching systems, banking systems, or health information systems which evolve naturally over decades. We outline two evolution experiments which aim to measure time and effort spent for certain evolution tasks using different software analysis and understanding strategies. Finally, our position is summarized by three theses.

1. Introduction

Experimental research in computer science in general and software engineering in particular is a relatively new area and perhaps controversial in nature. One area of controversy is its focus: software construction vs. software evolution. Currently computer science education prepare future software engineers with a background that encourages fresh creation almost exclusively. Moreover, software engineering research largely concentrates on the early phases of the software process and neglects, comparably, software maintenance and evolution where the critical aspects are analysis and understanding. As a consequence, experimental software engineering also focuses to a large extent on software construction as opposed to software analysis and understanding.

2. Concentrate on Software Evolution

We propose that the area of experimental software engineering focus more on software analysis and understanding to reflect the needs of software evolution properly. The task of implementing enhancements in systems which evolve naturally over long periods of time (*e.g.*, telephone switching systems, banking systems, health information system, or pervasive computer vendor products), is very difficult and requires enormous amounts of resources. In these systems, it is quite common that most of the time spent in implementing an enhancement is actually spent studying and analyzing the systems.

It is also worth pointing out that results of software analysis and understanding experiments designed for toy systems rarely scale up. Thus, evolution experiments should be performed in situ using large, industrial software systems.

We actually claim that it is easier for university researchers to perform maintenance and evolution experiments rather than software construction experiments because of the vast amount of data that is available. In addition, in our experience the results of maintenance and evolution experiments are almost always applicable to software construction in one form or another.

To illustrate our ideas, the next sections propose two evolution experiments which aim to compare time and effort spent for certain evolution tasks by applying different software analysis and understanding strategies.

3. Separation of Concerns vs. Tight Integration

In telephone switching systems new functionality is added periodically to reflect the latest market needs and trends. For example at Bell Northern research (BNR) almost all development is evolution. Their DMS telephone switching system currently consists of approximately twenty million lines of code. This system has to be continually enhanced with new functionality, adapted to new technologies, and improved to reflect the quality-driven development process. The DMS development process is designed for evolution because short design intervals constitute the critical competitive edge for the company. Thus, new releases are produced on a regular schedule (*i.e.*, every six months). A new release typically adds more than one million lines of code to the DMS software base. Thus, with every release the maintenance and evolution problem is compounded by an additional million lines of code.

Surprisingly, one of the reasons for this tremendous growth is well-established software engineering principles. Good software engineering practice advocates information hiding and separation of concerns. As a consequence, systems which have to evolve over a long period of time and on a tight schedule are enhanced by adding subsystems which interact with the rest of the system through a small and well-defined interface. To isolate the new code from the old code often large amounts of glue code have to be introduced. Such firewalls (*i.e.*, small interfaces) between new and old code result in great benefits during development and testing of the new functionality: they help to ensure that the old code is not affected (*i.e.*, the functionality of the previous version of the system is provably preserved). However, as soon as the new version has been released the problems with this strategy begin. The amount of glue code required to separate the new code from the old code is typically substantial and is often larger than the code that implements the actual enhancement. As a consequence, for all subsequent development, maintenance, and evolution the software engineers not only have to cope with the small enhancement but also with these large amounts of glue code. After a number of releases the resulting system resembles a quilt or a patchwork which exacerbates the maintenance and evolution problems considerably.

An alternative approach tries to minimize the amount of glue code required to add enhancements to the system. In order to eliminate the glue code the enhancements need to be tightly integrated into the existing system. This approach is only feasible if the software engineers are able to analyze the existing system with high confidence in a reasonable amount of time. In particular, they need to be able to determine the impact of changes on the entire system with high accuracy.

We are currently investigating how to conduct an experiment that compares these two different approaches to software evolution. The goal of the experiment is to measure the time and effort required to implement specific enhancements for different integration strategies (*i.e.*, tight integration vs. large amounts of glue code).

4. Tailor System Composition to Evolution Task

Banks have to update their systems regularly to implement new or changed business rules or tax laws. To determine the *extent* of a business rule or a tax law in a twenty to thirty year-old banking system is a non-trivial task. Large parts of the system have to be carefully investigated to determine the exact ramifications of such a rule or a law before it can be modified with high confidence.

Now suppose that the extent of a business rule or a tax law were concentrated in a single module, a subsystem, or a class. Note that such a system decomposition might violate software engineering principles such as few and small interfaces among subsystems. But given such a modularization of the system the modification task would be considerably less complicated since it would simply involve a single subsystem.

There are numerous reasons for why the existing code cannot be re-modularized to achieve the desired effect. However, one could build virtual system abstractions representing business rules and tax laws without changing the actual source code. One of the abstractions might be a subsystem decomposition by (sets of) business rule(s) and/or tax law(s). Reverse engineering technology could be used to identify such abstractions.

Over the past five years, we have developed a reverse engineering and program understanding system, called Rigi, which could be used to extract and store such system abstractions effectively without modifying the underlying source code [1,2]. In the last two years we started to apply this technology to real-world software systems and obtained some very encouraging results. In particular, we analyzed a health information system without any foreknowledge of the actual system. Once the analysis was complete, we presented the system abstractions we extracted from the source code to two maintainers of the system. Although the maintainers had never seen these structures and we had no foreknowledge of the actual application, we were able to talk with each other about the architecture of the system and its implications effectively. The system abstractions were in fact compatible with the mental model the maintainers had formed of the system over a number of years [3].

We are now planning an evolution experiment whose objective is to compare the time and effort it takes to identify and change a business rule or a tax law in a banking system given various kinds of system abstractions.

5. Conclusions

We conclude by proposing a major realignment of software engineering education and research to strengthen the foundations of software evolution. For the future of software engineering it is critical that we devote sufficient energies to software evolution commensurate with its socio-economic implications. Since experimental software engineering is a relatively new area, we have a chance to concentrate on evolution experiments and thus have the possibility of affecting computing practice significantly and effectively.

Thesis I *Shift experimental software engineering research efforts from software construction to software analysis and understanding.*

Thesis II *Concentrate on sufficiently large evolution experiments using real-world software systems.*

Thesis III *There will always be old software.*

References

1 H.A. Müller, J.S. Uhl: Composing Subsystem Structures Using (K,2)-Partite Graphs. In: *Proceedings of Conference on Software Maintenance - 1990*. San Diego, California, November 26-29, 1990. IEEE Computer Society Press: Order Number 2091, pp. 12-19

2 H.A. Müller, B.D. Corrie, S.R. Tilley, M.A. Orgun, N.H. Madhavji: A Reverse Engineering Environment Based on Spatial and Visual Software Interconnection Models. To appear in: *Proceedings of ACM SIGSOFT '92: Fifth Symposium on Software Development Environments*. Tyson's Corner, Virginia, December 9-11, 1992.

3 H.A. Müller, J.R. Möhr, J.G. McDaniel: Applying Software Re-engineering Techniques to Health Information Systems. In: *Proceedings of IMIA Working Conference on Software Engineering in Medical Informatics (SEMI)*, Amsterdam, October 8-10, 1990. In: T. Timmers, B.I. Blum (eds.): *Software Engineering in Medical Informatics*. Elsevier Science Publishers North Holland 1991, pp. 91-110

Yet Another Laboratory For Software Engineering

Eric Sumner, Jr.

AT&T Bell Laboratories

Abstract

The Software Production Research department is devoted to experimental research in large software engineering. It was formed in the Fall of 1990 at Indian Hill, the Illinois complex that houses many large software developments including that of the 5ESS® switch. In this position paper I describe a key mechanism for interaction between research and development, sketch three activities within the research department, and make some observations about experimental software research.

1 DEVELOPMENT PROCESS MANAGEMENT TEAMS

The development projects at Indian Hill invest 5% of their budgets in process management teams (PMTs) which are responsible for the cost, interval, and quality of each development process (e.g. design, testing, customer documentation, etc.). The teams are staffed by developers who typically have both project and PMT responsibilities. A close working relationship between the research department and the PMTs is achieved by assigning roughly one PMT intern to each researcher. Because the PMTs are process-based they are stable with respect to reorganizations caused by market forces on projects.

The PMTs observe, describe, measure, and analyze each development process. After constructing a baseline description, making measurements, and performing root-cause analysis on process deficiencies they conduct experiments on new process proposals. These proposals are documented in templates that include definition of the metrics which will be used to evaluate the experiment. If the experiment is successful, the PMTs are responsible for project adoption of the new process. Process descriptions, baseline measurements, and proposal templates are stored in a central database.

The research department engages in two types of activities. In the first, we attempt to improve the PMT methodology by inventing new approaches for observation, description, measurement, and analysis of large software system development. In the second, we attempt to improve the development methodology by inventing new processes and associated technologies for developing large software systems. Both types of research are greatly enhanced by ready access to the laboratory provided by the development projects and the PMTs. In the next section I describe two examples of the first type, and one example of the second type.

2 THREE ACTIVITIES

2.1 SeeSoft

The SeeSoft software visualization system allows one to view up to 50,000 lines of code simultaneously by mapping each line of code into a row of pixels. The color of each line indicates a statistic of interest, e.g., red lines are those most recently changed, violet are those least recently changed. SeeSoft displays data derived from a variety of sources, such as

- configuration management systems that track the age, programmer, and purpose of the code, e.g., control ISDN lamps, fix bug in call forwarding,

- static analyses, e.g. locations where functions are called, and

- dynamic analyses, e.g., profiling.

Potential applications for SeeSoft include discovery, training, code tuning, and, most relevant in the context of this paper, development analysis. There is wide variation in development methodology across projects at Indian Hill and the use of configuration management systems is ubiquitous. Therefore, analysts using SeeSoft can investigate the effect on software development of software age, size, language, and process without actively perturbing the system. This analysis is supported by an automated data-gathering system and by a new tool for rapid construction of C analyzers, known as ac. Useful ac programs may be very short (e.g. a program to calculate McCabe complexity is only nine lines).

2.2 Role-Based Process Description

We are investigating a method for process description based upon process roles, responsibilities, and collaborations among roles. Models are built quickly from data gathered in half-day interviews using a CRC card technique borrowed form object-oriented analysis. We have built models with 15 of the PMTs and also process owners from three other companies. A process-model evaluation environment is used to cluster and visualize the data. Roles are displayed as nodes and collaborations as colored edges, where the color is tied to either the type or intensity of the collaboration. Analyses of these models have yielded results that match PMT intuitions while giving them unforeseen process insights. The analyses also point to process characteristics that appear independent of organization and culture. For example, the coder is at the hub of almost every process.

This research has been strongly influenced by our easy access to the PMTs. Initially, we had focused upon a visualization environment for event-action process models. However, attempts to populate such models were frustrated by the discovery of a huge number of states. In addition, it was observed that ~50% of process execution involved inter-role communication which rarely included tangible artifacts. Therefore, we moved to a process characterization which stressed this inter-role communication. Each time we gather data on a new process we expand and modify our interview technique. Modifications are made when the PMTs have difficulty completing interviews or when the models are unable to answer their questions.

2.3 prl5

prl5 is a new language for specifying database integrity constraints. It is supported by tools that automatically generate C code that checks the constraints. Formerly, constraints were expressed in English and manually translated into C. In the last year a team of eight researchers and developers has defined prl5, implemented several processors for it, and developed documentation and training. Hundreds of developers are now writing prl5 code.

Because integrity constraints expressed in prl5 are only one tenth the size of those expressed in C, and because data integrity is critical to the high reliability of many telecommunications products, this collaboration may save the development organization tens of millions of dollars annually. The benefits for the research organization may be correspondingly large. Such benefits include

- new tools for developing tools, such as a*, a generalization of awk that operates on program parse trees (the source of ac);

- new insights into the design and implementation of specification languages;

- new algorithms for deriving constraints on database updates;

- a formal calculus for databases; and

- a system for reverse engineering of transaction-based C programs.

Benefits of this type are likely to accrue when a research organization has the opportunity to work on a problem from concept through development evaluation.

3 SOME OBSERVATIONS

That large software developments are fundamentally different from small developments is widely accepted. However, living and conducting experiments in such an environment serves to reinforce this lesson daily. For example, on a large project the average developer may write only a few lines of code for each formal meeting that he or she attends. Furthermore, large developments are complex and poorly understood. Thus extrapolating results from small experiments is risky, and we must have an active program of large experiments. Because large developments would be prohibitively expensive if their sole purpose were experimentation, we must conduct experiments in collaboration with industry.

If these collaborations are to be effective, they must be close. Analyses of development projects should consider as many projects as possible. Therefore, researchers must have efficient low-overhead means of data collection. Furthermore, because some data may only be correctly interpreted through follow-up conversation with the developers, both data gathering and follow-up must be timely. Experiments that attempt to introduce a new methodology bear the additional constraint that the new methodology is likely to require frequent and timely adjustments.

Close collaboration with industry, in which many of the issues are project-specific, may prove frustrating for researchers. In addition, effective experimental design is very difficult when research is not the primary purpose of a development. However, collocation and a strong process management infrastructure in development may mitigate these problems. In addition, significant research benefits accrue from building systems to be tested in an industrial setting. Finally, dealing with these problems may in fact be required for effective experimental research in large software engineering.

132

An Axiomatic Model for Program Complexity

Marvin V. Zelkowitz

Institute for Advanced Computer Studies and Department of Computer Science,
University of Maryland, College Park, MD 20742

Abstract. In this note we have proposed a set of axioms and a classification scheme that may be used to validate the effectiveness of proposed software productivity measures. We demonstrate the effectiveness of this model by applying a classification tree analysis for high cost modules on 16 NASA Software Engineering Laboratory projects and show that by prescreening the set of measures according to our axioms, we can improve upon the retrieval process.

1 Introduction

Just like there is no best automobile for every possible use and lifestyle, there is no universal program complexity measure that will provide all the information needed during a product development. Because of this, we have been developing a model of complexity where the user specifies a context where measurement is important, and thereafter proposed complexity measures can be evaluated as to applicability within that context.

We can classify software measurements as being *internal* i.e., those measurements depending solely upon the artifacts being produced (e.g., source code, design text, requirements documents) or *external* i.e., those measurements depending upon other factors such as process activities (e.g., computer time, error reports) or knowledge of the observer (e.g., educational level or experience of staff). While external factors provide potentially more useful information about the software development process and the set of *"ilities"* like *reliability, portability, reusability,* and *maintainability* that are of interest, they obviously are more difficult to objectively collect than static measurements of the products themselves.

Because of this, program complexity metrics have and are still being developed for analyzing software artifacts with the implied assumption that objects with a lower complexity (i.e., lower internal measurement) will have a lower external measurement (e.g., more reliable, cheaper to build, more desireable). Most program complexity measures have an ad hoc nature to their definition. What is needed is a more objective basis for deciding upon the potential effectiveness of such measures.

We have been developing a model for program complexity measures [1]. An important distinction between our model and others is that we view complexity as a relation between certain programs (i.e., meaning that some programs are inherently comparable and others are not) and a complexity measure is a "figure of merit" that can be applied to any specific program. Thus program complexity measures, being real numbers, permit any two programs to be compared and are therefore only an approximation to the real nature of program complexity.

Based upon a set of 5 axioms and a classification model based upon the proposed use for complexity, we can determine whether a proposed program complexity measure meets minimal criteria for such a measure. Given several such measures, we can determine which is more appropriate for specific measurement activities. This model addresses the 9 properties identified by Weyuker [2] as desireable for a program complexity meassure, and in one experiment this model has been tested on the classification tree analysis (CTA) model of Selby and Porter [3] using data from the NASA/GSFC Software Engineering Laboratory. We show that by eliminating ineffective measures, we can improve upon the accuracy of the CTA technique in identifying high-cost modules [4].

2   Summary of Model

The following is a brief summary of our model. Greater detail may be found elsewhere [1, 4]. Our goal is to determine a formal basis upon which we may determine whether a proposed measure of program complexity is potentially valid.

Consider a program as a hierarchy of modules consisting of instructions, data, and the underlying execution control mechanism. For this discussion, a syntax like Pascal can be assumed. We view complexity as an ordering among a subset of all programs U. A *complexity ranking* $\mathcal{R}$ is a binary relation on the set of programs. We write the complexity ranking between programs P and Q as $\mathcal{R}(P, Q)$, and we interpret $\mathcal{R}(P, Q)$ as P being no more complex than Q. $\mathcal{C}(P, Q)$ means that P and Q are comparable (either $\mathcal{R}(P, Q)$ or $\mathcal{R}(Q, P)$).

On the other hand, like in normal use, we view a complexity measure as a numerical value associated with any program. A *complexity measure* $\mathcal{V}$ is a function that maps every program into a real number: $\mathcal{V} : \mathbf{U} \rightarrow \mathbb{R}$.

This separation of complexity as an inherent property between some programs and its measurement is the crucial difference between this development and other complexity models.

Our 5 axioms are separated into 3 axioms concerning the underlying complexity ranking between 2 programs ($\mathcal{R}$) and 2 axioms concerning the measure $\mathcal{V}$ as an approximation to this ranking:

1. $(\forall P, Q) (\;\boxed{P} = \boxed{Q}\; \Rightarrow C(P,Q)\;)$ where $\boxed{X}$ is the function of program X. That is, if two programs have the same functionality, they are comparable. This is the basic assumption behind all of program complexity theory since the goal is to choose the program producing function $\boxed{X}$ with least complexity. Since this is undecidable in general, it simply demonstrates why practical and effective program complexity measures have been hard to find.

2. $(\forall P, Q) (IN(P,Q) \Rightarrow C(P,Q)\;)$ where $IN(P,Q)$ means that P is included in Q. A part of a program is comparable with the whole program.

3. $(\exists K \in I\!N)(\forall P, Q)((IN(P,Q) \wedge (dist(P,Q) > K)) \Rightarrow R(P,Q))$ where $dist$ is the number of nodes between P and Q in its syntax tree decomposition. This states that while complexity does not have to be strictly monotonic (e.g., a larger program may be less complex than a smaller program), at some point size does dominate complexity.

4. $(\forall P, Q) (\mathcal{R}(P,Q) \Rightarrow \mathcal{V}(P) \le \mathcal{V}(Q))$. If one program is less complex than another, its complexity measure must show that relationship.

5. $(\forall k \in I\!R)(\exists \delta > 0) (|\mathbf{U} - \{P : \mathcal{V}(P) \in [k - \delta, k + \delta]\}| = |\mathbf{U}|)$. This states that there must be more than one cluster point for such complexity measures.

Axiom 4 is the linkage between our complexity ranking and the usual notion of a complexity measure. It demonstrates another unique factor of this model– other models assume any two programs may be compared (i.e., the statement of axiom 4 would be "if and only if") while we assume that *if* two programs are comparable, then one has less complexity than the other. Determining whether these programs *are* comparable, is obviously the difficulty. But explicitly expressing this property demonstrates why such measures have been hard to develop.

In addition to the axioms which all complexity measures must adhere to, we considered a classification model for identification of specific measures for specific applications. Assessing complexity by using only syntactic components while ignoring interactions is a *context free* ranking. A complexity ranking $\mathcal{R}$ is *interactional* if it is not context free.

A complexity ranking is *primitive* if all programs with the same set of syntax nodes implies that the programs are comparable.

Without considering interaction, the complexity of the composite complexity is the sum of all the components complexities. However, due to interaction among component parts, the total complexity may be greater than the sum. Such a complexity ranking is called *overall*.

If we are allowed to modify the internal structure or reorganize the program according to some programming practices (such as modularization, data abstraction and information hiding), we may be able to lower interfacing complexity. Since the two programs are functionally equivalent, they are comparable in complexity (by axiom 2).

3 Application of Model

Sixteen software systems, ranging from 3 000 to 112 000 lines of FORTRAN source code, were selected from NASA ground support software for unmanned spacecraft developed at the Software Engineering Laboratory at Goddard Space Flight Center. Using estimating cost of producing a module as our goal, we applied this model to the 74 measures collected by NASA on each module. This resulted in 18 remaining measures. Applying Selby and Porter's classification tree analysis (a form of decision tree process for identification of high cost modules) on these 18 measures, rather than on the original set of 74, we showed that we needed smaller trees (9.1 versus 12.5 nodes) representing less data that needed to be collected. We had a slight improvement (from 69% to 74%) in making correct matches between predicted and actual costs and achieved improved consistency (correct identification of high cost modules) (from 38% to 50%). Both techniques achieved high identification of all modules (about 97%) and comparable identification of actual high cost modules at 35%.

While this does not prove the validity of this model, it does demonstrate that it is a reasonable step in trying to build a formal model of program complexity.

Acknowledgement

This research was performed jointly with Jianhui Tian, now with the IBM Laboratories, Ontario, Canada. This research was supported in part by National Science Foundation grant CCR-8819793 and National Aeronautics and Space Administration grant NSG-5123 to the University of Maryland.

References

1. J. Tian and M. V. Zelkowitz: A formal model of program complexity and its application. Journal of Systems and Software 17:3 253-266 (1992)
2. E. J. Weyuker: Evaluating Software Complexity Measures. IEEE Trans. on Software Engineering 14:9 1357-1365 (1988)
3. A. A. Porter and R. W. Selby: Empirically Guided Software Development Using Metric-Based Classification Trees. IEEE Software 7:2 46-54 (March, 1990)
4. J. Tian, A. Porter and M. V. Zelkowitz: An Improved Classification Tree Analysis of High Cost Modules Based Upon an Axiomatic Definition of Complexity. IEEE 3rd International Symposium on Software Reliability Engineering, Research Triangle Park, NC (October, 1992)

Support of Experimentation by Measurement Theory

Horst Zuse

Technische Universität Berlin (FR 5-3)
Franklinstraße 28/29
1 Berlin 10 (Germany)
Phone: +49-30-314-73439
Fax: +49-30-314-21103
Internet: ZUSE TUBVM.CS.TU-BERLIN.DE

1 Introduction

During the last years much attention has been directed toward the measurement of the properties and the complexity of software. The major goal using software measures is to get reliable software, an objective representation of the properties of software and the software development process by numbers, and a prediction which factors of software complexity have an influence to software maintenance complexity. Hundreds of software measures have been developed in order to determine the static complexity of single programs (intra-modular complexity) and of entire software systems (inter-modular complexity) during the phases of the software life-cycle. These investigations have been supported by experiments.

Since software complexity cannot be defined mathematically it is necessary to make experiments in order to get correlations between software measures and attributes of software like errors or factors of software maintenance. Validation of software measures is another important topic. However, to validate measures and to interpret correlations between attributes of software is not an easy task. We think, that measurement theory can help here to get better results.

Roberts /ROBE79/, p.2, describes some of the advantages of measurement: if we can measure things, we can begin to differentiate more than we can by simply classifying. For example, we can do more than simply distinguishing between warm objects and cold ones; we can assign degrees of warmth. Greater descriptive flexibility leads to greater flexibility in the formulation of general laws. This is also important for software measurement.

2 What is Measurement?

We introduce measurement as it is seen by Roberts /ROBE79/, Krantz et al. /KRAN71/ and Luce et al. /LUCE90/ very briefly. Measurement is a mapping of empirical objects to numerical objects by a homomorphism. Krantz et al. (/KRAN71/, p.33, line 13) write the following in the introduction of their book: *Here, by contrast, we are concerned almost exclusively with the qualitative conditions under which a particular representation holds.* That means, measurement is based on a homomorphism between the empirical und numerical relational systems related to a measure. Measurement theory gives qualitative (empirical) conditions for the use of measures and hypothesis about the reality.

Kriz /KRIZ88/ gives a good explanation of the benefits of measurement in general. Kriz introduced the following picture.

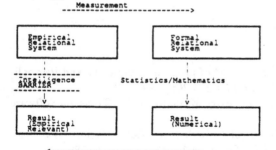

Figure 2.1: The measurement process as presented by Kriz /KRIZ88/. The empirical and formal relational systems are explained below.

Users want to have relevant empirical results of problems in reality. For example, users want to have relevant empirical statements about the complexity of programs. However, our human brain, in many of the cases, is not able to produce directly relevant empirical results. An exception is, for example, the length of wooden boards. In this case humans can make clear relevant empirical statements. However, considering the complexity of programs, the human brain is very often not able to make such statements. The relevant empirical statements related to software complexity can change over the time and people have different ideas of complexity. In many cases the human brain is unable to make relevant empirical decisions. Kriz calls this problem the "intelligence barrier". That means, in many cases, the human brain is not able to reduce informations without certain help.

In order to overcome the problem of the intelligence barrier measurement is introduced. Measurement is a mapping of empirical objects ("Empirical relational system") to numerical(mathematical) objects ("Formal relational system") by a homomorphism. Mathematics is used to process the informations. Doing this we get mathematical results ("Result numerical"). Now, the important step is to give the mathematical results an empirical meaning (empirical interpretation). The most important point of measurement is to give an interpretation of the numbers. In this case without an interpretation of the numbers it is not possible to make empirical statements. Measurement theory, as presented by Roberts /ROBE79/, Krantz et al. /KRAN71/ and Luce et al. /LUCE90/ gives the (relevant) empirical interpretation of the numbers by the empirical relational system. For this reason we introduce measurement theory.

Measurement is important in all sciences. Roberts /ROBE79/ supports this view and he writes in the introduction of his book about measurement: *"A major difference between a "well-developed" science such as physics and some of the "less well-developed" sciences such as psychology or sociology is the degree of which things are measured".* We mean that this is also true for software engineering.

3 Software Measures and Experiments

During the past many experiments related to software measures were done. These experimentations are close connected with the problem of the validation of measures. We now discuss some goals of experiments.

3.1 Goals of Correlations

The following list gives some goals of carrying out experiments in the area of software measures.

1. To get correlations between software measures and errors. These correlations should be used to make predictions of errors in the maintenance phase of a software system from early phases of the software life-cycle.
2. Correlations between software measures, software measures and factors of software maintenance or software measures and a software quality attribute.

However, the calculation and interpretation of correlations between objects is not without problems.

3.2 Problems with Correlations

Calculating correlations causes many problems. We will mention some of them here.

*   Using correlation coefficients the determination of the scale level is important and necessary. The question is: what is behind a scale?
*   The results of correlations coefficient can be differently if the scale level of the measurement process is unclear. That can lead to wrong results.
*   The correlations of the three most used correlation coefficients (Pearson, Spearman and Kendall Tau) can be differently if there are many programs in the same rank. In such a case it is necessary to analyze the reasons for that.
*   If the Pearson correlation coefficient is less than the Spearman and Kendall Tau correlation coefficients, a non-linear relationship between the variables is possible or there are problems with the level of scale.
*   The correlations between software measures are situation dependant. Correlations between software measures are mostly not high or low per se. It depends on the structure of the programs and the properties of software complexity measures.
*   Knowing exactly the properties of the software complexity measures an interpretation of the correlation coefficients related to the program structure is possible.
*   It is evident that a high correlation coefficient between measures is not a reason to replace a measure by another measure.
*   Correlations between software complexity measures and errors can lead to wrong results. It is not clear of what scale type errors are. A validation of software measures related to errors has to be done very carefully.

- Correlations between two variables (here software complexity measures or errors) is a necessary, but not a sufficient prerequisite for causal relationships. Correlations give indications where could be causal relationships. This indications should be checked by precisely prepared experiments. A correlation coefficient can be interpreted in the following ways, if x and y are the two variables:

1.   x influences y causally.
2.   y influences x causally.
3.   x and y are causally influenced by further variables.
4.   x interacts with y causally.

Mostly, there are correlations of the type 3. That is important if we consider, for example, the correlations between errors and software measures. This correlation can be caused by further variables, for example, deeply nested loops.

In general we say that there should be a hypothesis why there could be correlations between objects or the attributes of objects. Only a mathematical correlation is not helpful, an empirical interpretation is necessary.

4 Validation of a Software Measure

Validation of measures is a difficult task. We give a definition of validation by Fenton /FENT91/, p.82: *Validation of a software measure of the process of ensuring that the measure is a proper numerical characterization of the claimed attribute; this means showing that the representation condition is satisfied.*

It is important to notice that a measure has to be validated related to an attribute, like errors or factors of software maintenance or another software quality attribute. For example, it makes no sense to validate the cyclomatic number because it is a value of a mathematical function without any empirical meaning.

For example, validating the Measure MCC-V=|E|-|N|+2 of McCabe related to errors in the maintenance phase would mean: Under the assumption of transitivity and reflexivity the Measures of McCabe can be used as an ordinal scale, if and only if for all flowgraphs P,P' ∈ P, the following three conditions hold /ZUSE91/, p.161, /ZUSE91a/:

e1:   If P results from P' by inserting an edge, then P is more complex than P'.

e2:   If P results from P' by inserting an edge and a node, then P and P' are equally complex.

e3:   If P results from P' by transfering an edge from one location to another location, then P and P' are equally complex.

The conditions e1, e2, and e3 describe the ranking order of flowgraphs by the Measure MCC-V=|E|-|N|+2. This concept describing the ordinal property of measures by such elementary conditions was introduced in /ZUSE89/ and applied in /ZUSE91/. This concept makes it easier to understand the idea of complexity behind a measure. Of course the Measure of McCabe can also be used as an ordinal scale if the user accepts the ranking order of the flowgraphs by the measure.

Validating the Measure of McCabe related to errors would mean that the number of errors has something to do with the three conditions e1, e2 and e3. We think this is questionable. In the case of e1 there could be a relation between errors. However, related to e2 the measurement values of the Measures of McCabe remain unchanged and the number of errors could increase. With condition e3 flowgraphs can be modified but the complexity remains unchanged. Here we see a benefit of measurement theory because measurement theory gives the conditions of a measure for an ordinal scale which makes the property of the Measure of McCabe more clear.

In the case that the three conditions could be validated by an experiment the Measure of McCabe would be validated as an ordinal scale.

Another important question is whether it is possible to validate the Measure of McCabe as a ratio scale. The conditions for the ratio scale can be found in /ZUSE91/, p.49-57. What are the conditions for the validation? The answer gives measurement theory. Having established a concatenation operation of flowgraphs then the Measure MCC-V2=|E|-|N|+1 of McCabe is validated as a ratio scale if it is validated as an ordinal scale /ZUSE91/, p.49-57, /ZUSE91a/. Here we see the a further benefit of measurement theory because measurement theory gives the conditions of a measure for a ratio scale und supports validating a software measure.

5 Results of Measurement Theory

Measurement theory related to software measures is discussed in detail in /ZUSE89/, /ZUSE91/, /ZUSE91a/ and /ZUSE93/. We now summarize the results.

- Measurement theory deals with the connection of the empirical world and the world of numbers.

- Measurement theory gives hypotheses about reality by the empirical relational systems.
- Measurement theory gives the conditions for scales, among others, via Theorem 4.1 /ZUSE91/, p.50.
- Measurement theory gives hypotheses about experiments in form of axioms. It helps to figure out contradictions done by experiments.
- Measurement theory gives the empirical interpretation of the meaning of numbers by the empirical relational systems.
- Measurement theory allows to formulate more precisely the terms complexity, understandability and comprehension of software.
- Measurement theory helps to understand requirements for software measures. For example, it can be easily shown that Weyuker /WEYU88/ requires with the property P9: $\mu(P1 \circ P2) > \mu(P1) + \mu(P2)$ the ratio scale. Considering the admissible transformations of the nominal, ordinal, interval and ratio scale, the statement above is only meaningful for the ratio scale /ZUSE91/, p.45. However, Weyuker is rejecting the ratio scale with the properties P7 (weak commutativity) /ZUSE91/, p.57, and P6a, P6b /ZUSE91a/, /ZUSE93/. The properties P6a and P6b are identical with condition C1 in /ZUSE91/. Condition C1 is also a prerequisite for the ratio scale. This shows that measurement theory can help to get more clearity considering conditions for software measures. It also helps to figure out contradictions.

6 Experiments in the Future

We mean that measurement theory (among others) can help to support experiments in the future. Since measurement theory gives a better understanding of the properties of measures by axioms and gives hypotheses about reality, experiments can be better understood. The question for measurement scales is a major question because behind the scales are properties of measures and hypothesis about reality.

7 References

/KRAN71/   Krantz, David H.; Luce, R. Duncan; Suppes; Patrick; Tversky, Amos:
Foundations of Measurement - Additive and Polynominal Representation, Academic Press, Vol. 1, 1971

/KRIZ88/   Kriz, Jürgen:
Facts and Artefacts in Social Science: An Ephistemological and Methodological Analysis of Empirical Social Science Research Techniques. McGraw Hill Research, 1988

/LUCE90/   Luce, R. Duncan; Krantz, David H.; Suppes; Patrick; Tversky, Amos:
Foundations of Measurement, Vol 3, Academic Press, 1990

/ROBE79/   Roberts, Fred S.:
Measurement Theory with Applications to Decisionmaking, Utility, and the Social Sciences Encyclopedia of Mathematics and its Applications Addison Wesley Publishing Company, 1979

/WEYU88/   Weyuker, Elaine J.:
Evaluating Software Complexity Measures IEEE Transactions of Software Engineering Vol. 14, No. 9, Sept. 88.

/ZUSE89/   Zuse, Horst; Bollmann, P.:
Using Measurement Theory to Describe the Properties and Scales of Static Software Complexity Metrics Sigplan Notices, Vol. 24, No. 8, pp.23-33, August 1989.

/ZUSE91/   Zuse, Horst:
Software Complexity: Measures and Methods, DeGruyter Publisher 1991, Berlin, New York, 605 pages, 498 figures.

/ZUSE91a/ Zuse, Horst; Bollmann, Peter:
Measurement Theory and Software Measures. In: Proceedings of the International BCS-FACS Workshop (Formal Aspects of Computer Software), May 3, 1991, South Bank Polytechnic, London, UK", by T.Denvir, R.Herman and R.Whitty (Eds.), ISBN 3-540-19788-5, will appear in October 1992, Springer Publisher, Springer Verlag London Ltd, Springer House, 8 Alexandra Road, Wimbledon, London SW19 7JZ, UK.

/ZUSE93/   Zuse, Horst:
Properties of Software Measures. Will Appear in SOFTWARE QUALITY JOURNAL, 1993.

Session 3 Summary
Procedures and Mechanisms for
Measurement/Experimentation

Barbara Kitchenham

National Computing Centre
Oxford Road
Manchester M1 7ED

The purpose of this session was to discuss the procedures and mechanisms that can be used for measuring software items and undertaking software experiments. As agreed earlier in the workshop, the term experimentation covers both informal investigations as well as formal experiments.

The specific questions that were addressed by the session were:

- What models and measures exist?

- How should we collect and validate data?

- How should we specify objectives and context characteristics?

- How should we perform measurement and experimentation?

- How should we design experiments?

- How should we determine appropriate measures for a given objective?

The comments made on these topics in session 3 and throughout the workshop are summarised in the following sections.

What models and measures exist?

Throughout the workshop, it was emphasised that there were no "magic bullets". In this context, it was agreed that there were no models, measures or "metrics" that were appropriate in all situations.

The main interest of the workshop participants was the use of models from measurement theory. Measurement theory can be used to ensure that:

- complex metrics are constructed correctly (e.g. we do not add a ratio scale measure to an interval scale measure);

- the methods of data analysis applied to sets of data are valid (e.g. we do not derive the mean of a set of ordinal scale metrics)

- axiomatic representations of "ideal" metric properties are well-formulated (e.g. that sets of axioms that are meant to describe the properties of complexity metrics are internally consistent).

Thus, measurement theory can be used to ensure the internal validity of metrics. Horst Zuse gave a practical example of the use of measurement theory by demonstrating that Weyuker's complexity metric axioms [1] were internally inconsistent.

It was perhaps surprising that no mention was made of the statistical models (other than reliability models) or formal experimental design either in this session or during the workshop as a whole.

In terms of actual measurements, the most frequently referred to measure seemed to be lines of code. Although there are numerous criticisms of lines of code, many participants admitted that they used lines of code quite succesfully as long as they ensured that the metric was fully defined. Manny Lehman suggested that even simpler counts such as the number of modules were extremely useful for studies of system evolution.

How should we collect and validate data?

Warren Harrison suggested that the development of low-level primitives derived from programming languages to represent software programs that could be used to generate "new" metrics. The use of a "language" for representing programs would encourage industry to make software available to academic researchers because it would allow confidentiality to be maintained. It would also encourage independent validation of metrics because proposed metrics could be tested on a number of different dataset.

This approach was quite controversial. A number of participants mentioned the need to consider design and specification metrics rather than concentrating on code metrics. In addition, the approach could not be applied to 4GLs or graphical langugaes.

Later presentations and workshop discussions considered other aspects of metrics validation. In particular the issue of statistical validation was discussed. This involves confirming that metrics related to software design or code are correlated with process metrics such as the number of faults in programs or the amount of effort required to develop programs.

There was some concern about the issue of re-validation. If we use our metrics to identify potential problem modules and intervene to alleviate those problems we expect to remove the relationships. The participants disagreed as to whether this just meant that trigger levels at which intervention occured would change or whether re-validation would demand different types of analysis and/or the collection of additional contextual data.

How should we specify objectives and context characteristics?

Vic Basili (in session 1) and Richard Selby (in session 3) both presented the Goal-Question-Metric paradigm as the main mechanism for specifying objectives supported by the framework for measurement and experimentation [2].

Walter Tichy suggested that there was a major flaw in framework with respect to a method for comparing tools with one another. Both Selby and Basili suggested that tool comparisons was just as specific focus, but Tichy argued that the framework did not adequately support objective comparisons of tool performance independent of the tool development process. Discussions later in the workshop suggested that benchmarks might be used to undertake this form of investigation.[*]

How should we perform measurement and experimentation?

Several speakers addressed the topic of how we should undertake experiments. Chris Kemerer advocated bridging the gap between academic research and industrial problems by usign practitioners as experimental subjects in formally designed experiments that address industrial concerns. Hausi Müller suggested that the ongoing evolution of large projects over many years provided a ready made "software laboratory" where realistic experiments could take place.

Ross Jeffery discussed the need to rethink our entire research philosophy and move away from positivist to interpretive research. He suggested that interpretive studies would be generalisible if such studies are applied to a wide number of organisations.

How should we design experiments?

In an earlier session, Feldman pointed out that we need to distinguish between formal experiments and informal quantitative investigations. It was agreed that this was an important point and that part of Basili et al.'s framework referred to informal investigations not formal experiments. Within session 3, nothing was added to this topic, however, later in the workshop, Walter Tichy raised the issue of benchmarking as a means of performing objective comparative studies.

How should we determine appropriate measures for a given objective?

The only suggestion from the workshop with respect to this issue was to apply the GQM paradigm to derive appropriate measures from specific research questions.

Conclusions

There does not appear to have been a great deal of progress with respect to the methodology of running experiments since Basili et al.'s paper in 1986. Nonetheless, there does appear to be an attempt by several researchers to involve industry and academia in joint experimental studies that should help to reduce the criticisms of lack of relevance and scalability often levelled at software engineering experiments.

---

[*]Report from an ad-hoc meeting on issues of benchmarking is included as an appendix to this Session 3 summary.

However, in order to involve industry in experimentation it is essential that industry accept software measurement as a basic software development technique, and it is clear that industry is not yet committed to software measurement. Getting industrial take-up of software metrics thus remains a major problem.

References

[1] Weyuker, E.J. "Evaluating software complexity measures", IEEE Transactions on Software Engineering, vol SE-14, no. 9, 1988.

[2] Basili, V.R., Selby, R.W., and Hutchens, D.H. "Experimentation in Software Engineering", IEEE Transactions on Software Engineering, vol SE-12, no. 7, 1986, pp. 733-743.

Appendix: Report from an ad-hoc meeting on issues of benchmarking

---

Improving the Experimental Method in Software Engineering Research

Walter F. Tichy (ed.)

University of Karlsruhe

A discussion group addressing the question of how to improve the experimental method in Software Engineering research met on the fourth day of the workshop. The motivation was that there were few solid, experimentally validated results available in the field. Earlier in the workshop, it had been noted that only 18\% of the papers published in IEEE Transactions on Software Engineering in the past year contained non-trivial quantitative evaluation. Papers on hypothesis testing were totally absent. Since Software Engineering is not based on theory alone, the small number of empirical results points to a serious weakness of the field and deprives industry of potential benefits.

Since experimentation in Software Engineering appears more difficult than in some other areas of Computer Science, the meeting addressed the question of how to obtain useful, hard results where theory does not reach and experimentation is required. The following seven recommendations emerged.

Recommendation 1: Do not attack too big a problem at once.

For example, trying to improve the entire software development process or developing a global cost estimation model seems hopeless, simply because the effect of any one method or tool is likely to be small and easily swamped by variations in many other, uncontrollable variables.

Instead, tackle smaller, well-defined problems. A sharper focus yields sharper results.

Recommendation 2: Develop benchmarks for comparing the performance of methods and tools.

Benchmarks are an important tool in other areas of Computer Science, where they are used routinely to quantify the improvements obtained with new approaches. They could be used in Software Engineering as well, for obtaining objective data on the quality of proposed methods and tools. A detailed discussion of the issues surrounding benchmarks follows this list of recommendations.

Recommendation 3: Intensify benchmarking efforts in the following areas:

- Testing methods and tools;

- Software design methods and tools;

- The effect of software architecture on evolvability;

Progress in these areas is likely to accelerate as soon as benchmarks and experimental setups exist that do not require human interaction. Such benchmarks seem possible for testing tools today. Benchmarks for design and software evolution appear much more difficult.

Recommendation 4: If no performance measure for a tool or method exists, refrain from stating any claims about performance.

Recommendation 5: Reject any paper submitted to an archival journal that merely presents a software or hardware design without some form of quantitative evaluation, unless the article presents a solution to an as yet unsolved problem. Publish and discuss designs with qualitative evaluations at conferences.

Recommendation 6: Take evaluation seriously.

Start with yourself, your colleagues, and students. Building yet another system without any plans for evaluation does not constitute acceptable research. Instead, devise benchmarks or obtain them from others; use the benchmarks to quantify results; formulate hypotheses and use benchmarks in experiments to support or reject the hypotheses.

Recommendation 7: Identify examples of outstanding experimental work for study.

The work of Knight and Leveson on multiversion programming (IEEE Tr. on Software Engineering, Vol SE-12, No. 1, Jan. 1986) is one such example.

Notes on Benchmarks

The lack of published papers with quantitative evaluations and experiments indicates that it may be difficult to devise effective benchmarks in software engineering. The following observations about benchmarks are important.

1. Benchmarks must define an objective performance measure.

    Performance is interpreted in a broad sense. Performance is not limited to the execution speed of a program. For example, the performance of a speech analyzer relates to the number of inputs correctly parsed; the performance of a document retrieval system describes the fraction of relevant documents retrieved, etc. The execution speeds of these applications on a given hardware platform have become secondary.

    The performance measure must also be objective, i.e., it must yield the same results under the same conditions, independent of the experimenter.

2. A benchmark suite should be portable to different environments. Thus, the suite should specify its exact purpose, the performance measures applicable, plus all relevant environmental conditions and assumptions, so that nearly identical conditions can be constructed when using the suite in other laboratories.

3. A benchmark suite should in some way be representative of the intended application domain. However, it is usually neither possible nor necessary to achieve perfect representativeness. Instead, results should be reported on individual benchmarks in the suite, so that users of the results can choose a subset for interpretation.

4. Benchmarks allow a separation of the subjective and the objective part of an evaluation. The composition of the benchmark suite, the specification of the context, and the choice of performance measures are subjective. Once these choices are made, the performance on the benchmark can be measured objectively. Such separation keeps the subjective part out of the experiment.

5. Tools are usually easier and faster to benchmark than methods, because methods require human participation and compensation for human variation, while a tool can be executed automatically and repeatedly.

6. Benchmark suites must evolve continually, otherwise overfitting occurs (i.e., tools and methods work well only on the benchmarks). The need for evolution has been demonstrated by the benchmark suites for computer hardware, which evolved from simple MIPS ratings through the Whetstone and Dhrystone benchmarks to the SPEC benchmarks.

7. The effort to compose a benchmark suite and to construct synthetic benchmarks may be significant, but the effort can be shared among multiple laboratories.

The importance of benchmarks has been recognized in a number of areas within Computer Science. In these areas, benchmarks are used routinely for evaluation. Considerable resources are being spent on collecting and evolving them. The following are examples where the benchmarks effectively take the human out of the loop and thus allow relatively simple, objective, and cost-effective measurements.

- Operating systems: Workloads (synthetic or observed) are used to study paging behavior or file access behavior. Example performance measures are the page fault rate or the average file access time.

- Speech analyzers: Large data bases with speech samples are used to both train and compare speech analyzers. These benchmarks fix the domain of discourse, the size of the vocabulary, the number and characteristics of speakers, and a great number of other parameters. The performance measure is the error rate (the fraction of words not recognized correctly).

- Information retrieval: A benchmark consists of a sizable collection of articles, a set of queries to be run against the collection, and the sets of articles considered relevant to each query. The performance measures are recall (what fraction of the relevant articles has been retrieved) and precision (what fraction of the retrieved articles were relevant).

- Compilers: A benchmark consists of a number of programs to be compiled and run. The performance is the runtime and space consumption of the compiled programs. Runtime and space consumption of the compiler itself are usually less important.

- Software configuration management: A benchmark consists of the version history of an entire system or a subsystem. Interesting performance measures include compression rates achieved with delta storage or the number of compilations performed by various selective recompilation tools.

- Computer algebra: A benchmark consists of a set of algebraic problems, specified in a mixture of prose and mathematical notation. Performance measure are the number of problems solved correctly, or the size parameter of certain problems on which the algebra system fails (usually because of exponentially growing space in the solver.)

Conclusion

All seven recommendations were discussed in a plenary session, where the idea of benchmarking sparked a lively debate. The objection that experimentation takes too long and may prevent academicians from publishing large numbers of papers quickly was brushed aside as a problem with the academic reward structure. This problem should and could be solved, as other fields, such as experimental physics, have solved it.

Constructing benchmarks, performance measures, and proper laboratory conditions for experimenting with testing, design, and software evolution were recognized as quite difficult, but an important and necessary step to improve the state of the art in Software Engineering research.

Participants of the discussion group: William Agresti, Norbert Fuchs, Barbara Kitchenham, Bev Littlewood, Anneliese v. Mayrhauser, Hausi Muller, Adam Porter, Walt Scacchi, Richard Selby, Walter Tichy, Stu Zweben.

Session 4:

[Measurement-Based] Modeling

Session Chair: Anneliese von Mayrhauser

Keynote: Vincent Shen, Stephen Thebaut

Position Papers: Lionel Briand
                     Giovanni Cantone
                     Dan Hoffman
                     Bev Littlewood
                     Anneliese von Mayrhauser
                     Markku Oivo

Task-Specific Utility Assessment Models and their Role in the Development of Software Engineering Handbooks†

Stephen M. Thebaut and Vincent Y. Shen

Department of Computer Science
The Hong Kong University of Science and Technology
Clear Water Bay, Kowloon
Hong Kong

Abstract. We argue that research in software engineering: research and development has reached a plateau of sorts, and that the time is right to prepare for an undertaking it should greatly benefit the software producing community: the development of software engineering handbooks. The role of engineering handbooks is described, as are two of the ways they might be used: facilitating reuse and aiding in the identification of tools, methods, and techniques well suited to particular development tasks. Towards this goal, we propose a cooperative undertaking aimed at creating what we call Software Engineering Utility Assessment Models. These would serve to specify sets of related software engineering tasks and their associated attributes in order to allow for both the categorization and comparison of new and existing tools, methods, and techniques. Some initial insights regarding the steps to be explored in their development are illustrated by way of a simple example.

1. Introduction

The enormous cost of producing software has focused the attention of the computing community on the software development and maintenance processes. This cost is well known both in absolute terms and as an ever increasing component of the cost of any computer-based problem solution. The discipline of software engineering has been established in an attempt to counteract these cost trends. As a general discipline, engineering has always relied heavily on theories, measurement, and models to help in the design, manufacturing, and maintenance of products. In keeping with this tradition, software engineering researchers have devoted considerable effort on quantitative measurements of the cost and quality of software products in the last decade by developing models of the software development process and by proposing methods for their evaluation. As a tribute to the software metrics field, Boehm [1] summarized its useful results in an article published in 1987. The following is a restatement of Boehm's original list of relationships and our comments on their validity a few years later.

(1)   Finding and fixing a software problem after delivery is 100 times more expensive than finding and fixing it during the requirements and early design phases.

† This work is supported in part by Hong Kong Research Grant Council under No. HKUST 624/94 and by a Hong Kong Telecom Caltex Fellowship.

Task-Specific Utility Assessment Models and their Role in the Development of Software Engineering Handbooks[†]

Stephen M. Thebaut and Vincent Y. Shen

Department of Computer Science
The Hong Kong University of Science and Technology
Clear Water Bay, Kowloon
Hong Kong

Abstract. We argue that research in software engineering metrics and measurement has reached a plateau of sorts, and that the time is right to prepare for an undertaking that could greatly benefit the software producing community: the development of software engineering handbooks. The role of engineering handbooks is described, as are two of the ways they might be used: facilitating reuse, and aiding in the identification of tools, methods, and techniques well suited to particular development tasks. Towards this goal, we propose a cooperative undertaking aimed at creating what we call *Software Engineering Utility Assessment Models*. These would serve to specify sets of related software engineering tasks and their associated attributes in order to allow for both the categorization and comparison of new and existing tools, methods, and techniques. Some initial thoughts regarding the steps to be employed in their development are illustrated by way of a simple example.

1. Introduction

The enormous cost of procuring software has focused the attention of the computing community on the software development and maintenance processes. This cost is still growing both in absolute terms and as an ever-increasing component of the cost of any computer-based problem solution. The discipline of software engineering has been established in an attempt to counteract these cost trends. As a general discipline, engineering has always relied heavily on metrics, measurement, and models to help in the design, manufacturing, and maintenance of products. In keeping with this tradition, software engineering researchers have devoted considerable effort on quantitative assessments of the cost and quality of software products in the last decade by developing models of the software development process and by proposing methods for their evaluation. As a tribute to the software metrics field, Boehm [1] summarized its useful results in an article published in 1987. The following is a restatement of Boehm's original list of relationships and our comments on their validity five years later:

(1) *Finding and fixing a software problem after delivery is 100 times more expensive than finding and fixing it during the requirements and early design phases.*

---

† This work is supported in part by Hong Kong Research Grants Council grant No. HKUST 14/91 and by a Hong Kong Telecom Senior Fellowship.

Most of the major software development organizations have established good tracking systems for software defects. Although the factor of 100 could be disputed, there is general agreement that the later a defect is discovered, the more it will cost.

(2) *You can compress a software development schedule up to 25 percent of nominal, but no more.*

The "nominal" schedule referred to is based on Boehm's COCOMO cost estimation model [2], and may not be generally accepted. However, there is no question that a development schedule cannot be compressed arbitrarily, even with unlimited human resources and environment support.

(3) *For every dollar you spend on software development you will spend two dollars on software maintenance.*

The definition of software maintenance remains elusive. For the most part, people do not "maintain" software in order to make it perform like it did when first released, but to remove defects and to support new functionality. In general, there are significant, on-going expenses associated with such activities, and the longer a system remains in use, the greater these expenses tend to be.

(4) *Software development and maintenance costs are primarily a function of the number of source instructions in the product.*

In the context of cost estimation models, at least, there would seem to be general agreement on this. Very few people today are still looking for a "better" single predictor of cost.

(5) *Variations between people account for the biggest differences in software productivity.*

There is general agreement on this as well, although people are still looking for tools and techniques that will allow everyone to perform like a superstar.

(6) *The overall ratio of computer software to hardware costs has gone from 15:85 in 1955 to 85:15 in 1985, and it is still growing.*

This is almost certainly true for new or specialized applications running on popular platforms today, but the growing emphasis on software reuse may be an important factor in halting or even reversing this trend in the future.

(7) *Only about 15 percent of software product-development effort is devoted to programming.*

There is general agreement that programming is a relatively small component in system development. It may even be further reduced in the future through the use of higher-level development tools.

(8) *Software systems and software products each typically cost three times as much per instruction to fully develop as does an individual software program. Software-system products cost nine times as much.*

There is no question that software-systems which contain many software modules written by different people are more costly to produce than individual programs, and that systems developed for external use are even more costly. But whether the nominal factors of increase are three and nine, respectively, is disputable.

(9)   *Walkthroughs catch 60 percent of the errors.*

Most major development organizations have incorporated inspections or structured walkthroughs in their quality assurance process. This is a direct consequence of Boehm's first relationship: it is important to find the defects as early as possible, and inspections are clearly effective in doing so. But whether the 60% figure is accurate or not would be difficult to prove.

(10)   *Many software phenomena follow a Pareto distribution: 80 percent of the contribution comes from 20 percent of the contributors. For example, 20% of the modules contribute 80% of the cost, 20% of the errors consume 80% of the cost to fix, etc.*

Conjectured relationships such as these are never meant to be precise, but they are probably just as valid as similar ones in other fields.

Our general agreement with (and lack of refinement of) Boehm's five-year-old set of relationships today, suggests that research in software metrics and measurement has reached a plateau of sorts. We have collected a lot of data; we have confirmed a few hypotheses; and we have learned that most metrics-based models need to be calibrated for the specific environment in which they are to be applied. But on the whole, we have produced relatively little in recent years to significantly help our "user" community of practicing software engineers. We think it is time to focus our efforts on an undertaking that could provide them with a great deal of help.

2. Software Engineering Handbooks

Literally hundreds of tools, methods, and techniques have been developed in recent years which have been purported to be of potential value to software engineers. Many have been promoted with claims that the tasks with which they are concerned can be undertaken more easily, more efficiently, more reliably, more quickly, etc., than would be possible without them. We believe most of the software engineering community do not take these claims seriously. Most of the claims are not supported with the kind of evidence that stands up to critical scrutiny. Even if there is evidence of a tool's value in the context of a given methodology, there is no guarantee that it will be of value in another. There is also relatively little methodological uniformity in software engineering today compared with other engineering disciplines.

An engineering discipline is one that stresses the identification of an optimal solution strategy for a given problem based on certain requirements, constraints, and preferences. Attributes within the solution space are often numerous and conflicting. In construction projects, for example, engineers select materials based on such considerations as cost, strength, longevity, ease of handling, etc. Each of these may be assigned a particular weight in keeping with the given application and circumstances. In addition, there are often choices to be made with regard to the construction techniques or procedures to be employed. For example, some building components may be either pre-fabricated and shipped to construction sites or built on site with or without the aid of specialized equipment and/or craftsman.

In the better established engineering disciplines, the problem of choosing among alternative solution strategies has been greatly facilitated by the use of engineering handbooks. In civil engineering, for example, handbooks such as [3] describe the important characteristics of standard building materials and specify the tools and techniques that are known to be effective. Some engineering handbooks even provide risk analyses based on previous engineering experience.

With very few exceptions [4,5], software engineers do not have the benefit of such handbooks today. There are no widely available catalogs which give the important characteristics of generic software components,[1] or which identify the tools and techniques that are best suited to particular software engineering tasks.

Fortunately, the research community has made significant progress in developing a software reuse technology. Private catalogs of reusable software components have already been developed within some organizations, and we think it is only a matter of time before such catalogs become available to software engineers in general.

On the other hand, relatively little progress seems to have been made in developing useful criteria for selecting among the many competing tools and techniques available to software engineers. This is somewhat ironic given the maturity of the software metrics and measurement field today, and we think it is a situation that can and should be changed. In what follows, we propose a strategy for effecting this change.

3. Software Engineering Utility Assessment Models

As suggested in the previous section, we think an important and necessary step toward the goal of compiling engineering handbooks for practicing software engineers is development of a framework for objectively assessing the relative utility of software engineering tools, methods, and techniques. We therefore propose a cooperative undertaking aimed at the development of software engineering *Utility Assessment Models (UAM's)*. UAM's would serve to specify sets of related software engineering tasks/functions and their associated attributes in order to allow for both the categorization and comparison of new and existing tools, methods, and techniques.

Most software engineering activities tend to fall neatly into one or more generic task areas: requirements determination and analysis, system design, program implementation, verification and validation, and maintenance. Thus, an initial approach might be to develop a separate UAM for each of these areas. A tool

---
1. With the possible exception of those associated with mathematical, statistical, or other special purpose software libraries.

or method purported to be useful in a given area could then be evaluated on the basis of the UAM for that area. The results of such evaluations would permit meaningful comparisons among available tools or methods based on their strengths and weaknesses in various task areas. Thus, software engineers could utilize the results of several, possibly independent assessments – as captured in a corresponding handbook, perhaps – in making decisions regarding the tools or methods to employ. The contents of such handbooks could also evolve in a systematic way as the assessment technology, and our experience with it, develop over time.

We have only recently begun to explore the problem of UAM development, and our ideas concerning this process, therefore, are formative. In the next section, our initial thinking regarding the steps that might be employed in their development are illustrated by way of a simple example.

4. A UAM for the Requirements Area

A preliminary step in developing a UAM is identifying the activities associated with the area. For example, the following is a partial list of activities associated with the requirements determination and analysis area:

(1) identifying relevant system requirements sources,

(2) getting the right people involved and motivated,

(3) developing and utilizing conceptual models,

(4) eliciting overlooked system requirements,

(5) organizing system requirements according to functions, associated attributes, constraints, and preferences,

(6) identifying, analyzing, measuring, and reducing ambiguity, inconsistency, and incompleteness in system requirements,

(7) producing a system requirements document, and

(8) capturing the system requirements' rationale and determination process.

Some activities, such as (1) for example, may primarily involve tasks that are *not* easily facilitated with automation. Thus, the UAM would primarily support the evaluation of manual methods or strategies associated with this activity. Other activities, such as (3), may involve tasks that *can* be facilitated with automation, so the UAM would also support *tool* evaluation for this activity.

The next step in the development of the UAM would involve identifying the tasks or functions associated with individual activities. Again, consider activity (3), developing and utilizing conceptual models. Possible tasks for this activity may include selecting an appropriate approach (i.e., dataflow, state machine, object-oriented, etc.), identifying possible viewpoints (i.e., users, sensors, other computer systems, etc.), specifying/representing the model elements, analyzing the model statically, analyzing the model dynamically, etc.

Following the identification of tasks, pertinent attributes and attribute measurement scales would be specified for the purpose of evaluating the methods, strategies, and tools purported to assist with these tasks. Consider, for example, the dynamic analysis task. Attributes and measurement scales for this task might include:

(1) modes of execution supported (interactive, batch, programmed),

(2) automatic temporal verification (supported, not supported),

(3) maximum number of model elements supported (number of rules, states, objects, functions, etc.),

(4) automatic prototype code generation (supported, not supported),

(5) performance analysis (supported, not supported),

(6) animation (supported, not supported).

Based on such a list, a software engineer who is in need of a requirements modeling tool which supports dynamic analysis could select from a set of previously evaluated tools by weighting the attributes according to the particular application. By extension, once a UAM has been developed for the requirements determination and analysis area (employing, undoubtedly, many of the requirements engineering tasks with which it is concerned!), it could serve as a basis for characterizing both the value and niche of a given tool, method, or technique in the context of activities associated with this area.

5. The Challenge

We believe that the software engineering community has accumulated enough experience to begin the development of useful task-specific UAM's. This would require the cooperative, consensus-building effort of groups of researchers and the use of state-of-the-art measurement and modeling techniques. If successful, it should eventually be possible to compile software engineering handbooks which facilitate both software reuse and the identification of tools and techniques that are well suited to particular software engineering tasks.

Before the goal of producing useful software engineering handbooks can be fully realized, however, a number of issues related to their actual development will need to be addressed.

One such issue concerns the appropriate form and content of software engineering handbooks. A revealing way to view this problem is to imagine how one might go about transforming a software engineering textbook into one or more software engineering handbooks. What material would be kept, and what would be deleted? What information would need to be added?

Another issue concerns dealing with the *volatility* of information that might be included in software engineering handbooks, as compared to that for other engineering disciplines. How often would information need to be updated?

Our current thinking is that a useful software engineering handbook should provide the following:

(1) regularly (perhaps yearly) updated, concise, operational descriptions of state-of-the-art software engineering techniques and methods,

(2) critical attributes and appropriate measurement scales for specific software engineering tasks, products, or functions (i.e., the product of UAM development),

(3) requirements (in terms of attribute values) for representative application classes,

(4) scenarios which provide overall examples of integrated development strategies, including the use of compatible techniques, methods, and tools, for representative application classes, and

(5) useful decision-making guidelines (based on multiattribute utility theory) to assist in the selection of tools, systems, development platforms, etc., based on comparative analyses of attribute values and project priorities.

The compatibility of this view with the current state of the software engineering discipline, however, is not clear. In any case, we believe these and related issues should be addressed before attempts are made to actually produce software engineering handbooks.

What we have proposed here would not be an easy undertaking, but the effort spent would almost certainly make the fruits of our research more useful. It is increasingly apparent that, as researchers working in an immature field, we must seek every opportunity to earn credibility for our results. The development of UAM's, as a step toward the goal of compiling engineering handbooks for practicing software engineers, constitute one such opportunity.

References

1. B.W. Boehm, "Industrial Software Metrics Top 10 List," in V. Shen (Ed.), Quality Time, *IEEE Software*, 4(5), Sept. 1987.

2. B.W. Boehm, *Software Engineering Economics*, Prentice-Hall, 1981.

3. F. Merritt (Ed.), *Standard Handbook for Civil Engineers*, 3rd Ed., McGraw-Hill, 1983.

4. C. Hollocker, *Software Reviews and Audits Handbook*, John Wiley, New York, 1990.

5. G. Parikh, *Handbook of Software Maintenance: A Treasury of Technical and Managerial Tips, Techniques, Guidelines, Ideas, Sources, and Case Studies for Efficient Effective, and Economical Software Maintenance*, John Wiley, New York, 1986.

Quantitative Empirical Modeling for Managing Software Development: Constraints, Needs and Solutions

Lionel C. Briand

Software Engineering Laboratory
Computer Science Department
University of Maryland
College Park, MD, 20742

1 Introduction

In order to plan, control and evaluate the software development process, we need quantitative models. Because of our current lack of understanding/experience and the high complexity of the modeled processes, it appears very difficult to build theoretical models (e.g. SLIM for development resource management). Therefore, based on collected historical data, we attempt to build multivariate empirical models valid in a specific environment. Because the available information is always incomplete, these models are by nature stochastic. We need models to be able to predict but also to understand. Being able to interpret the generated models is therefore indispensable in order to take preventive / corrective actions and elaborate better standards for the development of software systems within an organization. Basili has introduced a paradigm of measurement based, improvement-oriented software development, called the Improvement Paradigm [B85, BH88]. This paradigm provides an experimental view of the software activities with a focus on learning and improvement, implying the need for quantitative approaches for the following uses:

- building predictive models of the software process, product, and other forms of experience (e.g., effort, schedule, and reliability) based upon common characteristics.

- recognizing and quantifying the influential factors (e.g. personnel capability, storage constraints) on various issues of interest (e.g. productivity improvement, effort estimation) for the purpose of understanding and controlling the development.

- evaluating software products and processes from different perspectives (e.g. productivity, fault rate) by comparing them with projects with similar characteristics.

2 Requirements for an Effective Modeling Process

2.1 Constraints Related to Software Engineering Data

In the text that follows, we refer to the variable to be assessed as the "Dependent Variable" (e.g. productivity, fault rate) and the variables explaining the phenomenon as

"Independent Variables" or "explanatory variables" (e.g. personnel skills, data base size).

Model building to support software engineering can be difficult due to the following inherent constraints:

• C1: It is very difficult to make valid assumptions about the form of the functional relationships between variables and the probability distributions of variables on their ranges. Therefore the capabilities of classical statistical approaches seem limited.

• C2: In the field of software engineering, we are often faced with data sets that contain both continuous and discrete explanatory variables (e.g. lines of code, team experience, application domain). There are several statistical modeling techniques that deal with these different types of variables (e.g. least-square regression versus ANOVA) [A90,DG84]. However, building models (e.g. cost models) requires the use of both types of variables.

• C3: Because of the lack of precision in the data collection process and because of unexpected events (e.g. unstable requirements) in the development process, extreme/ atypical explanatory/dependent variable values occur. In software engineering, it is usually the case that a large number of factors (which vary widely from one environment to another) can affect the dependent variables. Therefore, information that could help to validate and understand atypical vectors is not always available. Also, the fact that we are working with a large number of explanatory variables makes it difficult to distinguish between those vectors that are atypical (i.e. outliers in statistics) and those which actually represent the main trends of the data set.

• C4: The interrelationship of explanatory variables can affect the understandability of models, but is not always harmful to their accuracy (e.g. regression models [DG84]). On the other hand, very complex interdependencies may exist. For example, the structural complexity of a piece of software can be a very significant factor of productivity if the programmer is inexperienced with the application domain and programming language. However, complexity has a milder impact on productivity if the programmer is experienced. Thus, the impact of complexity on productivity is dependent on the ordinal explanatory variable "programmer experience".

• C5: An explanatory variable may be a much stronger factor (i.e. disturbances are small) on a particular part of its range/value domain, a phenomenon known in statistics under the name heteroscedasticity. It is easy to see that the accuracy of a model that does not consider such issues may be significantly affected and the model may not provide pieces of information very important to decision making.

• C6: Missing information is a common problem in software measurement. There are several causes of this: limited budget for data collection, collecting data is time consuming, collecting some of the data is technically impossible (e.g. no tool) or not humanly desirable (e.g. engineer's work evaluation), and our lack of understanding of the problem, due to the newness of the software measurement field and the wide variability from one development environment to another. All of the above can generate incompleteness in the data collection process. For example, suppose we wish to predict project productivity according to collected physical features of the system and predefined quality requirements. Also, suppose we do not have any information about team experience related to the programming environment and the application domain. This information might be somewhat irrelevant (i.e. the variance of the prediction is small) if the structural complexity of the software and the required reliability are low. However, if high reliability on a complex software system is expected, then low experienced people are likely to generate large schedule and/or budget slippages and make any prediction based exclusively on other criteria meaningless.

2.2 Requirements to Alleviate These Constraints

Matching the constraints, we can define requirements for effective data analysis or empirical modeling procedures as follows:

- R1 [matches C1]: The data analysis procedure should avoid assumptions about the relationships between the variables and the probability density distribution on the explanatory and dependent variable ranges.

- R2 [C2]: The modeling process needs to capture the impact of, and be accurate in, integrating all explanatory variables regardless of their type, i.e., discrete, continuous. Also, the constructed models need to provide a consistent way of interpreting each variable's effects on the dependent variable.

- R3 [C3]: It is preferable to use modeling techniques that are robust to outliers, i.e. a small number of data vectors cannot change dramatically the characteristics of the model.

- R4 [C4]: We need a modeling technique which accounts for interdependencies among the explanatory variables, i.e., which produces, despite interdependencies, a readable and interpretable model. The modeling technique must address the issue of interdependencies by providing the context within which each parameter of the model appears to be a relevant and significant piece of information.

- R5 [C5]: heteroscedasticity can be addressed by determining on which part of its range/value domain an independent variable strongly affects the dependent variable of interest.

- R6 [C6]: Missing information obviously reduces our ability to predict and learn. We need to better understand whether or not the lack of a piece of data is an obstacle to assessment. This means that we need a model that not only generates predictions but provides some insight into the reliability of each individual prediction, rather than a global reliability of the entire model.

3 Modeling Approaches

In order to construct quantitative empirical models, three main modeling strategies are available in the literature:

- Least-square and logistic regression analysis.

- Machine learning models, e.g. classification/decision trees

- Neural Networks, e.g. back-propagation model

Only the two first approaches have been extensively used despite a few attempts of building network based models [TTT91]. This stems mainly from the high difficulty to interpret network models which do not provide much insight into the studied issue. Regression models are very powerful when their underlying assumptions are met. However, these assumptions are rarely met in our field: functional relationships are unknown, interdependencies between variables supposedly independent are numerous and variance is not constant in the sample space (i.e. homoscedasticity). As a consequence, regression coefficients are rarely interpretable in isolation. Moreover, they do not handle discrete explanatory variable in a satisfactory manner and the variable selection processes (i.e. backward, forward, ...) appear very often to be unreliable heuristics especially when interdependencies among explanatory variables are numerous. Therefore, this modeling approach does not seem always suitable to complex software engineering stochastic modeling despite its great effectiveness for simple problems (e.g. few independent numerical explanatory variables).

On the other hand, classification tree models [PAF82, SP88] have shown useful qualities:

- They provide an easily interpretable symbolic representation: a decision tree.

- They handle effectively both symbolic and numerical variables.

- They take into account, to a certain extent, interdependencies between explanatory variables, i.e. there is a notion of context: what is significant in which context?

However, it has been shown [BBT92] that the partition tree structure forces the modeling process to include irrelevant or not statistically significant pieces of information in the generated tree. Moreover, relevant pieces of information may also be ignored. These characteristics stem from the fact that partition trees were usually developed on large data sets and used in contexts where they were first validated (and pruned) by experts. In a software engineering context, data sets are often small and models are used to gain expertise. As a consequence, interpretation of partition trees may, in this context, be difficult and its accuracy may be affected.

At the University of Maryland, within the framework of the TAME project, we have developed an alternative modeling approach (called OSR: Optimized Set Reduction) and a tool to support it. Despite the fact that this is partially a machine learning approach [BFOS84], the modeling process is not constrained by a tree or any other structure: a set of logical expressions (i.e. patterns) providing statistically valid and easily interpretable information is generated [BBT92, BBH92, BP92]. Based on the specific needs described above, we want to address the weaknesses of currently used techniques. Our goal has been to combine the qualities and expressiveness of classification trees with the rigor of a statistical basis in order to tackle issues such as:

- dealing with partial information

- providing support for quantitative interpretation and simplification of the generated patterns

- providing pattern-based mechanisms for risk analysis, decision making and quality evaluation.

- take into account heteroscedasticity

- dealing with model input / output uncertainties

Results have shown [BBT92, BBH92, BTH92] that OSR patterns had a comparable accuracy to regression-based models. More importantly, the models generated by OSR appeared much easier to interpret and therefore could facilitate any preventive/corrective action aimed at optimizing the development process.

References

[A90]   A. Agresti, Categorical Data Analysis, John Wiley & Sons, 1990.

[B85]   V. Basili, "Quantitative Evaluation of Software Methodology", Proceedings of the First Pan Pacific Computer Conference, Australia, July 1985.

[BFOS84] L. Breiman, J. Friedman, R. Olshen and C. Stone, Classification and Regression Trees, Wadsworth & Brooks/Cole advanced books & software, Monterey, California, 1984.

[BH88]   V. Basili and H. Rombach,"The TAME Project: Towards Improvement-Oriented Software Environments", IEEE Trans. Software Eng., 14 (6), June, 1988.

[DG84]   W. Dillon and M. Goldstein, Multivariate Analysis: Methods and Applications, Wiley and Sons, 1984

[BBH92]   L. Briand, V. Basili and C. Hetmanski, "Providing an Empirical Basis for Optimizing the Verification and Testing Phases of Software Development", IEEE International Symposium on Software Reliability Engineering, North Carolina, October 1992.

[BBT92]   L. Briand, V. Basili and W. Thomas, "A Pattern Recognition Approach to Software Engineering Data Analysis", IEEE trans. Software Eng, Special issue on software measurement principles, techniques and environments, November 1992.

[BTH92] L. Briand, W. Thomas and C. Hetmanski, "Modeling and Managing Risk Early in Software Development", Submitted to conference publication.

[BP92] L. Briand and A. Porter, "An Alternative Modeling Approach for Predicting Error Profiles in Ada Systems", EUROMETRICS '92, European Conference on Quantitative Evaluation of Software and Systems, Brussels, Belgium, April 1992.

[PAF82] H. Potier, J. Albin, R. Ferreol and A. Bilodeau, "Experiments with Computer Software Complexity and Reliability", Proceedings of the Sixth International Conference on Software Engineering , (1982)

[SP88] R. Selby and A. Porter, "Learning from Examples: Generation and Evaluation of Decision trees for Software Resource Analysis", IEEE trans. Software Eng., 1988.

[TTT91] K. Torii, Y. Takada and M. Thompson, "Better Predictions Even in Reduced Input Variable Numbers Using Neural Networks in Software Development", Proceedings of the sixteenth annual software engineering workshop, SEL, NASA GFSC, December 1991.

Software Business, Concurrent Engineering and Experience Factory Relationships[*]

Giovanni Cantone

Laboratory for Computer Science, University of Rome "Tor Vergata"
Roma 00133, Italy

Abstract

In order to define a general framework for reasoning about the technical, managerial, organizational and technological changes needed by the software business today, a business model is firstly shown and applied to software business. Advances in both the production and the development businesses, and some inter-relationships, are then briefly considered.

1 Introduction

One of the main aspects of the software engineering research at the present age is the investigation of relationships between the software factory organization and performance results in terms of products quality and cost. Due to the complexity of analysis and to the lack of experience that the human had with the field, such an investigation, similarly to other main software engineering research, has to be carried out by an experimental approach and driven by a closed loop improvement paradigm [1]. Based on these concepts, a flexible and reuse oriented conceptual architecture for the advanced software factory and, a logical process for designing and implementing such a factory were both investigated by [3]. The instantiation of such a "Reference" factory to particular cases calls for investigating some aspects related to the business environment and trend of the particular firm.

The today organizational challenges of industries other than the software one depend on factors like both the "size" of the factory and the "characteristics" of the target customer. For instance, in order to produce airplanes, ships or cars, the factory organization strongly depends on the exclusive, limited or masss target of the product. Moreover, it can be observed that the organization has to change in the long time, due to competitive innovations, and furthermore has change in the short time, due to the customization needs.

Some questions which call thus for an answer are i)- which relationships, if any, between the application domain and target, and the factory organization, i.e. what flexibility for the short time improvement? ii)- how to detect, filter and measure changes into the environment long term dynamics, in order to actuate the long term improvement organization? iii)- due to the pervasive nature of the software, are multiple implementation models expected for the software factory organization?

---

[*] Work partially supported by "Progetto Finalizzato Sistemi Informatici e Calcolo Parallelo" of CNR under Grant NO. 90.00705.PF69.

In the following sections a general framework for answering to the above questions is considered.

2 Modeling Businesses

In order to arrange with success any business, the software one included, a deep understanding of both the business framework, environment, andBusinessEnvironment context is needed. In the this paper, for the sake of brevity, the word "consumers" will be used to denote both consumers, customers, clients, users, and so on, while "producers" will be assumed to include the chain of people and functions that support a product from the production to the distribution to consumers.

Business Framework (BF). This term is herein used to denote boundaries of the abstract multi-dimension domain where both producers and consumers apply for some kind of business, say for instance the software business, the mission-critical software business, and so on.

The dimensions of a BF include attributes of both i)-consumers, say for instance, their number, their average knowledge degree about both what they could get from a product and which will never be got by some type of technology, and so on; ii)-producers, say experiences, models, techniques and tools for the software factory organization, for processes, for products, and so on.

Some normalization can be applied to the BFOs dimensions. A BF can be partioned in classes by ranges of attribute values.

Business Context of a producer at some time (BC). This term is herein used to denote any point (or sub-domain) inside the boundaries of a business framework, i.e. any tuple of attribute values (resp. sub-ranges), one value for each dimension of the framework. Such a point is labeled by both the producer ID and the time t. At any time, there is a single point for each producer. The measure of the time shows some granularity, say years, depending on the business dynamics; moreover, t may represent a range rather than a single time.

The business context of a producer changes in time, due to changes in the attribute values, say for instance the number of customers, the average price of products, the re-arrangement of the factory organization, number, reliability and performances of sub-contractors, and so on.

Business Environment at the time t (BE). This term is herein used to denote any max-set of Business Contexts that share a partition of the business framework at the time t, so having that BE is a class of BF at the time t. Note that some BE could be empty at some t. Moreover, it is assumed that an upper bound exists, at any time, of the cumulative value of any attribute: say, for instance, the cumulative number of potential customers into an application domain, the number of available skilled Ada programmers, and so on.

Business environments change in time, due to business context changes and to their propagation because of the attribute cumulative scarcity.

165

Both the internal states of producers, and their relationships with the environment may be affected by a context change, and vice versa. Moreover, any change in the environment affects at least a producer context, and vice versa; typically but not necessarily, somebody do down whenever somebody goes up.

In order to hold or enhance the present positions, each producer is expected to execute some tasks in parallel, including both a tactic task, and a strategic task. The former is aimed at updating the internal state of the producer in relation to the short term dynamics of the business environment (say new behaviours of customers, new organizational concepts, practices, or experiences, and so on). It receives data from BE, processes them by the current model of BE, and takes actions to change its internal status sufficiently quickly to save or enhance the present position in the business environment, relationships with both actual and potential customers included. The latter is a long term task aimed to improve and possibly simplify the business environment by moving the producer point to better positions inside the business framework boundaries. Experiences gained by running these tasks can be used to improve the currently available models of BE.

2.1 Business Life-Cycle

Let's consider a simplified planar model of a business framework, the Business Life-Cycle (BLC). Its partitions are called Stages. Proceeding from the worst to the best stages, a business life-cycle can be sequentially modelled as the following part of this paragraph shows.

Embryonic Stage. This stage is characterized by the following attribute values. High technology. Very skilled and smart workers. Brand new and trade-marked prototypes, or rough rather than fine products. Very low prices, to take away competitors from an expanding market or, as usual, very high prices because of a small sized market, respectively. Null, negative, or positive profit rates, depending on the business luck. USA leaded such a stage in the software business. Questions: Due to software pervasivity, is the Embryonic Stage a persistent stage of the software business? Will there always be needs for some form of plus or minus "exclusive" software? If yes, what organization for the embryonic production?

Growing Stage. This stage may follow the previous one. It is characterized by a relatively known production process, while more and more marks expire. Pioneers, innovator leaders, and skilled workers transform prototypes or rough products into industrial products, whose final destination is the market of the general purpose customers. These, in turn, may be more and more interested in, and possibly attracted by, the new product; they can't be completely aware of the products advantages and limits. Unbelievably high profit rates may be gained. This stage was leaded by USA in the software business. Questions: Due to software nature, is the Growing Stage a persistent stage of the software business? Will there always be an increasing demand for today "exclusive" software? If yes, what organization for the growing production?

Imitation Stage. This stage follows the previous one, because high profit rates call for imitators, i.e. people who are able to replicate, to adapt, sometimes also to improve processes and products. After some time, due to effects of competition, both prices and products go down and, almost every potential customer is motivated to buy products, get related experiences, understand advantages and limits of both technology and products. Due to the too high competition effort, the business may be, or typically is, involved with some crisis.

Imitators are not necessarily messengers of negative perspectives. On the contrary, some of them lead the transition to the next stage. Starting from the sixties, the imitation stage was more and more leaded by Japanese in almost all kinds of businesses, software businesses included.

Questions: Due to software nature, is the Imitation Stage a persistent stage of the software business? Will there always be a very increasing demand for to-day "scarce" software? If yes, what organization for the imitating production?

Maturity Stage. In this stage, all and only the firms that "must" be in the business can be found in the mature business environment. Thus, a simplified business environment is established. Its structure is hierarchically re-arranged by a limited number of firms, each leading few stable sub-contractors, and so on. Profits are established around the regular rate. Products are standardized and customized. Competition is mainly driven by prices and quality. Due to the regularity of the profit rate, both large scale economies, and the improvement of related organizations, processes and technologies are mainly followed by production business, say production of cars or of electronic apparatuses, where unskilled workers are very welcome. Software technology is a development rather than a production process. Some effects of this and other particularities of the software technology will be considered in the following sections. Question: assumed that a persistent Maturity Stage for software business is expected, what organization for the maturity production?

Revitalization Stage. This stage may both precede and/or follow, the Maturity stage. Old products are moved to show a new look. It is a temporary stage which does not affects the final destination of the firm. Questions: Due to software nature, is the Revitalization Stage a persistent stage of the software business? Will there always be a very increasing demand for changing interfaces, reversing/reengineering software, and for other forms of the software gerontology? If yes, what organization for the revitalizing production?

Declining Stage. In this stage, slowly but inexorably the business declines.

3 Software business and its environments today

Software business is the business of an industry. Consequently, it shows similarities with remaining industrial business. On the other hand, software is both a specific, difficult and not a very visible matter, a permeating product, and a development not a production process [2]. Consequentially, the software business is very dissimilar from other kinds of business.

At the present time, due to world-wide occurring transformations, it can be guessed that the the advanced software business is trying to overcome the imitation and the revitalization stages, and to gain the maturity stage. By such a guess, the market's underlying activities should be selecting the next generation of leader-firms, primary-contractors, and sub-contractors, from both the old pioneers, the relatively younger imitators, and the incoming corporations.

In order to win the challenge associated necessarily with such a selection, some concepts, requirements and supporting technologies have to be necessarily met, that are common to any business in part, software specific in the other part. The general requirements are: ability of the firm both to combine technical and managerial solutions, to continuously pursuit the improvement of processes and product needs, to re-arrange both products, processes and human relationships into a flexible organizational framework, so that this can be feed back [5] by quality, cost and performance results. For any business, challenge supporting technologies are measurements and reuse of both parts [6, 7, 9] and experiences [3]. These technologies are normally applied to repetitive "production" works. They need to be evaluated and possibly adapted to the software business, i.e. a "development" business. Quoting such an evaluation [2], modeling results in a key technology of the software business, because software modeling is software modeling, iteratively. Note that modeling may be expensive and, software modeling costs cannot be distributed on the re-production costs, because the reproduction cost of software practically equals zero, and division is not defined on zero.

4 Enhancing the software business environment

To advance software factories is one of the main tasks that software engineering has to faced. Complexities related to analysis and synthesis of such a task prove once again that experimental rather than formal approaches will continue to characterize future software engineering trends.

Software Factory Engineering [7] is the new engineering which consists of methodologies, tools, environments, and guide-lines for constructing advanced software factories. It is both aimed at improving software quality and cutting high percentages off of the software equipments' development and customization costs and times.

Experience Factory. By a management perspective on the future engineering of software [4], the advanced software factory is a closed loop system able to learn from experience [2]. Factory data, once modeled, are measured in the operating factory, collected, analyzed, packaged and reused [1]. One of the higher forms of reuse is obtained by feeding back factory models of processes and products by filtered experiences, in order to obtain improved models. Based on these concepts, the Reference factory was proposed [3] as conceptual, logical and an organizational model of the flexible software factory. Main lessons, which are expected to be learned by on-going simulated or "in-vivo" experiments of Reference factories, include effects of the factory's organization and communication models on quality, speed and costs of software products and processes.

Concurrent Engineering. In the past, concurrent engineering concepts were mainly applied to the production of electronic devices [8]. Moreover, software factory engineering and concurrent engineering were almost un-related engineering. In the following, some positions are shown in order to framework an investigation on relationships between concurrent and software factory engineering. Concurrent engineering in software factory receives its results from the application of concepts and models of cooperation, parallelism and concurrence to software factory engineering, specially to software factory organization. To overlap Research and Development, Design, Implementation and, Marketing of a product is one of the main aims of the software factory's concurrent engineering. In particular, factory processes, the above named higher level ones included, are requested to collaborate with each other in order to meet the customer's needs and desires and to anticipate, detect and, possibly insulate and remove bottle-necks and problems affecting quality or costs. The implementation of such a maximum parallel cooperative approach requires, as a side effect, that both the models of interaction, and the implementation of the factory processes are substantially changed. In particular, interfaces of the possibly remote factory processes are requested to be integrated into each other, and to be real-time conversational rather than batch interfaces, as usual in "sequential" software factories. Moreover, tasks whose executions depend on human work, are requested to be implemented in terms of multi-functional, tightly interacting team-work rather than batch teams.

Acknowledgments

Some parts of this paper are very much related to researches performed in association with Victor R. Basili at the the Department of Computer Science and the Institute for Advanced Computer Studies of the University of Maryland at College Park, and to some meeting with Giuseppe Iazeolla at the Laboratory for Computer Science of the University of Rome at Tor Vergata, respectively.

References

1. Basili V R: Software Development: a Paradigm for the Future. Proc.s of COMPSAC, Orlando, Fl., Sept. 1989.

2. Basili V R: The Experience Factory: Packaging Software Engineering Experiences. June 1992, Un-published lecture notes.

3. Basili V R, Caldiera G, Cantone G: A Reference Architecture for the Component Factory. ACM TOSEM, V. 1, No. 1, 1992.

4. Basili V R, Musa J D: The Future Engineering of Software: A Management Perspective. IEEE Computer, September 1991.

5. Cantone G: Advanced Software Factory: Experiences and Models. Proc. of CQSO91: European Observatory on Software Engineering: Case and Software Quality. Milano, I, Oct . 1991.

6. Cusumano M A: Japan' s Software Factories: A Challenge to US Management. Oxford Univ. Press, 1991

7. Fujino K: Concepts of Software Factory Engineering. NEC Research & Development, No. 94, July 1989.

8. Rosenblat A, Watson G F: editors: Concurrent Engineering. IEEE Spectrum, Special Issue, July 1991.

9. Matsumoto Y, Ohno Y: Japanese perspective in Software Engineering, Addison-Wesley, 1989.

Establishing the Fundamentals of Software Engineering

Daniel Hoffman

Department of Computer Science, University of Victoria, Victoria, BC V8W 3P6, Canada

Abstract

There is a crippling lack of agreement as to what constitutes the fundamental techniques of Software Engineering. In industry, there is little use of explicitly defined methods. Academic proposals, though promising, have seen little industrial use and evaluation. Pilot projects in industry can help establish the fundamentals by showing which techniques are effective in various situations. The critical question is: how should these projects be organized and instrumented so that the results are convincing and widely applicable?

1 Introduction

The SEI's Process Maturity Model [1] is controversial when viewed as a means for quantitatively comparing software development organizations. However, one result from the surveys to date appears irrefutable: very few software development organizations have achieved Level 3: *Defined*. In other words, most use the "traditional approach": no explicit methodology at all.

Similarly, at the February 1992 Dagstuhl workshop - *Future Directions in Software Engineering* - there was little agreement on the fundamentals of Software Engineering. As a researcher in software development methodology, I look to the measurement community for help in establishing these fundamentals. Without them there is no Software Engineering.

2 Academic Proposals

Academic Software Engineering research focuses on (1) tool development and (2) formal methods. The tools are built with and primarily support current practice, which relies on superior programming skill rather than on an explicit methodology. Humphrey warns that, in Levels 1 and 2, sophisticated tool support is ineffective or even harmful [1]. While it is clear that better tool support is needed, it is not clear what kind of support will be effective.

Current methodology proposals overwhelmingly favor formal methods, with little supporting evidence for this choice beyond the failures of current practice. Formality is emphasized despite the fact that formal methods are extremely expensive to apply. While more formality is surely needed, we first need to know which formalisms to apply, to what development tasks, and at what cost.

There is a critical gap in our knowledge: we do not know much about software development using methods that are defined and disciplined, though not highly formalized or automated. Very few organizations have achieved Level 3; fewer still have published detailed findings. The resulting lack of consensus undermines education, professional standards, and tool development. Most software engineering courses depend more on the skill and experience of the instructor than on sound fundamentals. While there is need for professional certification, there is no agreement as to what skills should be required. Good tool development projects are ineffective because it is unclear what methods should be supported.

3 Pilot Projects

For the past ten years, I have been attempting to determine the best techniques for three aspects of software development: module specification, verification, and testing. I have restricted myself to techniques usable in industry now, with existing tools and modest mathematics. I would like to gain experience with these techniques in an industrial setting. My goal is to demonstrate the feasibility of the techniques and to learn their strengths and weaknesses. I plan to run a series of pilot projects, adapting selected techniques to the company environment and applying them to a small number of work products.

4 Open Questions

The invitation to this workshop proposed that "It is no longer sufficient to devise new languages and techniques..." and that "we need to provide the means for understanding weaknesses and strengths of existing techniques." Regarding industrial pilot projects, these proposals give rise to a number of questions.

- How should the projects be organized, so as to provide meaningful results?

- Can we expect pilot projects to provide meaningful *quantitative* results?

- If so, what should be measured and how should the data be interpreted?

- Put another way, what is required of pilot project so that the results are considered sound and useful?

I look forward to hearing many answers to these questions. These would be extremely useful to me, and, I think, to others embarking on industrial pilot projects.

References

[1] W.S. Humphrey. *Managing the Software Process*. Addison-Wesley Publishing Company, 1989.

Measurement-Based Modelling Issues - The Problem of Assuring Ultra-High Dependability

Bev Littlewood

Centre for Software Reliability
City University
Northampton Square
London EC1V 0HB, UK

1 Introduction

It can be shown that the problem of assuring ultra-high reliability of software is very difficult. Essentially, if we need to convince ourselves that the failure rate is extremely low, it is infeasible to do this by direct observation of the failure behaviour and subsequent statistical analysis. Whilst it seems likely that we can never obtain scientifically meaningful measures of reliability at the levels sometimes required (e.g. 10^{-9} failures per hour for the A320 flight-critical control system), there is a great need to be able to improve on the present state of the art. One way forward is to incorporate into our judgements of software reliability information from other sources than direct observation of failure behaviour; experimentation is one such source of information. In this note, I will first consider some generic problems of experimentation in software engineering, and then discuss how we might use experiments to address the special problems of evaluation of very high reliability.

2 Some general problems of experimentation in software engineering

Experiments in software engineering have tended to suffer in varying degree from several problems:

- Hypotheses have rarely been stated clearly and unequivocally at the outset of the experiment. Indeed, the *outcome of the experiment itself* is often allowed to influence the construction of a more formal hypothesis.

- Factors influencing the response variables have often not been identified and hence controlled.

- The applicability of the results in wider contexts than the narrow confines of the experiment is often questionable.

- Extensive replication is often prohibitively expensive.

- Attempts to avoid these problems of statistical design often make the experiments unrealistic in software engineering terms.

The key issues seem to be *identification* (of all factors that *might* influence what is being measured) and *control*. In the case of the former, we seem to be in a worse position than in most other areas of scientific experimentation. For example, there is little agreement on the attributes of the software development process that might influence something as fundamental as final product reliability. To some extent we can overcome the problem of unknown factors by randomising the application of those treatments whose effects are of interest to us, but this may need extensive replication.

There are some problems where replication is not too difficult. Examples include comparisons of the efficacy of different testing techniques, where the replication will be of the test runs, and not of the software development. Even comparisons of different development methods need not always involve duplication of work: for example, it should be possible within an organisation to randomise the application of candidate treatments to, say, different modules and see their effect upon, say, module fault count or reliability.

In many cases, replication problems will make true experiments infeasible. The best we may be able to achieve here are *case studies* lying somewhere between simple anecdote and hard science. My own view is that case studies have been denigrated for somewhat the wrong reasons. They are usually much more representative of real-life software engineering than most controlled experiments. The impression they give of being scientifically disreputable is often because of the poor quality of the *measurement* that is carried out, rather than problems of statistical control. Thus they often seem to be concerned with complexity measures, measures of usability, and similar dubious concepts.

A continuing difficulty is that much of the work in this area is conducted by computer scientists with little or no statistical training. For the most part, the statistical apparatus to be used will be very simple, and this is a virtue. Some of the most disreputable work I have seen was trying to use fancy statistical techniques to make up for a basic paucity of evidence: this is just another version of GIGO.

Perhaps a useful output from this meeting would be

- a list of statistical techniques that are likely to be useful in this area (and maybe a list of ones to be suspicious of, e.g. most multiple regression, factor analysis)

- a list of some of the important problems that could be addressed, via experiment and case study, *and have a high chance of success*

- some guidance on matching of experimental and statistical techniques to problems

3 Relevance of experiments to the problem of assuring high reliability

Our concern is primarily one of *evaluation* when the reliability goal is a very high one. The issue is, ultimately, one of judgement; in what follows I shall look at a few potential sources of experimental evidence for such judgements.

Relationship between process and product attributes. If we had good scientific evidence for the efficacy of different software development procedures in delivering final product attributes, such as reliability, it might be reasonable to have confidence in a particular product if we knew such procedures had been used. In fact, such evidence is not available, and I remain sceptical whether it ever will be. There is a sense in which this is the key problem in experimental software engineering: after all, if we cannot have quantified confidence in our 'engineering' practices, how can we claim that we *are* engineering software? Unfortunately, all the difficulties of experimental software engineering seem to be present here: poor identification of the likely interesting process attributes and thus imprecise definition of hypotheses, presence of confounding factors such as special attributes of a particular application, difficulty in realistic replication.

Expert judgement. It seems inevitable that this will continue to form an important input into decisions as to whether or not particular systems are sufficiently reliable to be deployed. My suspicion is that such judgements are biased towards over-optimism - certainly there is evidence of this in other fields, where experts tend to believe too strongly in their own competence. This seems an ideal area for experimental investigation: we can formulate the hypotheses precisely if we restrict ourselves to reliability evaluation, replication over many experts should be relatively easy. It may even be possible to take a small team of experts (even a single expert) and 'recalibrate' their judgements by learning about their bias over many judgements.

Design diversity and fault tolerance. Whilst there is evidence that the use of design diversity can increase reliability when compared with single versions, there is equally evidence that this increase is not as great as might be expected under naive (and incorrect) assumptions of independence of the failure processes. This means that it is imperative, for an evaluation of a particular system, to know what degree of dependence exists between the failure processes of the versions. Once again, this is an area that lends itself to experimentation, and some good work has already been conducted. It may be possible at least to obtain some bounds on the claims that can be made for the use of design diversity.

Case studies and operational data. The general area of safety-critical systems is one where it ought to be possible to impose mandatory reporting requirements so that case studies would have a surfeit of high quality data. Amazingly, even scandalously, this seems not to be the case. Although not strictly an issue in experimentation itself, there is a great need to encourage the collection and publication of raw data from these important application areas

Accelerated testing. Most testing of software is intended to *achieve* reliability, rather than collect data suitable for measuring it. Typically, inputs are chosen which are expected to be 'stressful', in the sense of being more likely to seek out bugs than operationally typical inputs. If we could perform 'accelerated testing' (in the hardware terminology) on software, and still obtain accurate measures of reliability from the resulting data, we would be able to assure higher reliability levels than is possible with current techniques such as operational testing. This seems a suitable topic for experimental investigation, since useful results can be obtained from replication of the test runs (i.e. without replication of program development).

Finally, it should be said that in order to exploit the data that comes from experiments and case studies, it is necessary to develop new means of combining disparate information. Thus in order to judge whether a particular safety-critical system is sufficiently reliable to deploy, we need to combine information from testing (including accelerated testing), about the development methods and techniques used, about the architecture (possibly including design diversity). At present, such judgements are made by informally combining informally expressed evidence - a process that is sometimes referred to as 'engineering judgement'. If, as I believe, we can express the different kinds of evidence more formally - in particular, quantitatively - then we must also take the opportunity of developing formal ways of composing the different strands of evidence. Only then will we be able to claim that our judgements about these important systems warrant descriptors such as 'scientific' and 'engineering'.

The Role of Simulation in Software Engineering Experimentation

A. von Mayrhauser

Colorado State University, Computer Science Department, Fort Collins, CO 80523

Abstract

Software engineering experimentation should develop beyond statistical analysis of data and analytic models. We must become more active in developing a viable discipline of simulation to aid experimental software engineering. This will require developing standard modeling components, connections, tools, and a body of knowledge to interpret modeled phenomena.

1 Existing Models and their Limits

Existing models of software engineering (sub)processes or products are analytic or statistical.

To make analytic treatment possible, our models tend to lump many factors together. Yet we cannot reason about differences due to factors that we do not model. Where we do explicitly consider a factor in an analytic model, analytic treatment may only be possible for a limited set of behaviors for a factor: e. g. all software reliability models make specific execution assumptions for the code. These assumptions only cover a small range of known testing strategies.

Practitioners often apply models even when assumptions are not met. They may use a statistically derived model with data values that lie outside the range of data used to build the model. Or they may use a model with data collected differently or based on different metric definitions. They may use an analytic model in a situation when model assumptions cannot possibly be met. Sometimes the results are good. Sometimes they are abysmal. We do not always understand why.

Even for our existing models, we frequently do not understand enough about their ranges of applicability or accuracy. The best we have is an ever growing collection of papers that compare performance of various models on some, often quite aged data sets. A mature discipline must do better than that.

To isolate the effect of various options or factor levels (e. g. testing strategy) we may need to explore (run experiments as it were) a variety of scenarios "with other factors being the same"; no real software development organization would willingly do the "same" project several times except for varying the factor we are interested in. Even if they were, control of other project factors is at best tenuous. We can, of course, collect data from different projects and use the (larger amount of) data to help us control for differences in projects.

In view of known scarcity of good data this does not seem like a formula for success. Another sore point is the quality of data from different sources.

2 Simulation as an Alternative

Traditionally, simulation models are used when analytic treatment is either impossible or intractable. I believe, we have not sufficiently explored the possibilities of simulating the software development process and its resulting software product. Yet many practical questions could be more easily answered by simulation. Let me explain the possibilities with an example.[1]

A frequently asked question at the end of the design phase is "will the software be of sufficient quality if we go forward with this design"? This question asks for a mapping between design and software reliability. At the design stage we can identify structural properties and error characteristics. These can be used to automatically generate code and seed it with faults. An execution harness controls execution behavior (representing the testing strategy). Executing this simulated code produces a failure pattern, the key ingredient in estimating software reliability.

Researchers in Software Reliability Models have shown an increased interest in the effect of testing strategies. Such testing strategies are easily investigated with the simulated code. Not so for analytic models. They rely on very limited assumptions. Further, a simulator can easily vary the other components (structural properties, error characteristics, and debugging behavior). A simulator can model a variety of strategies and properties. We may only need to collect data for a single project type. The data is then used in different scenarios. In the example above we may collect data from one project for one test strategy, then use the same input data, but apply a different testing strategy in the model.

In summary, simulation holds the promise of flexibility in analysis, more realistic models, and, through self-driven simulation, data leverage. It does not, however, guarantee quality of data used to drive the simulator.

3 Challenges

It would be nice to say that simulation as a means to further experimental software engineering had come of age and all we have to do is apply it. Reality, however, tells us otherwise. First, any model simplifies the world by extracting and modeling relevant aspects while ignoring others to keep the model simple. We do not know enough about the software development process and all its variables (human and otherwise) to identify which variables should be modeled for what types of questions. Second, we need to build a discipline of simulation in software engineering experimentation with standard components, connections, and hierarchical structure, tools and a body of knowledge. A discipline that has developed such a structured modeling approach is performance analysis. The world is described in terms of workload descriptions, sys-

---

1. A. von Mayrhauser, J. Keables; "A Simulation Environment for Early Lifecycle Software Reliability Research and Prediction", International Test Conference, 1992, Sept. 21-25, Baltimore, MD.

tem components ("servers") and their interconnections and rules of operation (the system description). Many such models are hierarchical and it has been well established what type of information belongs to which level. We still have a long way to go in our discipline. It is not clear what a simulation discipline and standard building blocks are for simulation (indeed any modeling) as part of software engineering experimentation.

Above, I used software reliability modeling as an example. Possible input descriptions in this case might include

1. Program/design descriptors. Examples are structural, data and data flow properties, interface and connection/inheritance information. When we start with a design, we also need code expansion rules.

2. Error characteristics. This includes faults and fault types, where they will be located (not necessarily only as fault frequencies).

3. Execution pattern. This could be explained in terms of operational profile, testing strategy, even the execution history of an early prototype.

4. Fault-failure relationship. Traditional descriptors are fault exposure, but we should also be able to model cases when a failure is not traceable to a fault, as in the case of a missing function.

5. Debugging behavior. Debugging can be complete, incomplete, and even introduce new faults.

These input descriptors are used by the following simulation components:

Code generator: This component uses (1) and (2) above as input and produces code with faults.

Execution harness: It uses (3), (4), and the output of the Code Generator. It produces desired execution patterns and appropriate failures.

Debugger simulator: Debugging behavior (5) and the failures generated by the Execution harness drive this component.

Reliability model(s): This last component uses the output of the Execution harness and the Debugger simulator to assess the reliability of the simulated code. \end{description}

To complete a Meta-model, we must associate each of these component types with well-defined sets of information, rules for usage, and applicability. Information exists at various levels of detail and comes from different phases of the life cycle. This helps to structure modeling information in a hierarchical fashion. Once we can classify our data and measurement needs with respect to the modeling components that use them and the output they can produce (level and accuracy), we will have made an important advance towards a mature modeling discipline.

Multiple Viewpoints of Software Models

Markku Oivo

Technical Research Center of Finland (VTT)
Computer Technology Laboratory
P.O. Box 201, SF-90571 Oulu, Finland

1 Introduction

In order to effectively use any kind of knowledge involved in software engineering we have to have powerful means to model, package, manage, and reuse the information. We need a consistent internal knowledge representation mechanism, and at the same time we have to provide different viewpoints of the internal models for different types of users. Combining measurement information in the same models as products, documents, and processes allows us to integrate the metrics in the development process.

Most of the objects in software engineering need to be viewed from different viewpoints. A software module may have different attributes when viewed from developer's, tester's, manager's, or customer's viewpoint. Certainly there are many common attributes as well, but having all the attributes visible for everyone would make the object overwhelmingly complicated and difficult to comprehend. Hence, we need a mechanism for looking at objects from different viewpoints.

2 Modeling

Object-oriented techniques provide powerful and natural methods for modeling many software engineering applications. They yield themselves naturally into taxonomic classification and the inheritance mechanism makes it easy to incrementally define and maintain objects and their features. However, there are situations when the traditional object-oriented modeling and inheritance lattices are not sufficient [2].

We have introduced a meta-model concept which allows us to describe and build customized models of software engineering elements using pre-defined components. The modeling mechanisms can be used to model qualitative and quantitative aspects of various software engineering artifacts. Model building is based on *object-oriented modeling*, *inter-object relationships*, and a *dynamic viewpoint* mechanism with a highly *selective inheritance* [2]. In addition to the basic object-oriented modeling techniques, we use inter-object relationships to construct models consisting of various types of objects and to define the relationships between them. Dynamic viewpoints with selective inheritance are used to view the models from various perspectives and to control their inheritance via the relationships.

We have demonstrated the modeling principles in a prototype called ES-TAME [2] which has been developed and used in the context of top-down goal-oriented characterization of software engineering activities [1]. We are using reusable and tailorable object-oriented models to represent the software engineering elements. We have implemented a viewpoint mechanism with selective inheritance which will address the problems described earlier.

3 Measurement Viewpoint

In this section we will concentrate in describing a simple example of measurements and their connection to our modeling methods. However, the overall context for the measurements is defined in the top-down goal-oriented GQM paradigm [1, 2].

We can consider metrics as one viewpoint of the software engineering elements. For example, when we are sketching data flow diagrams we may not be interested in measuring the design quality before we reach a certain phase in the analysis and design process. When we are ready to measure the quality, we can simply change the viewpoint of the design tool and take a look of the diagrams from the measurement point of view. There is no need to quit the design tool and start searching for proper metrics tools. We simply change the viewpoint of our diagrams and the dynamic inheritance mechanism automatically provides us all the necessary measurement tools and methods defined in our generic object-oriented models.

3.1 Measuring Coupling

Let us consider the coupling of data flow diagram elements as a simple measure of modularity in design level quality metrics. The basic measurement methods, user interface components, and visualization techniques for coupling related tasks are fairly independent of the analysis and design methodology. Only the actual method for searching the connections between the modules and their classifications must be implemented for each design methodology. All design methods which include a notation for nodes (e.g. transformations in data flow diagrams) and links between nodes (e.g. data flows in data flow diagrams) are modeled in a similar way in our underlying object-oriented models. Consequently, the searching process is similar.

We have implemented the coupling methods in a generic class called *Coupling* which provides most of the functionalities needed to measure design level coupling regardless of the details of the design method. It also includes the user interface as well as visualization tools for the results of the metrics. The results of the coupling metrics are automatically displayed as various graphical charts and numerical data.

The *Coupling* class provides the generic methods for classifying the coupling attributes (e.g. data coupling, control coupling, external coupling, common coupling, content coupling) as well as the slots for maintaining them. Connections can be classified automatically or interactively with the user. The results are stored in the appropriate slots of the design model. In addition, we provide a mechanism for propagating the lower level measurements to the upper levels and vice versa. This is very useful in hierarchical systems like data flow diagrams. We can propagate, summarize and manipulate values between various levels of the hierarchical data flow diagrams.

We have demonstrated that our measurement principles are independent of the design method by using the same general purpose methods for measuring coupling in structured analysis and design method as well as Jackson's JSD method. The system automatically adjusts to a new methodology and creates new attributes and links in the models. When we change the viewpoint of the design models to measuring their quality we inherit appropriate methods in each design model element (for example, data flow diagrams). Only a few specific analysis and design methodology details have to be tailored and refined in the metrics methods which are inherited from the generic coupling models.

3.2 Packaging Measurements

The modeling scheme allows us to package the measurement results into an active knowledge base rather than a passive data base. The measurements are stored in the objects themselves. They remain in the object even when we change our viewpoint away from metrics. The measurement results are accessed again when we change the viewpoint back to metrics. The objects which are to be measured include the results from the previous measurement sessions and this information is reused whenever possible. This is especially important when we use metrics which require user involvement (e.g., subjective metrics). We can save time and effort by avoiding questions and measurements which were already used in earlier sessions.

Furthermore, the packaging and modeling methods allow us to take advantage of the results of other measurements. For example, if we have measured the number of source lines (KLOC) in the product measurements and given it as a value of the size attribute in the product model, we can link the corresponding KLOC attributes of the resource estimation and defect slippage models to the product model's KLOC attribute. Thus we maintain the KLOC value in one place only and changing the metrics can be automatically updated in the other models. This would be impossible to implement with multiple inheritance because these models are conceptually totally different and belong to different class hierarchies.

References

1. Basili, V.R. & Rombach, H.D. The TAME Project: Towards Improvement-Oriented Software Environments, IEEE Transactions on Software Engineering, Volume SE- 14, No. 6, June 1988, pp. 758-773.

2. Oivo, M. & Basili, V.R. Representing Software Engineering Models: The TAME Goal Oriented Approach. IEEE Transactions on Software Engineering, Volume 18, No. 10, October 1992.

Session 4 Summary
[Measurement-Based] Modeling

A. von Mayrhauser

Colorado State University
Computer Science Department
Fort Collins, CO 80523

In the software engineering field we find two major types of models: of the software process and of the products the process generates.Processes and products may have attributes which are useful to model. Examples are cost and effort estimation, productivity predictions, sizing models like the function point method, reliability growth models, fault predictors, performance models of sytems, etc. More recently we have developed more elaborate process models (e. g. [1], [7]) to help us control and improve the way we develop software.

A critical issue for developing and refining high quality models of process or product lie in the proper parameterization (modeling the right thing) and appropriate model validation (modeling accurately). For this we need proper design of experiments to define and collect data. We also must analyze the data appropriately and after building our models, validate them. The level of model, whether it is a rule of thumb, an analytic (closed form), or a simulation model, depends on the needs of the real world, the availability of data, and the desired accuracy for the model. We may not always be able to build a model. If not, are there alternatives? Even when we build models, they usually are not general, but work better in some contexts than others. We therefore must find out through rigorous experimentation what range of applicability our models have.

Lessons Learned in the Last Ten Years

Since models are so multi-faceted, we cannot expect consensus on the way to parameterize, build and validate models. When discussing the issues, the following points emerged:

There are many useful models

Some are considered useful from the practitioners who have been applying them for a long time, mostly with success. Examples of such models are COCOMO [2], SRM [10], Waterfall and Spiral Model [3], and a variety of product modeling techniques that fall into the general category of structured analysis, data modeling, etc. [5]. We also find business models (risk analysis, utility assessment frameworks, decision making methods using measurement levels of a variety of metrics, etc. [13]).

Models come at various levels of maturity

Existing models are not always considered useful from a theoretical or research perspective. They may lack rigorous development and validation. They may be used in a context for which they were not developed, but we know too little about the risk (of inaccuracy) involved. Model building ranges from shot-gun statistics to elaborate theories. Thus while we have agreement that useful models exist, there is disagreement as to which are currently useful.

Good models are difficult to build

There are a variety of reasons for this. First, metrication may be difficult. Human judgement is fallible. Experimental control may be hard to impossible. Especially at the project level, good data is hard to come by. Without them good models are difficult to build.

We have learned that it helps to narrow the focus. This can happen by either staying with a specific context (company, application area, development platform, etc.) or a narrowly defined modeling domain (e. g. reliability modeling [9]).

While the modeling community has always had strong proponents for scientifically respectable model validation, this still is not common practice. We must push for validation more strongly than we have been.

Key Points of Dissent

Large scale model validation

The scientific prescription for proper model development is to provide a precise description of goals, assumptions, results, and the evaluation mechanism. In reality, however, it may be difficult to define and metricate parameters, to control experiments used to define and validate a model. This makes it very hard to package a model with demonstrated utility. Demonstrated utility should include independent validation, specification of range of applicability and model limitations, demonstrated functionality and assessment of usefulness for classes of possible users [12].

Models come in a variety of types. They range from pilot studies and prototypes (models of solutions to product issues [8]) to process and business models [6], and to integrated models that combine process and product issues [11]. It is not clear whether one methodology for developing and validating models is possible or even desirable. This controversy could also have been titled "Scientific respectability versus real needs". While we know that models with restricted scope are more easily validated, they are also more restricted in their applicability. The point was made [9] that in the interest of scientific respectability, we should try to build less grandiose models, even if it restricts impact on practical work. Not everybody agreed.

In the discussions there was significant disagreement as to the general feasibility of large scale validation. This disagreement centered on two issues: whether and to which degree an engineering handbook could be built and whether the necessary benchmarking was possible to conduct the experiments.

Is an Engineering Handbook possible

As for the handbook controversy, some participants questioned whether we have the necessary knowledge to do the job. Others brought forward pieces of evidence that parts of such handbooks had been developed at companies, for the governement or military, and for restricted model domains at universities.

Can and should we benchmark

The dissent about benchmarks centered around the basic feasibility of benchmarking for models in the software engineering domain. Some participants, while acknowledging that it would be difficult to do, nevertheless pointed to an existing dicipline of benchmarking in other fields, like performance analysis, with existing methods and rules of workload characterization and modeling that could be adapted at least to some areas of modeling in software engineering.

Key Issues of Next Five Years

Build a set of models that cover relevant aspects of the real world they purport to model

In particular, this includes building models that relate technical process and product to business issues. This also speaks for further investigation into process-product relationships. Process and product models must interface with each other. If possible they must provide various views of process and product [11].

Further, it addresses the issue of model realism. We may have to find new approaches to existing model types (such as using simulation for software reliability estimation, rather than analytic modeling).

This also implies establishing proper context for the use of a model before it is developed, then deriving parameters based on the needs of the context (applying a GQM paradigm as it were).

Develop techniques to cover situations where model building is difficult

An example of such work is [4], techniques for building empirical models when regression assumptions don't hold. Another example is [8], dealing with assessing the value of prototypes as models of desired functionality.

Reward application of sound experimental techniques

To put it even more bluntly: every new model, every technique must be accompanied by objective, quantitative validation and assessment of its usefulness. This requires active cooperation by editors, program committees, etc. (There was considerable frustration that "inventing somethin new" all too often still does not require experimental evidence that it works).

Inevitably, this will lead to models with better scientific justification, a first step towards obtaining the material that would go into an engineering handbook.

For currently existing models: conduct experiments as needed to quantify what models can and cannot do

This is probably one of the more difficult to sell to researchers. One, the proper rewards are missing for repeating existing experiments. On the other hand repeatability is important. Second, validating an existing technique or model may also be difficult to sell as research, even though, from an experimental point of view, it is.

Specific Modeling Studies

Not everybody supported all points, but each point had a significant measure of support.

1. Move forward with building, using and evaluating process models. Participants disagreed as to the proper experimental paradigm. There was also concern that we need to understand the range of applicability and the robustness of lower level (product) models better that are used as components in the process models.

2. Evaluate models and package them with the results. This way potential users know exactly what a model can and cannot do and when best not to use a particular model [12].

3. Define benchmarks for specific scenarios to evaluate models. To do this for reliability models is much easier than for process models. We can expect results here to first come for the more focused model types.

4. Emphasize building of models to include factors relevant to software development, but usually considered outside the software domain. Examples are models of the business environment and its relationship to the production process [6].

5. Develop new techniques to make metrication possible where current techniques fail (cf. [4]).

References

[1] Basili, V., Rombach, D.; The TAME Project: Towards Improvement Oriented Software Environments", *IEEE Transactions on Software Engineering SE-14*, 6(June 1988), pp. 758-773.

[2] Boehm, B.; "Software Engineering Economics", Prentice Hall, 1981.

[3] Boehm, B.; "A Spiral Model of Software Development and Enhancement", *Computer 21*, 5(May 1988), pp. 61-72.

[4] Briand, L., "Quantitative Empirical Modeling for Managing Software Development", *Workshop on Experimental Software Engineering*, Sept. 1992, Dagstuhl, Germany.

[5] Nerson, J.-M.; "Applying Object-Oriented Analysis and Design", *CACM 35*, 9(September 1992), pp. 63-74.

[6] Cantone, G., "Software Business, Concurrent Engineering and Experience Factory Relationship", *Workshop on Experimental Software Engineering*, Sept. 1992, Dagstuhl, Germany.

[7] Curtis, B., et al.; "Process Modeling" *CACM 35*, 9(September 1992), pp. 75-90.

[8] Hoffman, D., "Establishing the Fundamentals of Software Engineering", *Workshop on Experimental Software Engineering*, Sept. 1992, Dagstuhl, Germany.

[9] Littlewood, B., "Measurement-based Modeling Issues - The Problem of Assuring Ultra-High Dependability", *Workshop on Experimental Software Engineering*, Sept. 1992, Dagstuhl, Germany.

[10] Musa, J., Iannino, J., Okumoto; "Software Reliability Modeling: Theory and Applications", MacGraw-Hill, 1986.

[11] Oivo, M., "Multiple Viewpoints to Software Models", *Workshop on Experimental Software Engineering*, Sept. 1992, Dagstuhl, Germany.

[12] Shen, V., "Towards the Development of Task-Specific Software Engineering Utility Assessment Models", *Workshop on Experimental Software Engineering*, Sept. 1992, Dagstuhl, Germany.

[13] von Mayrhauser, A.; "Software Engineering: Methods and Management", Academic Press, 1990.

Session 5:

Packaging for Reuse / Reuse of Models

Session Chair: Frank McGarry

Keynote: Kevin Wentzel

Position Papers: Albert Endres
                      Stuart Feldman
                      Claus Lewerentz
                      Frank McGarry
                      Norm Schneidewind

Software Engineering Models Using and Reusing

Hewlett-Packard Laboratories
1501 Page Mill Road, Palo Alto, CA 94303
Telephone: 415-857-6018; Fax: 415-852-8526
Email: wentzel@hpl.hp.com

Abstract

Process, organizational, analytical, and technological models for improving
software engineering, work are developed as a result of research in software
engineering. These models have a variety of uses in the research community and
the software development community, however, models must be tuned for a particular audience and goal. Portfolios of models must be developed with selection
criteria to indicate where each is applicable. The concept of "model" goes
beyond these meanings as it extends into models/processes for technology transfer and for evaluation of transfer.

1 Background

The word "model" has many meanings even in a limited context like software engineering. A model is much more than a matrix or a formula to be applied to metrics.
Process, organizational, analytical, and technological models are frequently developed
for software engineering, but these models must be linked to and supported if they are to
be reused effectively.

2 What do we mean by "Model"?

Webster's New Collegiate dictionary defines two distinct meanings of "model" as follows
[Web]:

1: A set of plans for a building. 2: Copy, image. 3: Structural design. 4a: a miniature home on the model of an old farmhouse. 4: a miniature representation of something; also a pattern of something to be made. 5: an example. 6: representation o
simulation as a pattern or thing that serves as a pattern for imitation. 7: one who
poses for an artist. 7: Archetype. 8: one upon whom something important is modeled; one who is employed to display. 9: kinds or duty that may pose design
of clothing 10b: a type or design of product. 10a: one or a person. 11: a description or analogy used to help visualize something that cannot be
directly observed. 12: a system of postulates, data, and inferences presented as a
mathematical description of an entity or state of affairs.

Archetype, Model, Example, Pattern, Blueprint, Ideal, kind of meaning, example
something set or held before one for guidance or imitation.

Software Engineering Models, Using and Reusing

Kevin D. Wentzel

Hewlett Packard Laboratories
1501 Page Mill Road, Palo Alto, CA 94303
Telephone: 415-857-4018, Fax: 415-857-8526
Email: wentzel@hpl.hp.com

15 October 1992

Abstract

Process, organizational, analytical, and technological models for improving software engineering work are developed as a result of research in software engineering. These models have a variety of uses in the research community and the software development community, however, models must be tuned for a particular audience and goal. Portfolios of models must be developed with selection criteria to indicate where each is applicable. The concept of "model" goes beyond these meanings as it extends into models/processes for technology transfer and for evaluation of transfer.

1 Background

The word "model" has many meanings even in a limited context like software engineering. A model is much more than a metric or a formula to be applied to metrics. Process, organizational, analytical, and technological models are frequently developed for software engineering, but these models must be linked and supported if they are to be reused effectively.

2 What do we mean by "Model"

Webster's New Collegiate dictionary defines the noun meanings of "model" as follows [Web]:

1: A set of plans for a building 2: Copy, Image 3: Structural design (built his home on the model of an old farmhouse) 4: a miniature representation of something; also a pattern of something to be made 5: an example for examination or emulation 6: a person or thing that serves as a pattern for an artist; one who poses for an artist 7: Archetype 8: an organism whose appearance a mimic imitates 9: one who is employed to display clothes or clothing 10a: a type or design of clothing 10b: a type or design of product (as a car or airplane) 11: a description or analogy used to help visualize something (as an atom) that cannot be directly observed 12: a system of postulates, data, and inferences presented as a mathematical description of an entity or state of affairs

syn: Model, Example, Pattern, Exemplar, Ideal, shared meaning element: something set or held before one for guidance or imitation

For software engineering work, the last two definitions seem particularly applicable.

- As defined in (12), we use models as analytical tools for describing and applying the results of research.

- As in definition (11), we use models as description tools (abstractions) which help others understand and "visualize" artifacts of the software engineering discipline which cannot easily be directly observed.

2.1 Models in Software Engineering

There are several uses of models in software engineering. Notice that the first three listed here are models having to do with processes and the last is a model of a software system.

- Analytical models: Systems of metrics, measurements, formulas, graphs etc. which can be used to analyze the results of an experiment or a software development activity. We often use analytical models in software engineering research to compare experimental results to previous practice or to a control (when available). In main line software engineering, we frequently use analytical models to monitor a process, predict process results, or to attempt to convince others of the advantages of a particular new technology or process. It is critical that analytical models answer questions that are important to the audience. Data collection should be unobtrusive. The model results must be displayable in an understandable manner which connects easily to the reason behind use of this analytical model.

- Process models: We can use many techniques, (dataflow, decision tree, flowchart ...) to describe processes for software development and maintenance. These models are used to allow an observer to get an overall view of a process. They can also be used to guide a user through a process. Analytical models which show how to evaluate and monitor the effectiveness of the process should be referenced.

- Organizational models: Software engineering is performed by organizations of people. We can define organizational models to show reporting structures, where in the organization the responsibilities for particular activities are positioned, interdependencies (Who does what for whom?), and communication structures. These can be used to communicate researchers ideas on structures and to guide a group in setting up their organization for most efficient work. Organization models must be implementable, they must be able to be evaluated, and they must be oriented toward solving a real problem, not dealing with management legacies and fiefdoms.

- Technology/architectural models: Software technology is very difficult to visualize. Unlike computer hardware, it can't be walked around and looked at. It is difficult to pull the panels off and poke around inside. We must use models of many kinds (including organizational and process models) to show the construction and operation of an application or system. Some prototypes can be

192

viewed as models of systems user interfaces which can allow a user to have early input into a system under development. Technology models can help a user configure a system. They can help a developer build, extend, or maintain a system. When combined with analytical models, they can be used to predict capacity, performance, and resource requirements of a yet to be built system. It is critical that technology models show a level of detail appropriate for the target audience and that they are up-to-date and accurate.

3 Using Models

In software engineering we use analytical models for monitoring productivity and quality. We also use analytical models to predict project duration and cost [GC87]. We use Technology models to show the architectures of software systems at levels from a simple architectural overview to detailed process models showing the flow of data and control through the system. To be successful, models must be

- useful - they must solve a problem.

- intuitive - the target user must be able to understand and interpret the models.

- predictive - users should be able to use the models to plan their future activities..

3.1 Different Goals Require Different Models

Often, models must be selected and presented for a particular audience. In the Software Reuse Department at Hewlett Packard Laboratories (HP-SRD), one of the our activities is collection of metrics and construction of a portfolio of analytical models to measure and demonstrate the costs and benefits of systematic software reuse. Because different organizations may adopt reuse for different reasons, or evaluate reuse results toward different goals, one model of reuse benefit will not be enough. In our research, we are developing a portfolio of cost-benefit models for reuse. We will need to catalog these models in a way which allows us to select the appropriate ones for a particular situation and audience.

In interviews with organizations around HP who are currently using or considering reuse, we have heard many different business reasons for the interest in reuse including:

- *Develop with fewer people* - This is a common reason for reuse. The organization is under cost pressure and views reuse as a way to develop new products with fewer engineers than would be required if all software was being developed from scratch.

- *Save on maintenance costs* - This organization had many years of experience with maintenance of existing products and sees maintenance costs growing and often diverting resources from new development. Reuse is viewed as a way to amplify the effectiveness of maintenance effort since it will apply to several products instead of a single one.

- *Develop more quickly* - Once a base of reusable software components, and a standard application architecture is in place, new products in the line can be developed more quickly by combining components from the library with application specific components within the framework of the standard architecture.

- *Develop custom applications* - An organization interested in development of many similar applications customized for particular customers can use a standard architecture and component library to build most of each application, developing new components which are added back into the reusable component library as necessary. This is a direction of the Japanese "software factories" [Cu91].

- *Standardize the product line* - A collection of divisions developing products which fit into the same product line heard it's customers asking for standardized interfaces. Reuse of interface programming is seen as a way to satisfy this customer need.

- *Certified software* - A division was under increasing regulatory pressure to certify it's embedded software. Since the volume of embedded software is growing rapidly, reuse of previously certified components in new developments is a way to decrease the certification and testing effort and the cost of new product introduction.

- *Effectively apply more resources to a development effort* - A division was looking for a way to defeat the "Mythical Man-Month" [Br75] principal that adding engineers to a late project makes it later, and be able to apply more engineering resources to a development project to get it to market sooner. A reuse organization split into producers and consumers of reusable code was viewed as a better way to organize the development effort.

- *Ensure quality of software in ROM* - Embedded software, delivered in read-only-memory (ROM) must be free of serious defects. A division sees a risk in its reliance on embedded software in that if a serious defect is delivered, it will be extremely expensive to replace the ROMs in all units. Software reuse is viewed as a way to build software from previously debugged components lowering the risk of delivering defects in products.

Many of the above justifications for reuse have been seen before in a general description (ie: lower costs) however we saw different twists in the reasons each group gave us for considering reuse. For example, the *"Certified software"* and *"Ensure quality of software in ROM"* reasons can be classified under *"reuse to improve software quality"*, however the specific interests of the organizations were different. Different evaluation models and different presentations of reuse results may be required even for these organizations with very similar goals.

3.2 Different People Require Different Models

From our work in software reuse, we have found that communication of the benefits and effects of reuse will involve different presentations to different staff members. A technical argument which may interest a development engineer will probably not impress a general manager who is more interested in financials than computer science. Since a successful reuse program requires business as well as technical support, we must construct models to show both the business and technical implications of reuse clearly. We need to analyze the issues each member of the organization considers important and be able to show convincing benefits of reuse tailored to individual interests.

- Engineering staff - Reuse is often viewed by software developers as taking away their creativity. We must be able to show them that through reuse they can be more creative by reusing previous work to allow concentration on the "interesting" parts of the problem. Productivity models may be convincing here. Technology models are essential to engineering staff.

- First level management - Project managers must understand the true cost of newly developed code as compared to reused code. This true cost includes not only development cost but testing, packaging, and maintenance costs. Frequently decisions to develop vs reuse are made on incomplete data so models showing relative costs, productivity, and quality will be important to this audience.

- Middle level management - Because reusable components are a long term investment in a corporate asset, middle level managers, with a view that spans multiple projects must look for the payback across a collection or series of projects. This means that reusable software must be viewed as an investment to be amortized over future uses, not as a cost to a single project [BB91]. A longer term, cross project financial model for reuse which will accurately show the costs and benefits of the reuse program is needed. This model becomes more complicated when reuse spans organizations as well as projects. These managers will also be involved in building software engineering organizations, organizational, and process models will be important to them.

- Higher level management - Higher level managers will look for the secondary effects of reuse. Products will get to market faster, R&D expenses will be paid back more quickly, new products can be proposed and developed without expanding development staff. The product portfolio can be expanded to include products which could not have been developed before.

We must define a payback model for reuse which takes issues such as time to market into account. It must also facilitate recognition of the contribution of the design and develop with reuse paradigms to expanded and more flexible product portfolio.

4 Connecting Models

Models seldom stand alone. In an effective software engineering setting, we are able to connect appropriate architectural, organizational, process, and analytical models to work toward a particular goal. Here is another example from the software reuse domain.

In a particular organization, the reason for adopting reuse was to decrease the time from recognition of a need for a particular product to getting that product on the market. With a goal of *minimize time to market*, the models chosen for the development environment might include:

- Architectural - Standard, reusable product framework populated by software components drawn from a portfolio of carefully developed, highly cohesive components.

- Organizational - Develop specialists. Component producers develop (with input from component consumers) frameworks and components for the product line. Component consumers are application domain specialists who use the frameworks and collections of components to develop new products based on market requirements. The roles and relationships between the producers and consumers are well defined.

- Process - Optimize development concurrency by separating roles. Design products with knowledge of the reuse portfolio to make sure that a minimum of new components need to be developed.

- Analytical - Measure effort, calendar time, and integration difficulty. Use this to predict time to market for new products, final test and integration time for product development, and critical dates for integration of other work such as documentation, training class preparation, and market introduction plans.

For a different overall goal, such as "Ensure quality of software in ROM" a different set of models may be needed. We must not only match models to particular goals, but we must be able to identify and build networks of models which will support a goal.

5 Reusing Models

We can get the most utility from software engineering models if rather than being developed only for a particular group, they are reusable. Reusable models have different requirements from single use models.

To be reusable, models must be:

- proven - They must have a track record which shows successful use. They should include analytical metrics. They should have clearly stated applicability limits.

- usable - The models should include assistance on how they may be applied to a particular situation.

- accessible - Models must be classified and stored in a way which allows users to find models applicable to their specific needs.

- supported - Models will change over time and use. There must be ways to manage and communicate model evolution.

One goal might be development of a portfolio or catalog of models. To develop an effective catalog, we need to determine the components of a catalog entry. An entry is much more than a single representation, it should include:

- A collection of representations and directions for applicability of the representations.

- A collection of "indications" and "counterindications". Few models are universally applicable. We need to tell where a model can be applied and just as important, where it is not suitable.

- Instructions for successful adoption. This may include process manuals, pictures, appropriate learning processes, or other material which an adopter can use to implement the model.

- Links to other models. A process model may have links to useful analytical models which can evaluate the process and to organizational models which are appropriate for groups adopting the process. An architectural model may have links to analytical models which are useful for benchmarking products developed in that architecture. An analytical model may have a link to a process for collecting metrics.

- Tools for facilitating use of the model. Appropriate tools have an impact on successful adoption of new processes, organizations, architectures and metrics. While tools will not but themselves ensure success, they are important.

- Usage history and collected evaluations of usage. Information on where the model has been used previously. Evaluations of success of the usage.

- User comments and suggestions. This is a more informal expansion on the above topic. It includes notes from other users of a particular model which can help in selection, startup and ongoing usage of the model. This implies that the catalog is dynamic enough to accommodate additions from users.

- Instructions for model evolution. Models are seldom static. Users need to know who to tell about suggestions for changes, and how to get or make modifications.

There are many possibilities for dramatic technological implementations of a catalog. Databases, hypertext and multimedia have great promise for organizing and linking the models and model components. Technology is not essential however and we should not let a lack of technology stand in the way of building a catalog. Paper binders with references to topics and ability to add and remove pages work.

6 Transferring Models

We should look at two different varieties of models when we talk about communicating and transferring models. Analytical, process, organizational, and technological models will be constructed and tested as a result of experiments, development projects, and from empirical data gathered in interviews and observations. If a model has proven useful and accurate over a series of experiments and real projects, it should become part of the portfolio of possibly applicable models for use in future work.

We will also need to look at *models for transfer of models*. There are several well known technology transfer models and some emerging ones. Some of the facets we might use for evaluating technology transfer alternatives are:

- coverage - How widely is the learning spread?
- detail - What is the depth of detail in the transfer? How well is the material understood?
- longevity - Did the transfer "take"? Will the material continue to be used over the long term?
- outcome - Were the expected benefits realized?
- cost - What is the cost in money, time, materials, tools, etc. for use of a particular transfer model. How can we evaluate the value received for the cost?

A few models for technology transfer are:

- Publishing - Models, results, and suggestions for implementation can be published in papers or books. Papers can be given at conferences and workshops. Wide coverage at low cost, but low detail. Usage is completely up to the receiver.
- Classroom teaching - Models, results, and suggestions for implementation can be discussed in detail in a class or tutorial setting. Longer classes allow a great deal of detail in discussion of the material. Coverage is not as wide as publishing, but detail is greater, and questions can be answered during the class.
- Project Based Training - A class can be tailored to a particular audience's interests. For example a class on object oriented design can be presented to a particular project team at the time they are ready to use the material. The class can use the teams application domain for examples and exercises. Because the training is both timely and focused, the detail and likelihood for successful usage are high. The coverage is narrow. The cost is high, especially if the class must be tuned to a particular domain.
- Tools - The target organization adopts and begins to use a tool which implements the model(s) being transferred. Tools will frequently help in getting a new model (process, technology, analytical) put into general use. A caution however: adoption of a tool without enough training and consultation may cause the tool and the model to be used incorrectly or incompletely and eventu-

ally abandoned. There are millions of dollars invested in "shelfware" tools in software engineering labs.

- Consulting - An expert works closely with an organization guiding the implementation of the material being transferred. Coverage is narrow but detail can be very deep. Since the organization receiving the material is getting close, individual attention, the chance for success and continued use of the material is much stronger than in any of the above approaches.

- Pilot projects - The expert works closely with the target organization through the implementation. Problems can be addressed as they are encountered. Systems and models can be tuned as appropriate. Coverage is narrow, probably limited to a particular project. The chance of success and continued implementation is high since the expert is available to help solve problems and customize the solution to the particular project. The project may develop a collection of experts who can help implement in other projects.

- Apprenticeship - People from the target organization work with an expert to develop their own skill in the technique being transferred. These experts can then go back to the their organizations to use their skills in a "pilot" or "consulting" mode with other projects. [Hav87] Broad coverage is a secondary effect as the apprentices are distributed. Since the (former) apprentices have a commitment to the technique and a deep level of understanding, chances of longevity and successful outcome are high.

- Experience Factory [BCC91] - An organization includes both developers and an "experience factory" who's job is to collect and package relevant experience in technology, process, analysis, and organization so that it can be used in other projects.

- Participatory Action Research [WFW92] - Experts can work with an implementing organization before the process to be implemented is completely designed and tested. In a Participatory Action Research activity, the expert researcher works closely with a project to change the project's organization and methods, to introduce new technologies, to monitor progress and results, and to adjust the models when measurements show that attention is needed. The result should be a model, an expert who understands it, and a project which has implemented and tested it and understands it in detail.

Selecting a good model for technology transfer is as important as the technology itself. Experience within HP has shown that a technology or process may be abandoned when the first attempt to use it fails. Usually, this results from usage attempts after a class or paper presentation without the long term commitment or deep understanding of an expert. In the few situations where an expert has worked closely with the implementing project, the project has a much greater probability of success in using the material. We need a portfolio of transfer models with selection criteria weighing the goals and constraints of the target and the provider.

6.1 Evaluating Transfer

Some organizations evaluate the success of their transfer. Schools have long used testing and grading to evaluate whether students remember/understand the material that has been presented. Tutorial presenters often collect "Feedback Forms" at the end of a session to measure the audience's opinions of the material and the presentation. While a "Feedback Form" will get an immediate opinion and can help improve future sessions, it will not measure whether the session has been an effective transfer. Visits or other evaluations at intervals of months or years after the transfer work could help determine whether a transfer was really effective. Some organizations do go to greater depths to measure the long term effects of their transfer and training. Hitachi for example tested program development time as a measure of the efficiency of training on a new tool (Eagle) and development process [TMTT92]. There is speculation that some organizations may not want to accurately access technology transfer efficiency since it might show that they are not effective [Hav87].

There is an opportunity for development of analytical models to accompany processes for technology transfer.

7 Conclusion

The word "model" has many meanings in the dictionary. It also has many meanings in software engineering research. We understand the concepts of process, organizational, analytical, and technological models for software engineering work but even those models must be tuned for a particular audience and goal. A software engineering research organization like HP-SRD must develop portfolios of models with selection and applicability criteria to indicate where each is appropriate. We must extend the concept of "model" beyond the above meanings into models/processes for technology transfer and for evaluation of transfer.

8 References

[BB91]   B. Barnes and T. Bollinger, "Making Reuse Cost Effective", IEEE Software, January 1991.

[BCC91] V. R. Basili, G. Caldiera, and G. Cantone, "A Reference Architecture for the Component Factory", ACM Transactions on Software Engineering and Methodology, Vol. 1, No. 1, January 1992, Pages 53-80.

[BR75]   Frederick Brooks, The Mythical Man-Month: Essays on Software Engineering, Addison Wesley, 1975.

[CB91]   G. Caldiera and V. Basili, Identifying and Qualifying Reusable Software Components, IEEE Computer, February 1991.

[GC87]   B. Grady and D. Caswell, "Software Metrics: Establishing a Company Wide Program, Prentice-Hall, 1987, Chapter 4.

[Hav87]   R. O. Havelock, "The Technology Transfer Strategies of R&D Consortia, Transferring Software Engineering Tool Technology (Workshop proceedings), IEEE Computer Society, 1987, Pages 136-153.

[TMTT92] M. Tsuda, Y. Morioka, M. Takadachi, M. Takahashi, "Productivity Analysis of Software Development with an Integrated CASE Tool", Proceedings 14th International Conference on Software Engineering, May 1992, Pages 49-58.

[Web]   Webster's New Collegiate Dictionary, G. & C. Merriam Co., 1979, page 732.

[WFW92] William Foote White, "Participatory Action Research", Sage Publications, 1991

9 Biography

Kevin Wentzel is a project manager in the Software Reuse Department in the Software Technology Laboratory at Hewlett Packard Laboratories. Together with Martin Griss, he has proposed and built a multidisciplinary team oriented toward experimental research in software engineering and software reuse. Prior to joining HP Labs, Kevin worked in various engineering and management roles in several HP divisions developing software products, software libraries for reuse, and software development tools. Kevin has worked at Hewlett Packard Company for 15 years.

Model Reuse and Technology Transfer

Albert Endres

IBM Development Laboratory
Böblingen, Germany

Abstract. Quantitative models are a widely accepted means to predict and to control software quality and development productivity. If these models are updated to reflect the positive effect of new processes or new technologies, and if the same models are reused by several projects, this will make the advantage of the new technology visible and will create pressure to adopt it. Thus, reuse of models becomes a vehicle for technology transfer.

1 Introduction

Models are descriptions of reality. They help to explain or understand certain aspects that may normally be obscured. In software engineering, an important domain of modeling is the development process. Graphical models, e.g. Petri nets, can be used to describe the interdependency of tasks. Quantitative models are the basis if predictions are made for development costs or for product quality. Such a quantitative model is typically a function relating some input parameters with some output parameters.

Models are a way to condense experience and to communicate this experience to others. The person who develops a model may use own experience or other people's experience. Of course, models are the more useful, the more people can use (reuse) them. Another interesting way to condense experience and to communicate it to others is through the definition of rules. This point is illustrated elsewhere [1].

2 What makes models reusable?

A model is reusable if it represents a good abstraction of a commonly occurring problem. This is not different from reusable software. An abstraction is well chosen, if it includes those entities that are essential contributors, and leaves out those which are insignificant. Those contributors that vary significantly must be parameterized, for others default or constant values can be assumed.

The most obvious parameter for both cost estimating and quality predictions is the size of a product. It is normally expressed in number of lines of code (LOC). The simplest models use just this parameter. It makes a model difficult to use if the number of parameters is too high or if their values cannot be derived easily. By standardizing on the processes involved or on the tools used, the number of parameters can be reduced. The LOC parameter is an example of a parameter that cannot be determined easily if we are early in a project. Therefore attempts have been made to substitute it by other parameters, e.g. function points. The great advantage of LOC is that toward the end of a project it can be measured easily, i.e. it can be used to compare planned and actual values.

In general, the model should rely only on such entities for which actual data can be collected during or after a project. The form of a model is not essential. In the case of cost estimating, a mathematical formula or a table will do. Simple curves or a bar chart can be used to visualize the data. Whenever the amount of data to be collected or to be evaluated exceeds the manual housekeeping limits, a programmed tool is justified.

3 When should we reuse models?

One should reuse models whenever predictions have to be made for the same type of activity. Models are helpful also when analysing empirical data. Unless we relate measured values to some expected (or predicted) values it is hard to see what they mean.

Models of the kind used in the software development process are also useful in controlling the progress of a project. By comparing actual versus planned (predicted) data we can determine the project's status. To be able to control an on-going project, the model has to be decomposed into the contributions coming from individual process steps or from different organisational units. The same models should be used by all projects of an organisation if possible. This allows to compare projects with each other and can trigger technology transfer (as discussed later).

When models are used to describe those aspects of a project that are critical for its success, the periodic updating of models is a way to express the progress that has been made from one project to the next. Models then serve as a mechanism to support the principle of continuous process improvement, which relies on the steps predict, measure and improve.

4 An example

To illustrate the previous points a simple example is given. Fig. 1 represents a defect removal model, i.e. it encodes the experience of some organisation with respect to error insertion and error removal. The assumption here is that over the life of a product 20 defects are inserted and removed per KLOC. With the currently used development process 17 of these are typically removed prior to shipment and 3 are found during the maintenance phase. The phase designations used in the example are the following:

Phase	Activity
I	Requirements Definition
II	Design, Specification
III	Coding, Documentation
IV	Test, Validation
V	Installation, Distribution
VI	Maintenance

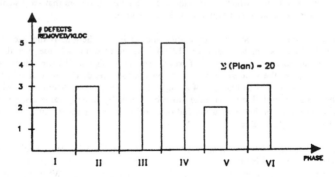

Figure 1. Defect removal model (current technology)

If appropriate data are collected, a comparison can be made between the prediction and the actual data. Fig. 2 shows such a comparison at the end of the project, i.e. after completion of the maintenance period. This comparison can be used to recalibrate the model so that better predictions can be made for the next project that uses the same process.

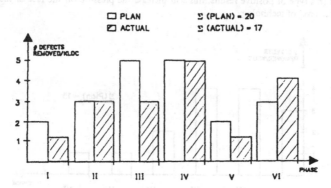

Figure 2. Plan vs. actual comparison (post-mortem)

As Fig. 3 shows, the same model can also be used for controlling the status of the project (in-process measurement). In this case, actuals are compared to that part of the plan only that has been achieved so far (plan-to-date).

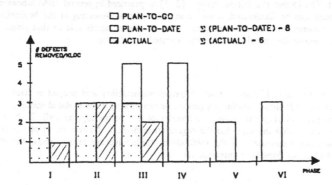

Figure 3. In-process measurement

By the way, exactly the same type of charts can be used to describe the cost predictions of a project, to perform post-mortem cost analysis or to exercise cost control while the project is still on-going.

5 The role of models in technology transfer

If new technology is introduced in the development process this should have a positive effect on some aspects, be it quality or cost. For two types of technologies, namely CASE tools and OOA/OOD methods, we know that they have a positive effect on the quality of the delivered code. This is paid for by some additional effort in the early phases. In terms of our defect removal model, this could result in a prediction as given in Fig. 4. Although the total number of defects handled during the life of the project only decreases from 20 to 15, the most dramatic change is predicted for the maintenance phase, i.e. a reduction by a factor of 3. By propagating this model instead of that of Fig. 1, all projects will see the benefits (and effects) of the new approach. It will create the competitive pressure that is needed for projects to evaluate new technology. As soon as a project has adopted this model, it can track its results against the new prediction. Whenever a project achieves this type of positive results, this will increase the pressure on the rest of the organisation to move to the same level of technology.

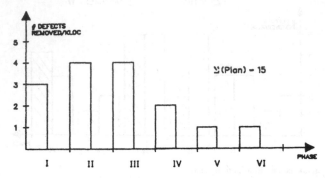

Figure 4. Alternate defect removal model (new technology)

If valuable new experience is made in one of the early phases of a project, the entire organisation should not have to wait until this project has completed all other phases of its lifecycle, before this new knowledge is being transferred. The Defect Prevention Process [2, 3] as practiced in several IBM laboratories shows how this learning process can be accelerated. It uses a so-called Kick-off-meeting at the beginning of each phase to communicate experiences from other projects as far as they are applicable to that phase. This procedure can be used to propagate the knowledge on newly updated models also.

6 Summary

The use of quantitative models does certainly improve predictability and project control. Models can also serve as a mechanism to facilitate continuous process improvement. If the updated models are propagated for use (reuse) by all projects, they can trigger the transfer of new technology as well. If chosen correctly they can bring across exactly that message that the organisation needs to be convinced of the advantage of new methods or new tools. Conversely, if the methods or tools advocate cannot show the effect on cost or quality models, he has not done his homework yet.

References

1. A. Endres: On the empirical foundations of software engineering, IBM Techn. Report TR-05.458 (1989)

2. C.L. Jones: A process-integrated approach to defect prevention, IBM Syst. J. 24,2 (1985)

3. R.G. Mays et al.: Experiences with defect prevention, IBM Syst. J. 29,1 (1990)

Packaging for Reuse and Reuse of Models

Stuart I. Feldman

Bellcore
445 South Street, Morristown, NJ 07960, USA
Telephone: +1-201-829-4305, Fax: +1-201-829-5981
E-mail: sif@bellcore.com

1. Introduction

A crucial stumbling block to effective reuse is understanding what material can be saved and transferred, and how it should be used. Even the apparently easy case of code reuse has proved to be extremely difficult, partly for organizational and sociological reasons, but also for serious technical ones. These include packaging the relevant materials, making sure that associated information is available without overwhelming the re-user, and assisting in transforming, evolving, and porting the code.

These difficulties and others clearly get in the way when discussing higher level abstractions, such as process and product models. These categories of model are essential and overlap. Architectures can be very hard to describe because of the risk of having too much detail (an implementation specification) or too little (a management presentation). Process descriptions needs to be detailed enough to be relevant to an organization, but without binding in all the working details (e.g., names of people fulfilling roles). Hard and fast rules are not however feasible.

2. What makes models reusable?

The key features that encourage reusability of a model are

1) It must be presented or made available in a sufficiently clear way that the potential customer can tell its relevance.

2) It should come with tools to utilize the saved information.

3) There must be a belief or demonstration that it is better to reuse than to start afresh.

The first topic addresses the representations of the model. There need to be several representations, depending on purpose and application. The people deciding to follow a particular model may be quite different from the ones who do the quotidian labor and the ones who ensure conformance to the goal. For many purposes, diagrams and pretty pictures are essential, since they capture the interest and enable discussions of details. Analytic frameworks and details are also very useful: Having a model that enables one to forecast resource needs and schedule and quality impacts can make choices clearer and also encourage use of a methodology. For an architecture, the content need to be available in a number of forms, ranging from object definitions and interface specifications to block diagrams and animations.

The second topic addresses information storage, representation, and processing. These issues are technical and even empirically testable. The existence of good tools and easy access to the information is very important. It is also necessary to be realistic about the size of this collection. In the near future, the number of detailed and reusable models will be measured at best in hundreds, so sophisticated search techniques are less important than the usefulness of the model and the availability of associated tools.

The third topic is the demonstrable superiority of using an earlier model. Most process model transfer probably happens through experience, general descriptions and prescriptions, and swapping of stories (later enshrined as 'best practice') rather than through a formal storage and transfer mechanism. Computer scientists are more comfortable with formalized and mechanized techniques, in part because they permit experiments and controlled studies to produce results that will be believed when there are changes of context. Until the variables are known and described, it requires an act of faith or intuition to believe that an earlier experience will apply to a new project. Similarly, adopting an architecture is frequently done on the basis of experience and informal criteria, rather than any mathematical analysis of the best fit to the problem. This approach is thoroughly justified, since we lack either data or method that would allow that job to be done convincingly for a complicated problem.

3. How would we organize and build up reusable model libraries?

As suggested above, organizing the library is less important than building it. Recording and analyzing a model is arduous and rarely rewarded, so the library will take a long time to grow to unmanageable size. We need an understanding of the tools that must accompany a model to make its use easily justifiable. Most new applications require changes from previous work, so it is essential to have adequate documentation of previous uses and information on which aspects or parameters are easy and which are hard to change.

However, the most pressing problem is getting sufficient information about what was done, and transmitting knowledge of the overall context and the inferences to be drawn from the choices.

4. What mechanisms are needed to support reuse of models across projects?

The biggest problems in practice are vocabulary and context: how much information is needed to understand what the model requires. Examples: What sort of organization implications does a particular process have? What tools are needed to take advantage of an architecture? What skills (process) are required to utilize an architecture (product) model?

The obvious approach is further to formalize the problem, to have cogent and abstract descriptions of what is being done and well defined terminology and interface definitions. Clearly such work needs to proceed, but there is a risk that a highly formal description will be of no practical interest to the people who make the choices.

5. Some Comments on Empiric Software Research Problems

5.1. The Problem: Lack of Published and Accepted Software-Related Data

There is a crying need for empiric validation of software engineering techniques, methodologies, and approaches. There are very few reliable studies based on real (as opposed to contrived or class project) software product and process data. Experience has shown that looking at the details of actual usage can yield counter-intuitive results and technologically significant insights. Examples include the lack of complexity of most manually entered expressions and the small amount of stack space required to support most programs; the first affects register set design, the second affects practical RISC architectures. For larger scale software and software development, we have few similar data.

The lack of hard data and good analyses impedes research and practical application of research: lack of good benchmark data and trusted comparative studies makes it unclear whether a new line is worthwhile, and without such data a hardheaded development manager will be loath to utilize a technique in a serious effort. There is of course a chicken-and-egg problem: if no one will try something first, then it never gets used.

5.2. Availability of Raw Data

A lot of information is available. Good development organizations keep careful records of the aspects of a project that matter to them: process records if reimbursement depends on them, product records if replicability and support demand them. Ideal data are rare, but information suitable for a great deal of research does exist. It can be difficult, tedious, and expensive to gather and analyze this information, and most development groups are more interested in fighting fires and meeting deadlines than in such analysis, but today's process-improvement culture makes these activities more welcome.

Practical difficulties in the way of such research include finding sources of information, getting access to it, getting adequate information to provide an adequate basis for analysis, restrictions on sharing or revealing proprietary data, and possible conditions on publication. Some of these problems may be less severe than people think. Bellcore's development organization would be willing to have researchers examine information and publish results with relatively few strings. Other companies would probably do the same, if the research activity could be expected to be of significant benefit and be relatively unobtrusive.

Research that requires active participation (controlled experiments rather than retrospective studies) are harder to arrange. There are excellent cases in the literature involving small projects, but few involving large projects or big software. There is some hope, but it requires much closer links to the target organization and a research goal that can be of direct and immediate benefit (such as justification for switching to a major new methodology).

5.3. Methodology and Samples

In order to form the basis of real engineering, the information needs to be relevant to current and future practice. Toy examples are fine for the first demonstration of a new idea, but analyses of large software systems are needed to be really useful. (It is possible to quibble about metrics and thresholds, but reports on a thousand-line student project will rarely influence people who manage dozens of programmers.) Furthermore, it is necessary to know something about the application and programming style to make a meaningful comparison between projects – kernel code for a real time operating system has little in common with screen specification code in a database application.

At present we have only crude ways to approach such problems of design of software experiments, data analysis, standardization, and presentation. We have even less understanding of ways to describe software process in complex and changing organizations, or of associating low-level actions with significant software tasks.

5.4. Examples

Studies of software products ("artifact research" or "software archeology") may be unfashionable, but we can learn a great deal of practical value. The engineering of support systems requires information on a variety of facts. For example, in practice,

what is the distribution of module sizes, cohesivenesses?
how complex are object (class) hierarchies?
how much use is made of multiple inheritance?
what is the distribution (dynamic and static) of uses of methods?

Related questions involve studies of the evolution of software

how do such parameters change as a project moves among phases?
how do the coarse-grained and fine-grained structures and change with time?
what cues are there in the software to suggest rewriting?

Information from other parts of the life cycle could provide information such as

effect of testing methodologies on faults reported from the field*
effect of module size, language choice, programming methodology on field faults?
relation between software metrics and field performance and faults

More process oriented questions, require capturing software engineering activity, not just results. The bounds of a position paper do not permit an enumeration of possible projects.

---

* A colleague recently showed me data from a real development project, demonstrating a significant relation between the amount of coverage achieved during unit testing and the number of errors uncovered during system integration. Different coverage measures may have usefully different relationships. Up to now most arguments encouraging use of such tools have been anecdotal or based on general arguments and faith, rather than based on clear evidence that would convince a skeptical manager that such tools actually pay off.

A Reuse Culture for Software Construction

Claus Lewerentz

Forschungszentrum Informatik Karlsruhe
lewerentz@fzi.de

Abstract. In this position paper we advocate the idea of creating a new style of
software construction that is based on the systematic reuse of application specific
collections of software components and design structures together with corresponding process models. On the structural level object oriented approaches
proved to be well suited for the specification and realization of such application
frameworks. On the management level a whole set of measures have to be taken to
foster the creation, propagation, and application of reusable software. Particularly
there are different processes for constructing general or application specific and reusable components or frameworks, and for the development of a particular application software system.

Reuse of Software Structures and Development Processes

Both the reuse of software and the explicit modelling of software processes is an ongoing debate for some years now. Despite of that we rather rarely find the systematic application of these ideas in industrial software production nowadays. From our point of
view the major impediments do not come from the basic technical means like modelling
methods, programming languages or tools, but lie in todays generally used single-piece
production style for application software. As done in other constructive sciences the experiences from building systems of a certain kind (e.g. interactive information system)
and for a particular application domain (e.g. financial management) have to be better
captured and packaged for reuse in future development projects with similar charcter-
istics. Today reuse often is restricted to rather low-level components like function libraries; only for some application fields there exist higher-level constructs.

Careful analysis and experimentation often reveals that only a limited number of
well-tried, successful, and robust components and design patterns are used to construct
software systems of a certain type. Specific patterns are found on any design level from
simple components to complex subsystems and entire system architectures. Such structures are either derived from some theory (which is missing for software engineering)
or from experience (backed up by qualitative and quantitative assessment) and serve to
guide new system development by restricting the degree of variation. To do so they
have to be easy understandable (i.e. not too complex, well documented), transferable,
adaptable, reliable, and trustworthy.

This is reflected by a component-oriented style of software construction, as proposed
in [2]. It aims to develop and to use prefabricated system skeletons, generic design patterns and reusable components for certain classes of application systems. This approach
promises to be an effective way to acquire, apply, and to evaluate structural design
knowledge and to create a marketplace for reusable software. From our point of view it
has to be supplemented by explicitly capturing process-oriented knowledge, that now
mainly exists implicitly in the structure of generic designs and components. Besides the

question 'What can I reuse?' one has to answer the question 'How can I reuse it?'.

Object-oriented techniques seem to provide a good basis to incorporate the different aspects into one comprehensive methodology that helps us to work out successful structures and processes.

Ingredients for a Reuse Culture

The following list sketches only major aspects of the desired development style.We use the term 'culture' to indicate that there are many aspects which are quite different from the current practice of software production (cf [1]). There are a lot more open questions than answers, but it seems worthwhile considering them.

Modelling Application Domain Specific Knowledge. To solve problems within a particular application domain (e.g. banking) it is necessary to identify and to understand the requirements, key notions and concepts of that domain. The application of object-oriented analysis techniques should result in the formulation of a minimal set of orthogonal concepts together with appropriate abstractions for common concepts. From this the design of an object-oriented class library is derived comprising interface and (multiple) implementation classes for each concept. In [5] it is demonstrated, how such a design strategy considerably reduces the amount of coding that had to be done for implementing a library of abstract data types. Such application domain specific libraries have to be evaluated, refined, and extended by an evolutionary process due to experiences gained from constructing application systems based on them. The thorough analysis of the Eiffel class library described in [6] quantifies the effects of systematic restructuring such an object-oriented library.

Development of General Application Designs. To facilitate the construction of certain application types, e.g. interactive graphical applications, so-called frameworks have been developed (e.g. ET++ described in [4]). Such class libraries contain sets of interdependent classes, that realize certain base functionality (e.g. window management) and provide useful subsystems or generic architectural patterns for this application type (e.g. model-view-controller). Even entire generic applications which define the basic behavior and interaction style of a whole class of applications have been developed. Such general application designs could be combined with an application domain specific library to create a generic application framework (GAF, cf [1]). Typically, specific strategies (process model) for developing particular applications from such GAFs are incorporated in the GAF design. These process models have to be documented and supported explicitly (cf [7]).

Both the development of application domain specific libraries and the development of general application designs are investments for future reuse and need much experience in the application domain as well as in system design. There is a need for many comprehensive collections of such application specific 'development kits'.

Formal Specification of Components. One of the essential requirements for reusable software libraries is the reliability of components. Supplier and user of the library are separated, correct use of parameterized (generic) components and composition of components imposes additional burden on the component supplier. A precise semantic definition of component interfaces is the basis for correctness. Further, formally defined and guaranteed compatibility relations for certain design patterns (cf. [4]) like between

211

concepts, interfaces and implementations are required. This can be achieved by mathematically founded development methods using logical specifications and proof techniques (e.g. refinement calculus). Such formal development approaches require a formal foundation of the modelling and implementation languages and also require additional support to be effectively usable. At least for certain application domains such rigorous approaches to reliability are necessary.

Classification and Retrieval of Components and Design Patterns. An essential factor for the success of reuse is an appropriate support for finding the right GAF and the desired components in the whole set of libraries. New approaches to documentation are necessary that take entire design patterns as described in [3] and [4] into account. Classification schemes (taxonomies) for application requirements together with expert system and data base support are required. The software information management is a real challenge.

Construction of Applications. An application is constructed by selecting an appropriate GAF and adapting or refining it according to the specific requirements. A crucial prerequisite is to understand the GAFs structure and how to specialize or extend it, i.e. the process model that is underlying the GAF. The evaluation of the derived applications and of the related construction process generates feed-back that leads to the evolution of the libraries.

Market-Place for Reusable Components. The component-oriented development style should change the way how industry produces software and brings it to market. It will create a need for new solutions in standardization, copyrighting, distribution, and prizing of software components. In the field of PC software we can already see the success of such strategies.

References

1. Bertrand Meyer: The new Culture of Software Development: Reflections on the Practice of Object Oriented Design, Proc. TOOLS '89, pp. 13-23, 1989
2. Dennis Tsichritzis, Oscar Nierstrasz, Simon Gibbs: Beyond Objects: Objects. In: D. Tsichritzis (ed.): Object Frameworks, Centre Universitaire d´Informatique, Univerity of Geneva, July 1992, pp 331-346
3. Peter Coad: Object-oriented Patterns, CACM Vol. 35, No. 9, pp 153-159, September 1992
4. Erich Gamma: Objektorientierte Software-Entwicklung am Beispiel von ET++: Klassenbibliothek, Werkzeuge, Design, Ph.D. thesis, 180 pp, Universität Zürich, 1991
5. Franz Weber: Reusable Software Catalogues, Technical Report FZI-ProSt/91-3, 6 pp, Forschungszentrum Informatik Karlsruhe, 1991
6. Eduardo Casais: Automatic Reorganization of Object-oriented Hierarchies: A Case Study, Technical Report FZI-ProSt/92-4, 19 pp, Forschungszentrum Informatik Karlsruhe, 1992
7. Jacky Estublier: Reusing Software Processes, in J.C.Derniame (Ed.): Software Process Technology, pp 156-158, LNCS 635, Springer Verlag (1992)

Experimental Software Engineering; Packaging for Reuse

Frank McGarry

NASA/Goddard Space Flight Center

For 16 years, the Software Engineering Laboratory (SEL) at NASA Goddard has been conducting experiments in software engineering technology toward a goal of understanding and improving the software process used on NASA projects. The SEL has combined the talents of personnel at NASA, the University of Maryland, and Computer Sciences Corporation. These three organizations have jointly participated in defining, executing, and analyzing over 100 software engineering experiments utilizing mid-sized NASA ground support systems as study cases.

The results of the studies have been published and widely distributed, but more importantly the results have been incorporated into the NASA development environment so that the development process has continually evolved and matured as a result of the experiments. The SEL has additionally analyzed the major lessons learned from 15 years of studies and has itself matured into an experimental environment, called an 'Experience Factory' (Ref. 1). Some of the major lessons that have been derived from the 16 years of effort in experimental software engineering include the following. Each has been supported with numerous experimental studies:

1. Measurement must be treated as a means-to-an-end and must not be treated as an end in itself.

    The amount of information that has been required to support the numerous experiments in the SEL has continually decreased over the years because of the increased emphasis on the 'Goal-Question-Metric' paradigm of Basili (Ref. 2). In many software environments, there is an excessive effort put towards defining new measures, and defining standards for measures, and developing tools to collect measures without clearly understanding why a particular measure would be needed.

2. Continuous/Sustained improvement should be the goal of any development organization; not technology breakthroughs as an answer.

    The SEL has concluded that although some specific software technologies may have more impacts than others, the overall philosophy of continuous, sustained improvement should be the over-riding goal of any development organization.

3. Concepts of the Experience Factory require both a production software organization element as well as an analysis element.

    Each element has a clear, well defined role and the identification of these elements must be kept separate. Successful studies cannot assume that the development organization will carry out both tasks successfully.

4. The major steps in successful experimentation in the Experience Factory Concept are (1) Understanding, (2) Assessment/Tailoring, and (3) Packaging

> Before any change or improvement can be expected within a software production environment, a well established baseline of software within the environment must be established. The *'Understanding'* is the most important yet most forgotten step. One must be able to characterize the process, as well as to define the characteristics of the typical product. Without this 'Understanding', no comparison nor improvement can be expected, since there is nothing to measure change against.
>
> *Assessment* entails the analysis and tailoring of specific software techniques to determine their compatibility with the production environment and *Packaging* includes the infusion of the identified improved process into a media for use by production projects (used as stand ards, training, and tools). This *Packaging* step is the key element of successful *reuse* of evolving models, relationships, and general experiences produced by the analysis of software engineering experiments.

This 3 step approach toward successful reuse of experiences and models is depicted in Figure 1.

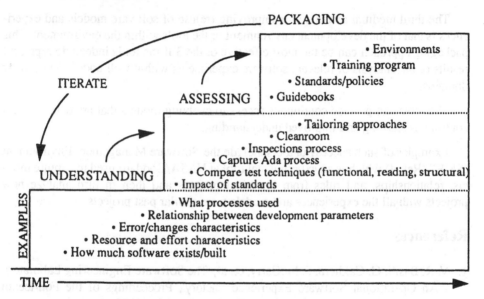

Figure 1: Steps in 'Experience Factory' Concepts - Packaging for Reuse

In software production organizations where the reuse of models and experiences are successful, *packaging* is supported with 3 approaches.

1. Process *Standards and Polices* -

Available, appropriate models and experiences are captured in written policies that define the process (development, management, assurance, etc.). The policies must be directed to specific domain characteristics and in that they must contain the characterization of the derived/models which have been produced by the continuous experimentation and improvement for the production organization. Examples of such successful packaging into relevant policies include the SEL series of policy documents which are used to support all mission operations software at NASA/Goddard (e.g. Ref. 3).

2. Training -

The second medium for packaging which assures the reuse of models in software production domains is that of 'Training'. Both formal and informal classes, workshops, symposiums, etc. can be a key element of packaging for reuse. Results of any experimentation, assessment and tailoring which may be represented as empirically developed models are effectively reused by incorporating these results into the standard training and development programs of organizations. Examples of such successful training programs include those which exist in the form of managers and developers classes and workshops within the SEL. The SEL has produced a series of classes directed specifically at the production domain which is studied to continually build improved models.

Domains with similar characteristics also make use of those SEL training tools.

3. Tools -

The third medium available for improving (re)use of software models and experiences is that of the development environment or the tools within the environment. This packaging approach can be the most effective of the 3 if the tools indeed do represent results of the analysis of relevant software experiments within well understood similar domains.

The tools can provide continuous access to evolving models that are derived from continuous learning and improved understanding.

Examples of such successful tools include the 'Software Management Environment (SME)' (Ref. 4) which is an experimental tool at NASA/Goddard used to capture models, relationships, and rules from historical projects and then in turn analyze new projects with all the experiences and models from similar past projects.

References

1. V. R. Basili, G. Caldiera, F. McGarry, et. al, 'The Software Engineering Laboratory - An Operational Software Experience Factory', Proceedings of the Fourteenth International Conference on Software Engineering, May 1992.

2. V. R. Basili and D. M. Weiss, 'A Methodology for Collecting Valid Software Engineering Data', IEEE Transactions on Software Engineering, November 1984.

3. L. Landis, F. McGarry, S. Waligora, et. al, 'Manager's Handbook for Software Development (Revision 1)', SEL-84-001, November 1990.

4. R. Handrick, D. Kistler, J. Valett, 'Software Management Environment (SME), Concepts and Architecture (Revision 1)', SEL-89-103, August 1992.

Experimental Designs for Validating Metrics and Applying them across Multiple Projects

Norman F. Schneidewind

Code AS/Ss Naval Postgraduate School Monterey, CA 93943, U.S.A

Abstract

We explain why it is important to validate metrics for use on multiple projects and how the risk of doing so can be assessed. We also point out that by prototyping the measurement plan on a project, we can eliminate the risk inherent in the process of validating metrics on one project and applying them on another project, where the two projects may have significant differences in application and development environment characteristics. In order to support the application of metrics across multiple projects, there must be reuse of methodologies, metrics, and metrics processes. A metrics methodology is reusable when there is a process associated with the methodology that can be applied across projects. Both the metrics and the process for applying metrics must be reusable. Metrics are reusable when validated metrics can be applied across projects, using the methodology. An example is given of assessing risk by using the confidence limits of a metric to evaluate the consequences of best-case and worst-case outcomes of using metrics on multiple projects.

1 Introduction

Validating metrics (i.e., showing that a metric's values are statistically associated with corresponding quality factor values [3]) and applying metrics across multiple projects and environments [4] is a very important and difficult issue in software measurement. It is an important issue because most organizations have a need to use metrics on multiple projects or in multiple environments. Secondly, it is desirable to validate metrics on one project (*validation project*) for their intended use on other projects (*application projects*). For example, our goal could be to achieve a specified quality, as measured by error count, on the application project but we can't wait until the software is delivered to find out whether we have met our goal. Therefore, if we have validated a metric on the *validation project* (e.g., size or complexity partitions the module set into subsets of "error modules" and "no error" modules" with acceptable statistical significance) and assessed the risk of using the metric on the application project (see below), we could use the metric as an *indirect measure* [1,2] of quality to monitor and control the quality of software during the design phase of the *application project*.

Validating metrics for application to multiple projects is also a difficult issue because many changes in process and product can occur within a single project. This problem is exacerbated with multiple projects because variations in product and process are even more significant. As a consequence of these differences, validation results may be project and *application dependent* [4]. Despite these problems we would like to capitalize on the results and experiences of earlier projects and apply them to new projects. Thus there is a need for reuse of methodologies, metrics, and metrics processes.

2 Reusable Methodologies, Metrics, and Processes

A metrics methodology is reusable when there is a process associated with the methodology that can be applied across projects. Both the metrics and the process for applying metrics must be reusable. Metrics are reusable when validated metrics can be applied across projects, using the methodology. However when using metrics on multiple projects, we must consider the risk of doing so (i.e., a metric that is valid on one project may not be valid on another project). The reason that metrics may give inconsistent results across projects is that applications (e.g., real-time), product characteristics (e.g., size), process maturity level (e.g., use of inspection), development environments (e.g., design methodology and programming language), personnel (e.g., skill and experience) may be project dependent and differ considerably among projects. In addition, on a given project, there could be a considerable time lag between the collection of a metric and its validation against a quality factor (e.g., reliability) such that the metric is no longer representative of the current condition of a product or process. These effects can be understood better by analyzing Figure 1, where the metric validation process is interpreted as follows:

- The events and time progression of the validation project are depicted by the top horizontal line and arrow. This time line consists of Project 1 with metric M collection in Phase T1 (step 1); factor F collection in Phase T2 (step 2); and validation of M with respect to F in Phase T2 (step 3).

- The events and time progression of the application project are depicted by the bottom horizontal line and arrow. This project is later in chronological time than the validation project but has the same phases T1 and T2. This time line consists of Project 2 with metric collection M' in Phase T1 (step 4); application of M' to assess, control, and predict quality in Phase T1 (step 5); collection of factor F' in Phase T2 (step 6); and revalidation of M and M' with respect to F and F' in Phase T2 (step 7).

- Metric M' is the same metric as M but, in general, it has different values since it is collected in a different project. The same statement applies to F' and F.

- An important element of this process is the construction and maintenance of a database of project characteristics and histories of metrics validation and application that could be retrieved for assessing the applicability of metrics on future projects.

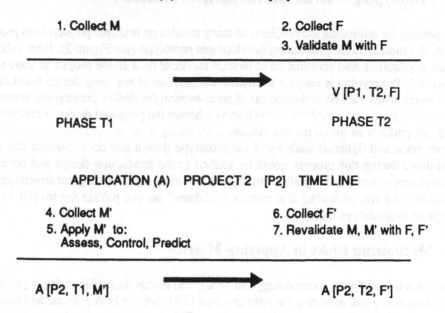

VALIDATION (V) PROJECT 1 [P1] TIME LINE
1. Collect M
2. Collect F
3. Validate M with F
V [P1, T2, F]
PHASE T1
PHASE T2
APPLICATION (A) PROJECT 2 [P2] TIME LINE
4. Collect M'
5. Apply M' to:
Assess, Control, Predict
6. Collect F'
7. Revalidate M, M' with F, F'
A [P2, T1, M']
A [P2, T2, F']

Figure 1: Metrics Validation Process

VALIDATE
APPLY
REVALIDATE
1. COLLECT M
2. COLLECT F
3. VALIDATE M WITH F
4. COLLECT M'
5. APPLY M' TO:
Assess, Control, & Predict
6. COLLECT F'
7. REVALIDATE
M, M' WITH F, F'
PROJECT TIME LINE
PROTOTYPE PHASE T1
DESIGN PHASE T2
TEST/OPERATIONS PHASE T3

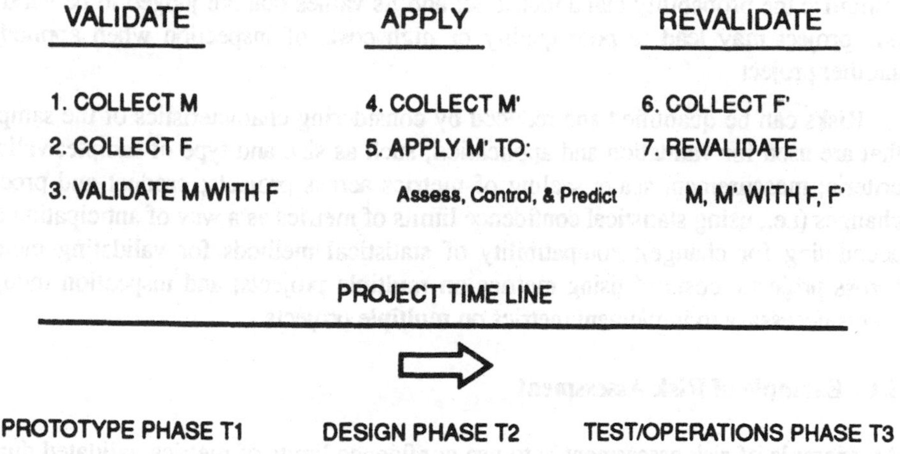

Figure 2: Metrics Validation Process with Prototyping

3 Prototyping Metrics and the Metrics Process

A process for mitigating the problems of using metrics on multiple projects is to prototype the measurement plan during development prototype (see Figure 2). Here validation, application, and revalidation of metrics all occur on a single project as shown in Figure 2. Prototyping is used for the traditional purpose of assessing design feasibility. However, when viewed in the context of *measurement feasibility*, prototyping assumes greater importance: in addition to evaluating whether the proposed design is realizable, we can perform an initial metrics validation by taking a sample of factors and metrics from static and dynamic analyses of the prototype design and code. Metrics that are validated during this process would be applied to the production design and code to assess, contol and predict quality. Prototyping a metrics plan has the great advantage of avoiding the risk of finding that metrics "validated" on one project are invalid when applied to another project.

4 Minimizing Risks in Applying Metrics

Our metrics validation methodology can be applied across dissimilar multiple projects *by recognizing and assessing the risks involved* [3,4]. We can both *estimate* and reduce the risk of using metrics on multiple projects. This is important for the metrics user who needs to recognize that the choice of metrics and their values can have a significant effect on the quality of software that is achieved and on the cost and amount of inspection that is incurred on multiple projects. Also, the tradeoff between quality goals and the amount and cost of inspection that is required to achieve those goals must be recognized. We have addressed these issues by developing a methodology for managing the risks associated with using metrics on multiple projects [4]. We want to minimize the probability that a metric set and its values that are judged to be valid on one project may lead to poor quality or high costs of inspection when applied to another project.

Risks can be quantified and reduced by considering characteristics of the samples that are used for validation and application, such as size and type of sample; validity criteria; measurement scale; scaling of metrics across projects; product and process changes (i.e., using statistical confidence limits of metrics as a way of anticipating and accounting for change); compatibility of statistical methods for validating metrics across projects; costs of using metrics on multiple projects; and inspection requirements necessary to implement metrics on multiple projects.

4.1 Example of Risk Assessment

An example of risk assessment is to use confidence limits of metrics validated during the *validation project* or *prototype* phase as the best-case and worst-case values to evaluate for the application project or production phase. That is, rather than confining the analysis to using an estimate of the critical value of a metric M_c in the *validation project* (i.e., a value that can discriminate between high and low quality software [3]) and assuming that value will apply in the *application project*, we base the analysis on assuming that the critical value M'_c will be at the limit. Then we can evaluate the consequences of $M'_c \neq M_c$, by evaluating the confidence limits $M'_c = M_c \pm \Delta$, where Δ is estimated from appropriate statistical analysis. We can then evaluate the consequences of this outcome on quality and inspection requirements. That is, if M'c is used to flag high complexity modules for inspection, $M_c - \Delta$ represents high quality and high inspection (more modules flagged than with Mc); conversely, $M_c + \Delta$ represents low quality and low inspection (fewer modules flagged than with Mc).

References

1. Martin E. Bush and Norman E. Fenton, "Software Measurement: A Conceptual Framework", The Journal of Systems and Software, Vol. 12, No. 3, July 1990, pp. 223-231.

2. H. Dieter Rombach, "Design Measurement: Some Lessons Learned", IEEE Software, Vol. 7, No. 2, March 1990, pp. 17-25.

3. Norman F. Schneidewind, "Methodology for Validating Software Metrics", IEEE Transactions on Software Engineering", May 1992, pp. 410-422.

4. Norman F. Schneidewind, "Minimizing Risks in Applying Metrics on Multiple Projects", Proceedings of the Third International Symposium on Software Reliability Engineering", Raleigh, NC, October 9, 1992.

Session 5 Summary
Packaging for Reuse

Frank McGarry

The focused topic of the fifth session was 'Packaging for Reuse', where five specific questions were addressed by the panel members.

- What types of information can be packaged?
- What makes models/processes reusable?
- How do we determine needs for reuse?
- How do we organize reusable libraries/processes?
- How do we determine domain dependencies?

In addition to the specific questions being addressed during this time period , other general, relevant points were discussed both at this session as well as during other sessions throughout the week. Overall, the panelists and general audience arrived at some specific points of agreement representing significant accomplishments, lessons learned and areas that required more development within the software engineering community. Presentations and general discussion continually addressed the point that although some significant progress has been made over the past 8 - 10 years relevant to 'packaging for reuse', there are still some key obstacles which limit the overall 'reuse' of results of experimental software engineering. Significant discussion were carried out addressing the fact that the major components that can be packaged include products (such as source code, or tools), process (such as development methods), models (such as defect models) and experiences (such as lessons learned on projects). The point that the key to effective packaging was to understand and apply reuse components in a specific context (or applications domain) was reiterated during the seminar. It was agreed that although progress has been made in developing concepts of domain dependencies for reusing models and processes, the software engineering community should accelerate its effort in developing approaches for characterizing and better understanding domains or contexts of software environments.

What types of information can be packaged?

Discussions which addressed the issue of 'types' of information that can be packaged indicated that the software engineering community has made significant progress over the past decade toward better understanding the fact that reuse addresses a much broader spectrum than only code. It was agreed that there are at least 4 major types of software elements that can be packaged:

1. Software Products (such as code, designs, or tools)
2. Models (such as defect models or life cycle models)
3. Processes (such as development methods)
4. Experiences (such as s lessons learned or people)

The maturing of the packaging concept was evident in the discussions where it was pointed out that 5 - 10 years ago, the complete focus was on packaging code only for reuse; but today there is a strong emphasis on developing models, tailor able processes, as well as software development experiences (through measurement).

It was also noted that successful REUSE implies a prior USE and with that realization, the software engineering community is increasingly demanding demonstration of evolving technologies before accepting it as something ready to be reused.

Although the software development community has demonstrated significant success in packaging code libraries for reuse, there has been more limited success in packaging processes and experiences. The success has been apparent in the realization that reuse can now focus on a broader spectrum than merely code, but the routine success of this broader reuse is still limited.

Some participants felt that there has been significant progress in packaging models (specifically reliability models and cost models) for reuse, but it was commonly agreed that the level of success was still not as high as that of code reuse.

Extended discussions also focused on approaches for packaging teams (personnel) that have gained certain levels of expertise in specific applications domains. All agreed that 'reusing people' would generate the highest payoff, but this goal was a management issue while the other approaches were more technical issues.

What makes models/processes reusable?

In addressing the question as to 'what makes models reusable?', the participants focused on 2 key points that drive the reuse:

1. Demonstrated 'Use' in the same context.
2. Convincing economic benefits.

Once again, the point of 'Use before Reuse' was emphasized and lengthy discussions focused on the need for products, models and processes to be understood and used in specific contexts before assuming they can be generalized or packaged. It was noted that attempting to (re)use any of the software artifacts when the context is not considered can be disastrous.

The discussants also agreed that a key to successful reuse is the economic advantage. Such demonstrated benefits as 'sooner, better and cheaper' are sample economic advantages that any organization would expect from reused artifacts. Several other related points were agreed as providing additional stimuli for reuse. These included:
- credible (having demonstrated benefits)
- accessible
- Artifact is Supported
- It is standardized
- It is competitively priced

Some of the progress that has been made over the past several years includes significant steps taken in better understanding of the need for tailoring artifacts to suit particular contexts which in turn has led to progress in relating specific products with specific software processes. The underlying key point was summarized as 'There is no single best method".

How do we determine need for reuse?

Discussion which attempted to address the question as to how we determine the need for reuse, converged on 2 major points:

1. Understanding/Observing
2. Pilot Studies

The discussions addressing this question continually emphasized the need for any organization to clearly understand their context and to then understand the need and/or potential application of software artifacts available for reuse. The understanding aspect often times needs to be supported with a class of projects called 'pilot studies' where experiments could be carried out with the major goal of providing insight into the characteristics of a particular software domain or to provide awareness into the potential impact of a software process or model or other reusable artifact.

How do you organize reusable libraries/processes?

Over the past 4-6 years, the focus of organizing software for reuse has matured from only developing code libraries to a focus of producing software standards, training units, tool sets and most recently in 'Cook Books'. With the realization that the potential for reusing software artifacts far extends beyond code only, the software engineering community has expanded efforts in developing approaches for effectively organizing reusable processes, models, and experiences.

The seminar discussions focused on the potential and critical need of being able to produce cookbook style documents which could capture relevant experiences as well as useful models which have been developed through the completion of both pilot project and software development projects in general. The participants essentially agreed that significant strides had been taken in developing effective training programs (derived from experiences available for reuse). These training programs were pointed out to be most effective when they encompassed lessons, models and processes developed from successful software development experiences. It was concluded that the software engineering community has made strides in using this vehicle to organize reusable software processes, but it was also pointed out that a significant amount of work was still needed in the training process itself.

It was pointed out that one of the most common means of organizing reusable software was to develop tools, tool sets, and finally full environments.

The use of standards was not extensively discussed but seminar participants agreed that policies and standards within development organizations must continually evolve to reflect observed best processes and must therefore play a key role in 'organizing software for reuse'.

The topic of software 'Cookbooks" was addressed repeatedly during the week and participants agreed that not only are such mediums feasible for capturing and organizing reusable materials, but they are most probably the most effective approach.

How do we determine domain dependencies?

The topic of software domains and 'Context' was one of the major points of review during the entire seminar. When the question of how can we determine domain dependencies for the purpose of 'packaging for reuse', 3 points were presented as aids in answering that question"

1. Pilot Studies
2. Cross-Project Metrics Validation
3. Application Frameworks

The use of pilot studies is primarily effective in gaining understanding of a software organizations characteristics' and in producing information as to potential effectiveness of evolving technologies. Through this understanding goal, the seminar participants agreed that the studies would therefore be effective in determining how the boundaries of software domains could be defined.

Lengthy discussions on the value and role of software metrics were held and it was pointed out that because of the existence of differing software domain characteristics, there needed to be a well developed metrics validation process which in turn could be used to determine software domain dependencies.

One briefing focused in a 'General Application Framework' which developed yet another approach for determining domain dependencies. This type of framework provides a means for 'reuse culture' that evolves and matures toward characterizing domains by continually receiving feedback from client users. One of the key points made in attempting to address the questions as to how domains can be characterized is to baseline a framework then to continually refine the domain definitions through actual use of such products as Code libraries and to observe successes, failures and needs of the using organizations.

From various discussions on the topic of 'packaging for reuse', a number of 'Lessons and Achievements' were captured along with a set of points describing 'Issues and Unresolved Points'.

Key Lessons Learned over the past decade include:

- There is no single best method.
- Reuse is rare and difficult outside a single context.
- Reuse of products (such as Code libraries) has improved significantly.
- Too limited a use of measurement analysis toward reuse.
- There is a significant need for both process and product measures.
- Models are of limited success when used in isolation. They must be used in conjunction with process.

- Research in this area (packaging for reuse) requires practical input and knowledge.
- 'Understanding' is the driving underlying need for any organization (understanding of their process, domain, and overall characteristics).
- Packaging must focus on more than merely 'Code packaging'.
- Reuse of 'People and Teams' is a major technology focus.

Key Opportunities for improvement include:

- There is too little effort put into baselining or <u>understanding</u> software and software processes.
- No agreements on how to effectively assess new technology.
- Effective packaging of models is still a problem across domains.
- Validation of metrics has not been addressed.
- There is no agreement as to standards for models, measures and processes.
- There is still difficulty in matching user goals to metrics.
- The software engineering community is not willing to take risk with change.
- Work is needed to help organizations determine 'return on investment' for reuse.
- 'Stories' and experiences from development organizations are major sources. (How do we capture these?)
- Approaches to defining domains/context for software reuse is still one of the most significant challenges.

Session 6:

Technology Transfer, Teaching and Training

Session Chair: H. Dieter Rombach

Keynote: Manny M. Lehman

Position Papers: John Marciniak
H. Dieter Rombach
Stu Zweben

Position Paper

M M Lehman

Detailed study of the significance of alternative views of software engineering and examination of the practical implications of each must here be restricted to the impact on education, training and technology transfer. In particular, the view taken will strongly influence the content, structure and organisation of software engineering curricula. It will, for example, direct their content more towards what might loosely be termed computing science - including programming methodology - or to an emphasise on issues in process and process support.

Software engineering, a new and fast developing technology, is still largely based on pragmatic experience accumulated over a wide spectrum of organisations, interests, objectives, countries, technical cultures and traditions. It has no solid scientific base or unified conceptual framework. There is no universally accepted definition. Authorities such as ISO and the IEEE have, indeed, proposed definitions but these cannot yet be taken as the last word. Researchers have not identified or agreed a set of views, concepts, processes, methods, procedures and tools that together comprise the technology. The industrial view is reflected in the fact that organisations advertising for staff appear to view Software Engineer as socially more desirable, and therefore more attractive, alternative to the classical job title of Programmer.

The most common view of the technology regards it as covering the design and development of well engineered software products, that is products having quality attributes appropriate for the intended application; in the words of Sommerville [SOM92] "the challenge for software engineers is to produce high-quality software". This view represents one extreme of a spectrum of which the other is represented by the present author's definition [LEH91]. That definition derives, in part, from a canonical model of software development [LEH84] which provides a paradigm covering the task of all involved with the evolution of specific software from a simple procedure to complete systems. The common activity implied by the paradigm should be identified by a common term. All developers are programmers, product engineers involved in the development and maintenance of specific software products. Their role is analogous to, for example, that of electrical and electronic engineers. In contrast, software engineers are concerned with the processes by which products are created and evolved, the processes of software evolution. Their responsibilities include design and development of such processes and their support, methods, procedures, tools, environments and so on. The primary focus of software engineers is on the means whereby products are developed and maintained satisfactory, a responsibility analogous to that of, for example, chemical and civil engineers. In this role the software engineer is not, in general, involved with a specific software product. Note, however, that in projects where the make up and control of process is critical, it may be appropriate to utilise process engineers of the right persuasion as project monitors and managers or, more generally, as consultants tailoring a process and its support to the needs of a specific product.

The proponents of these extreme, and of intermediate, views will agree that product and process related activities are strongly related; they cannot always be clearly differentiated. Nor can one, in general, be involved in the definition, design or support of, say, a development process if one has not had personal, direct and extensive development experience over a wide spectrum of products. Moreover, many of those involved in software development will, from time to time, take process related decisions and actions; what to do next, which language, method or tool to use? Even in a well defined development task on a specific product, individuals will, normally, interleave programming and software engineering tasks and activities.

The areas covered by the alternative views clearly overlap and many topics lie in their intersection. Consider, for example, methods for requirements analysis and specification. In terms of the author's preferred definition, design of a method or a comparative evaluation of alternative methods (in a particular environment) is a software engineering issue. Teaching a selected method and training in its practical use, on the other hand, belongs properly to programming methodology. Evaluation of its effectiveness in a particular development project is a borderline situation. Evaluation of all activity in program evolution is essential if quality software is to be produced and maintained. If students are to be taught how to critically evaluate, post factum, a requirements analysis for example it is valid to associate such teaching with programming (in the wider definition adopted here) methodology. If, on the other hand, the purpose is to provide understanding of evaluation and how it may be undertaken and supported the topic is closer to software engineering. Relative to the needs of education and training, the importance of the definition adopted is not so much for itself as in its reflection of the designer's understanding. It is equally important in conveying to the student the importance of process, and of the product/process dichotomy and of the relationships between them.

This same issue is also of significance when considering technology transfer and the introduction of advanced software technology into practice. Before considering this it is essential to understand the nature of the obstacles that must be overcome.

The switch to advanced software technology involves changes in the process of software evolution and in process support. This requires substantial training, changes in practices and attitudes by both technical and management personnel and major investment of time and funds. In particular it requires that both management and those technically involved fully appreciate the importance of process, its design, support and faithful execution.

Since both direct investment in technology improvement and indirect investment such as initial loss of production, cost of training and so on, must be approved by management, possibly senior management real progress cannot be made until these have been convinced of the commercial benefits to be obtained.

The cost-benefit analysis this requires is particularly difficult for software because:

-   the technology is new and there is no solid experience base for meaningful cost-benefit analysis and predictions.

- initial impact of the introduction of new technology is likely to increase costs, because of, for example, capital investment, training, lost production and lower productivity until new skills are mastered.

- local changes to process and the introduction of isolated methods or tools bring little visible benefit; they may even induce a net loss (eg. impact on other process steps, learning curve, capital investment). Visible benefit depends on the introduction of advanced technology over a major portion of the life cycle.

- much of the benefit due to the introduction of advanced technology will only become visible over time. It will accrue over years of usage as, for example, a consequence of reduced maintenance with simpler, speedier, less costly and more reliable changes when changes are necessary.

- many of the benefits will not be progressive, that is, arising from increased productivity, lower costs, higher product quality. Instead they will be anti-regressive [LEH74], that is due to fewer losses as a consequence, for example, of less application down-time, less delay in making fixes because of improved control over growth of system complexity and decline in documentation quality, fewer penalties arising in the application domain from software inadequacies, faults or weaknesses.

Software development has traditionally been treated as a people intensive activity. Thus even when potential benefit is demonstrated, management will oppose moves to a capital intensive approach. Until educated otherwise they will resist change and investment, despite the general trend to industrial mechanisation.

The total life cycle process and its support, or even that of a major portion, cannot be changed overnight and technology must be introduced piece meal because:

- people have to learn and acclimatise to new methods and tools.

- teaching, training and experience makings technology second nature takes time.

- ingrained habits and practices cannot change overnight.

- the size of investment required is such that management will wish to spread it, possibly over several years

- existing organisational investment in process, procedures, methods and tools must be protected and written off gradually before being replaced.

- introduction of change must be planned and spread to avoid disruption of committed production and to maintain corporate revenue.

Clearly the switch to advanced software technology requires a major investment in education and training. The need for education in such topics as formal methods, systematic requirements elicitation, formal specification or structured design and implementation is well recognised in universities and becoming so in industry. That for training and familiarisation in the use of specific methods and tools is also understood. The concept of an evolution process that can be modelled, reasoned about, evaluated and improved is slowly spreading. The (university) education and training of highly qualified professionals in the field of software engineering is in hand though in many instances there is room for improvement in structure and content. The greatest need, however, and that receiving the least attention, is the education and training of management. Only management can free up the resources, funds and time, that are essential for the transfer of advanced software technology and its successful introduction into practice. Management oriented courses demanding at any one sitting only the short periods available to senior and middle management, must be developed and widely disseminated. Such courses must:

> motivate the managers to come back for more

> describe the environment of software evolution

> convey the source and nature of the problems that arise in its implementation outline the principles and concepts that underlie advanced technology

> discuss what is needed to introduce it into practice

> and to derive significant benefit

> analyse the nature of the potential benefit from adoption of the technology

> outline strategies for its effective introduction

The needs are clear. Software engineering education and training emphasising the advanced thinking and concepts must be prepared and delivered. The targets include those who will become computer professional and other students who will become computer users or encounter computers in some other way in their occupation. It must also be directed to technical and managerial staff at all levels in industry, commerce, government and the wider community. But education by itself will not suffice. Any technology requires scientific foundations and a framework that defines and relates concepts and behaviours and reflects understanding of the phenomena and activities within the technology. Such an organised science is not currently available to the software engineering community, though elements do exist [LEH92]. To achieve further significant advances in the technology, to transmit it through teaching, training and technology transfer and to achieve effectiveness and quality in software evolution demands a systematic approach based on the scientific method. This requires systematic observation, experimentation, measurement and reasoning to develop deeper understanding and meaningful models of what is being done and what needs to be done in the field of software engineering. Regular patterns of behaviour and response must be identified. From these principles theories, models and laws must be derived and formulated. The beginnings are available [LEH85, 91], the time is ripe and the need is great. This is the challenge that this Seminar must address.

One final word. The views expressed here are based on the accumulated experience of over twenty years in industry, an equal number in academia, responsibility for the conception and setting up of a four year M Eng. degree in software engineering and the establishment of a software company developing and marketing advanced software technology. They represent solid experience not philosophical musings.

[LEH74] Lehman M M, Programs, Cities, Students - Limits to Growth, Imperial College, Inaugural Lecture Series, v. 9, 1970 - 1974. Also in [LEH85], pp. 42 - 69 and [24], pp. 133 - 163

[LEH84] Lehman M M, Stenning V and Turski W M, (1984). Another Look at Software Design Methodology, ICST DoC Res. Rep. 83/13, June 1983. Also, Software Engineering Notes, vol. 9, no 2, April 1984, pp. 38 - 53

[LEH85] Lehman M M and Belady L A, Program Evolution - Processes of Software Change, Academic Press, London, 1985, 538 p.

[LEH91] Lehman M M,Software Engineering, the Software Process and Their Support, IEE Softw. Eng. J. Spec. Iss. on Software Environments and Factories, Sept. 1991, v. 6, n. 5, pp. 243 - 258

[[LEH92] Lehman M M,Software Engineering - Theory and Practice, DoC Research Report 91/25, preliminary draft available

[SOM92] Sommerville I, Software Engineering, (fourth ed.), Addison-Wesley Publishers Ltd., Wokingham, UK, 1992, 649 p.

mml496 27/8/92

Prof. M M (Manny) Lehman Department of Computing Imperial College of Science, Technology and Medicine 180 Queen's Gate London SW7 2BZ, UK. Phone: +44 (0)71 589 5111, ext. 5009 Fax.: +44 (0)71 581 8024 email: mml@doc.ic.ac.uk

TECHNOLOGY TRANSFER

John J Marciniak

CTA INCORPORATED
6116 Executive Boulevard
Rockville, MD 20852

Abstract

Without the means to transfer technology we lose opportunity, not only of its application, but the means of evaluating its effectiveness. Numerous studies of technology transfer (most recently by the US DoD SEI) point to recommendations that are long term solutions. Yet, if we are to shorten the introduction of technology from its the often quoted 18 years to something much less, more effective methods must be employed. This paper discusses three areas where improvements to technology insertion are suggested: quantification of technology effectiveness, packaging, and motivation and incentive.

1 Introduction

This paper discusses three aspects of Technology Transfer: quantification of technology effectiveness, packaging, and motivation and incentive. While it will be more difficult to address the third, by addressing the first two we can provide a means for facilitating the third.

New technologies are historically difficult to transfer into practice. Indeed, even today, technologies that have been demonstrated over a decade ago still are not in widespread use. One example is Formal Inspections. Introduced by Fagen in 1976 [1] the practice still does not appear as a matter of routine in current development. Much of this can be ascribed to the continuing lack of discipline in present acquisition projects which allow disorderly practice to continue.

In a typical project environment, the engineering staff is reluctant to try anything new. Before the project starts there is better opportunity, however, sufficient resources to support training and practice are often lacking. Today, it seems that the only companies and organizations that can attack this problem are those that are rather large and can support staffs to work it, and academic or laboratory environments that are dedicated to the problem. In laboratory and academic settings, however, new technologies are typically demonstrated on projects of small scale, therefore, often accused of being non-appropriate to large organizations and projects.

A compounding factor is that even software technology is moving faster than staff software engineers can absorb it. In a typical organization people are struggling with the introduction of new languages (Ada), new paradigms such as OOD, and new CASE tools such RDD100. Setting up a new environment today is much more difficult than it was 10 years ago.

Process improvement programs, such as the US DoD SEI program based on Humphrey's Capability Maturity Model [2] have provided a mechanism to focus on improvement, forcing organizations to address critical software engineering issues such as measurement. While the model has a section on technologies and tools that section has not received wide attention or use. Its presence, however, provides the opportunity to focus on technology transition.

2 Technology Environment

There appears to be two types of technology shifts: those that represent a new paradigm, and those that represent a new method or change to an existing one. From the standpoint of technology insertion there are major differences between these two. The new paradigm shift is a revolutionary way of changing engineering practice and it would be difficult to propose a simple means for expediting its introduction. On the other hand one could argue that all new paradigms are not necessarily bonafide ones. Clearly, OOD is an example of one that is, however, the spiral model may be an example of one that is not.

Technologies that are steps along common practice are easier to accept and assimilate into practice than those that provide a radical new step. For example, Cleanroom, because it radically departs from the socially accepted mode of the programmer mindset, has been extremely difficult to introduce into practice even in IBM where it had its genesis. On the other hand, technologies that are a next step in a current practice are much easier to introduce. For example, software reliability engineering. Since testing software, with its concomitant accrual of errors (failure data) and using that data to manage the release and subsequent operation of the software was an early development requirement, reliability modeling was facilitated. Today, in the emerging field of measurement, this is the vogue form.

3 Approach

Technology transfer must be orchestrated through bite sized improvements to current practice and accompanied by measures or metrics to provide a means to quantify their effect. We first discuss the means or method for packaging "bites", then address motivation and incentive.

3.1 By bite sized we mean improvements that satisfy the following criteria.

1. There is a basis for the new technology that is accepted and understood practice.

2. They are incremental improvements, that is, the improvement is described as a change to accepted practice.

3. The change is accompanied by the tools for evaluating its effectiveness in employment. That is, the means of measuring its use are packaged with the change.

4. The change is accompanied by a description of its introduction into development practice.

To illustrate these criteria we employ the example of Formal Inspections. The basis for the technology is the walkthrough [3]. This method is clearly understood, accepted, and widely practiced. Thus, it represents a basis. The incremental improvement could be described, as it often is, by the term structured walkthrough, or perhaps formal walkthrough, instead of formal inspection which creates confusion on the part of engineering staffs who now have to try to understand a seemingly new technology. Thus, a structured walkthrough is an incremental improvement on the walkthrough.

The next step would be to provide the means of evaluating its effectiveness. This could be accomplished in a number of ways. Base values could be provided, whereby baseline metric data would be available from similar domain projects. These could be used to determine if the procedure was operating according to correct practice. Other data could provide a comparison to errors found in similar domains that are using the structured walkthrough. Measures could be suggested to evaluate the practice and the process it is applied against. Naturally, the organization may choose to perform parallel types of experiments to develop their own comparative data.

Lastly, the technology could be provided with a description of its use within the life cycle. Thus, it can be placed within conventional practice. That is, guidance can be offered about using the structured walkthrough - where, how many times, incremental application, etc. This kind of advice provides context for the engineer and manager who are attempting to deal with an "unknown".

3.2 For major revolutionary shifts in practice, technology transition is influenced by trial projects and other extraordinary means of introduction. This has been used within the US DoD to introduce Ada, albeit with differing results. The employment of "shadow" projects, where development is conducted in parallel with an ongoing development to draw distinction between existing and new practice is also useful.

Sometimes new technologies are really not that, but packaged in such a way that they appear to be new, radical departures from conventional practice. One example is the spiral model of development [4].

The spiral model has received tremendous attention, at least in those industries dealing with the US DoD. Its primary function is the introduction of successive prototypes and the reliance on risk management or abatement.

Today, many software engineers and acquisition managers have difficulty understanding the different process models and how to integrate them into a project. In fact, many will argue that the waterfall model [5] is "dead", and not useful. In fact it is used in many development projects. Missing in today's environment is an orderly way to get engineers and managers who understand the waterfall process to take the next step to an advanced process development model. A development model that uses the waterfall as a basis for a new process paradigm would have more chance of success than one that is a radical departure.

If the spiral model was described as an incremental improvement of the waterfall model, with accompanying information on how to apply it, insertion would be improved. The basis for the spiral model is grounded in the understanding of the waterfall process, risk management, and prototyping. Guidance on how to apply or use the model in current acquisition practice would provide the necessary context without degrading the effect or impact of the model. Metrics could describe how to evaluate the prototyping process to determine when risk had been reduced to an acceptable level in order to facilitate the decision of moving to successive layers of the model.

4 Motivation/Incentive

Motivation and incentive initiatives to introduce new technologies are principally focused at management. One example is the use of shadow projects, which attempt to demonstrate the benefit of new practices or technologies through parallel development. A better place, however, to provide incentive and motivation for technology insertion is in academia.

The concept of measurement, widely used in engineering practice, is deficient in software engineering practice. If engineering had this practice built into it the introduction of new technologies would not be the problem that it is today. If graduates were grounded in engineering practice they would be in a much better position to handle change.

We believe that it is important to provide an undergraduate program in software engineering. Without such a program basic methods of engineering construction are missing. When computer scientists enter an engineering environment they are not equipped to deal with engineering practice because they have not been exposed to engineering methods. If a software engineering program were offered at the undergraduate level, with the integration of measurement as a part of the engineering process, transfer of measurement technologies would be greatly aided.

5 Summary

There are a number of actions that may be taken to facilitate the transfer of technology into industrial practice. The paper suggests three courses. One is the concept of packaging to avoid the introduction of an alien technology into established engineering practice. By packaging new technology as an incremental change to existing practice, along with the context for its place in development models, the change can be more easily accepted.

Along with packaging, the integration of measurement into engineering practice provides the means to assess the success of the new technology. This provides engineering management with a basis for understanding the effect on process and product, thus reinforcing the advantage of its use. To facilitate the integration of measurement into practice we believe that software engineering should be offered as an undergraduate curriculum so that engineering processes can be reinforced in future systems developers.

References

1. M.E. Fagen: Design and Code Inspections and Process Control in the Development of Programs. In: IBM-TR-00.73, June 1973.

2. W.S. Humphrey, W.L. Sweet: A Method for Assessing the Software Engineering Capability of Contractors. Pittsburgh: Software Engineering Institute Technical Report CMU/SEI-87-TR-23 Carnegie Mellon University, 1987

3. J.J. Marciniak, D.J. Reifer: Software Acquisition Management. New York: Wiley 1990, p. 173.

4. B.W. Boehm: A Spiral Model of Software Development and Enhancement. IEEE Computer, Vol. 21, No. 5. California: May 1988, pp. 61-72.

5. J.J. Marciniak, D.J. Reifer: Software Acquisition Management. New York: Wiley 1990, pp. 4, 20, 23, 48.

Systematic Software Technology Transfer

H. Dieter Rombach

Fachbereich Informatik, Universität Kaiserslautern

W-6750 Kaiserslautern, Germany

Abstract

Transferring new technologies into a software organization can be expected to change the software processes used within this organization. It is unrealistic to expect project members to manage such changes on the fly and still fulfill their product-oriented project goals. Systematic software technology transfer requires a software engineering model which is based on sound scientific and engineering principles and clearly distinguishes between the roles of experience building versus application development on the one hand, and process engineering versus product engineering on the other hand.

1 Introduction

Software engineering as a subdiscipline of computer science has long been biased towards the creation of new software evolution principles, techniques, and tools and their application in the context of given (generic) process models. A typical definition reflecting this narrow view reads as follows: "Software engineering is the study of principles and methodologies for developing and maintaining software systems [Zel78]." This view is based on fundamental misconceptions regarding the nature of software and its creation. These misconceptions include the following:

- process is not a variable of software projects; therefore there is no need to choose and customize the appropriate processes for given project goals and characteristics

- principles, techniques, and tools are generally applicable; therefore there is no need to investigate their limits in different project contexts.

A detailed discussion of such misconceptions is contained in [BasRom87].

In the TAME project a detailed analysis of such misconceptions was performed [BasRom87], which resulted in a new software engineering paradigm [BasRom88]. This new paradigm:

- recognizes the need to reuse (with modification !) software experience such as process models, product models, quality models to the degree possible,

- facilitates necessary further learning without overburdening the product engineering oriented project members,

- enables the integration of measurement with specific improvement goals.

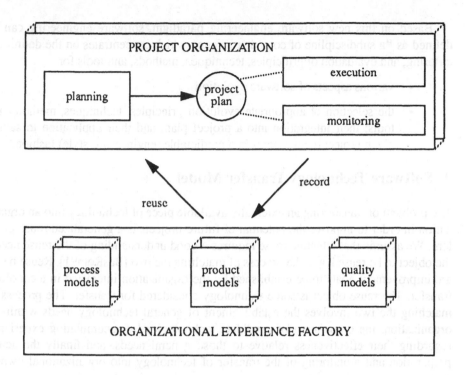

Figure 1: TAME Software Engineering Paradigm

This new paradigm (see Figure 1) distinguishes between those software engineering activities aimed at fulfilling requirements of a given project and those aimed at improving the scientific and engineering base for future projects. The project-oriented activities in the project organization can be divided into process engineering activities (especially those aimed at creating an explicit plan to achieve the given project requirements and those monitoring project execution) and product engineering activities (those aimed at fulfilling given product requirements according to plan). This distinction is similar to the separation between process and product engineering [Leh91].

The quality of the project-oriented activities depends on the ability to reuse prior experience such as process models, product models, or quality models. The creation of such experience does not happen as a side-effect of project-specific activities. A separate organization (here called the organizational experience factory) with specific qualifications and perspectives needs to be established. Their goal is to focus on the needs of the entire organization instead of individual projects. The activities in the organizational experience factory require sound mechanisms for monitoring all projects, analyzing those observations, building models, and packaging them for reuse in future projects. The overall improvement paradigm based on the scientific method and the goal oriented measurement approach used for monitoring project execution have been formulated as the quality improvement paradigm (QIP) and goal/question/metric paradigm (GQM), respectively [BasRom88, Bas92].

Based on this new software engineering paradigm, software engineering can be defined as "a subdiscipline of computer science which concentrates on the definition, tailoring, and evaluation of principles, techniques, methods, and tools for

- various aspects of software evolution

- the selection of appropriate evolution principles, techniques, methods and tools; their integration into a project plan; and their application to satisfy given project requirements in a predictable (engineering-style) fashion."

2 Software Technology Transfer Model

The problem of transferring an externally available piece of technology into an organization in order to improve the potential of future projects is a generalized reuse problem. We assume that effective reuse requires a good understanding of the reuse needs, the object to be reused, and the process of matching the two [BasRom91]. Reuse needs are improvement goals to be established by the organization interested in technology transfer. The reuse object is some technology considered for transfer. The process of matching the two involves the establishment of general technology needs within an organization, the preparation of candidate technologies by accumulating experience regarding their effectiveness relative to those general needs, and finally the actual preparation and monitoring of the transfer of technology into organizational ownership.

Assume, for example, the existence of a code reading method based on a stepwise-abstraction reading technique. We can assume that organizations have general needs for technologies enabling the effective detection of software faults. We consider it necessary technology preparation as a first step to perform an experimental study like the one by Basili and Selby [BasSel87] in order to provide evidence regarding the effectiveness of such a method. In a second step, an organization which has established problems with fault detection methods has to formulate its improvement goals relative to current baselines. It may be appropriate to perform another experiment or run a tightly controlled prototype project in order to validate the expectations and understand the implications of this new method on other aspects within the organization. Assuming that one can now package this method in terms of its impact on project characteristics of the interested organization, one is ready to think about introducing the method into real projects (this includes training, setting up of monitoring procedures, etc.).

The new software engineering paradigm discussed earlier provides the appropriate context for this kind of technology transfer.

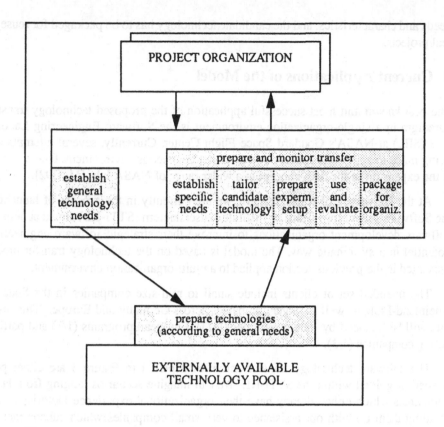

Figure 2: Technology Transfer in the TAME Software Engineering Paradigm

Figure 2 depicts our convictions that

- the recipient of externally available technologies should be the organizational experience factory and not the individual project
- the technology transfer process includes technology preparation, transfer preparation, and transfer monitoring/assessment.

Technology preparation includes all the activities needed to package "naked" technology with information regarding its effectiveness relative to general needs. Example activities include establishing such general needs, conducting experimental studies to derive evidence regarding the effectiveness of the candidate technology, adding documentation, preparing training materials, and building supporting (prototype) tools. Transfer preparation and monitoring includes all activities needed to move pre-packaged technology into organizational ownership. Example activities include the establishment of precise organizational needs, and of a measurement program suitable for stating these needs in a measurable way and for monitoring new technologies. In addition, further experimental studies may have to be conducted aimed at validating existing experience regarding the candidate technology relative to specific organizational needs and characteristics, and the candidate technology has to be packaged for reuse in real projects.

3 Current Applications of the Model

The best known and most successful application of the proposed technology transfer paradigm in a single-organization-environment is the Software Engineering Laboratory (SEL) at NASA's Goddard Space Flight Center. Currently, several attempts are being made to apply this concept to a more heterogeneous environment. One example is the expansion of the SEL concept to a wider range of NASA labs [McG92].

At the University of Kaiserslautern, we are currently in the process of launching the Software Technology Transfer Institute Kaiserslautern (STTI-KL) aimed at helping software development organizations to improve their strategic software engineering potential in a systematic way. The model is based on the technology transfer model presented in the previous section applied to a multi-organization environment.

The intended set of clients include small to mid-size companies in the State of Rheinland-Pfalz as well as larger companies across Germany and Europe. This institute will be financed by state government (1/3), European programs (1/3) and participating companies (1/3).

The software technology transfer activities depicted in Figure 3 are either performed or guided within the STTI-KL. We can imagine scenarios ranging from large companies which either already have their organizational experience factories or are building them up with our assistance to very small companies which subcontract all activities to us. The idea is to help companies build small experience factories based on the model presented. In the long-term, the STTI-KL will build its own experience factory enabling industry to draw from more powerful technology pools and us (i.e., academia) to continue our process of building ever more generalized models by being able to investigate the effects of different organizations.

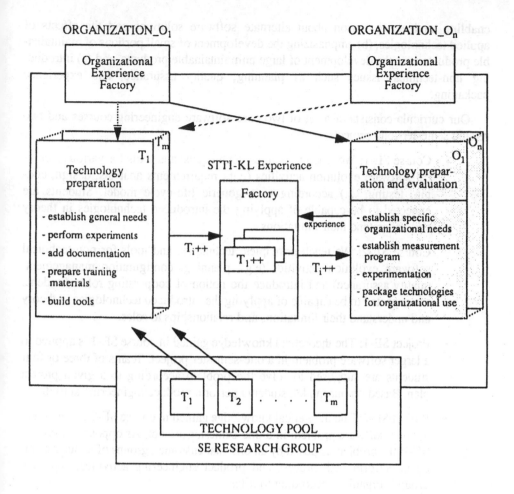

ORGANIZATION_O₁ ... ORGANIZATION_Oₙ

Organizational Experience Factory

Organizational Experience Factory

T₁ ... Tₘ

Technology preparation

- establish general needs
- perform experiments
- add documentation
- prepare training materials
- build tools

STTI-KL Experience Factory

Tᵢ++

T₁++

experience

Tᵢ++

O₁ ... Oₙ

Technology preparation and evaluation

- establish specific organizational needs
- establish measurement program
- experimentation
- package technologies for organizational use

T₁ T₂ . . . . Tₘ

TECHNOLOGY POOL

SE RESEARCH GROUP

Figure 3: STTI-KL Technology Transfer Model

4 Related Issues

It is clear that teaching and training are important activities in support of technology transfer. The role of training is outlined in the above STTI-KL model.

I will address the question of how the suggested software engineering paradigm change could and should affect our teaching curricula by outlining the graduate software engineering program at the University of Kaiserslautern. We are attempting to move away from just teaching technologies (i.e., implementation languages, design techniques, testing techniques). We want to emphasize the need for understanding the effectiveness of technologies by (a) replacing buzzwords by measurable definitions enabling students to reason about alternate software solutions and the effects of applied technologies, (b) emphasizing the development of small portions of maintainable products over the development of large unmaintainable products, and (c) introducing non-technical issues such as planning, quality assurance, and experience packaging.

Our curricula consists of a set of two core software engineering courses and two related semester-long projects:

- Course SE-1: We teach principles, techniques, and tools for various technical software evolution activities (e.g., requirements analysis, design, coding, testing, ...) according to a generic life-cycle model. Students are expected to be capable of applying the introduced technologies in theory and understand their limitations.

- Course SE-2: We teach principles, techniques and tools for non-technical software evolution activities (e.g., planning, configuration management, quality assurance) and introduce the notion of cooperating roles. Students are expected to be capable of applying the introduced technologies in theory and understand their limitations and relationships to roles.

- Project SE-1: The theoretical knowledge gained in course SE-1 is applied to a larger software problem in a one-semester project. Teams of three or four students are supposed to solve the problem according to a given project plan. Based on our model, students perform product engineering activities.

- Project SE-2: The theoretical knowledge gained in course SE-2 is applied to a larger software problem in a one-semester project. As opposed to project SE-1, the problem is posed by an external customer, groups of about ten students perform both process and product engineering activities, and each group is organized according to roles.

We believe that the separation of teaching and practical project courses into two consecutive semesters enables us to concentrate on theoretical software engineering aspects without the constraints imposed by a parallel project. We can afford to teach SE-1 in a bottom-up fashion. This means that we start with coding issues and slowly introduce issues related to design and requirements. This approach has the advantage of being able to build on the undergraduate experience of our students. Our curriculum also allows us to separate between product engineering issues in SE-1 and process engineering issues in SE-2.

References

[Bas92]   V. R. Basili: "The Experimental Paradigm in Software Engineering," Keynote, International Workshop on Experimental Software Engineering Issues, Dagstuhl Castle, Germany, September 1992.

[BasRom87] V. R. Basili and H. D. Rombach: "TAME: integrating measurement into software environments," Technical Report TR-1764, Department of Computer Science, University of Maryland, College Park, MD, June 1987.

[BasRom88] V. R. Basili and H. D. Rombach: "The TAME Project: toward improvement-oriented software environments," IEEE Transactions on Software Engineering, vol. 14, no. 6, June 1988, pp. 759-773.

[BasRom91] V. R. Basili and H. D. Rombach: "Support for comprehensive reuse", IEE Software Eng. Journal, Special Issue on Software Environments and Factories, vol. 6, no. 5, September 1991, pp. 303-316.

[BasSel87] V. R. Basili and R. W. Selby: "Comparing the effectiveness of software testing techniques", IEEE Transactions on Software Engineering, vol. 13, no. 12, December 1987, pp. 1278-1296.

[Leh91] M. M. Lehman: "Software engineering, the software processes and their support", IEE Software Eng. Journal, Special Issue on Software Environments and Factories, vol. 6, no. 5, September 1991, pp. 243-258.

[McG92] F. McGarry: "Experimental Software Engineering: Packaging for Reuse", Position paper, International Workshop on Experimental Software Engineering Issues, Dagstuhl Castle, Germany, September 1992.

[Zel78] M. V. Zelkowitz: "Perspectives on Software Engineering", ACM Computing Surveys, vol. 10, no. 2, 1978, pp. 197-216.

Effective Use of Measurement and Experimentation in Computing Curricula

Stu Zweben
Dept. of Computer and Information Science
Ohio State University
Columbus, Ohio 43210 USA
zweben@cis.ohio-state.edu

1 Introduction

Measurement and experimentation are standard ingredients in traditional science and engineering curricula. They form the basis for understanding and practicing the scientific method, and its lessons of hypothesis formation, design, validation and refinement. Though the emphasis on the various elements of the scientific method may be somewhat different in pure science than in pure engineering, the components of the method are similar [2].

While based mainly on mathematical elements instead of physical elements, computer science also has ample room for measurement and experimentation in its curricula. Parts of computing curricula involve the study of devices and switching circuits, where traditional engineering laboratory work of an empirical nature (particularly that of electrical engineering) is relevant. Within the software areas of computing curricula, too, there are many places to employ empirically-oriented labs to illustrate the scientific method. Recurring use of this paradigm within the curriculum is important, to facilitate its being learned properly.

However, it is important that measurement and experimentation be used in a sound manner with respect to educational objectives. These objectives define levels of mastery (called knowledge, comprehension, application, analysis, synthesis, and evaluation [1]) of a topic, ranging from simple knowledge of terminology to the ability to evaluate its utility. They build on one another, in the sense that one should not expect to achieve a higher level of mastery before achieving the lower levels. In our zeal to move software engineering more toward a true engineering discipline, to build computing curricula that have more of a solid software engineering component, and to put more "science" into computer science, we must be careful to organize our educational programs with these objectives in mind.

Below, I will give some examples of areas, within the software component of undergraduate computing curricula, where the incorporation of measurement and experimentation appears useful and consistent with curricular objectives. I will also give an example of what I feel is an inappropriate objective for undergraduate computing curricula with respect to software engineering issues.

2 Areas of Potential Use

One obvious area in which the notions of measurement and experimentation make sense is that of software testing. While we would like students to be able to write programs whose functionality is provably correct, in practice we're going to have these programs tested. Testing is, by nature, an empirical activity. It also is applied early in the curriculum, so that computing students can be introduced to systematic measurement and experimentation from the very beginning of their computing education. Unfortunately, only recently have introductory textbooks been giving some emphasis to the subject of systematically approaching testing. Also, there is not really a standard strategy for creating test cases. However, emphasis on the need to create a test plan, on commonly used strategies for testing based on elements of the specification as well as the code, and on the recording of the defects observed, would provide a natural application of the scientific method in computing, and would give students greater respect for both testing and computing as having a scientific and engineering flavor.

The study of algorithms and data structures provides other convenient places in a typical computing curriculum where measurement and experimentation can be used effectively. To complement functional correctness, we are interested in performance as an important issue in software development. While we'd like our students to be able to formally analyze the performance characteristics of the algorithms and components they write, empirical analysis provides another means of exploring these characteristics. Empirical studies also help illustrate intractability, and how performance of an otherwise good component can be adversely affected by poor implementations of components on top of which it is layered. Sorting and searching techniques, also introduced early in the curriculum (and normally revisited later in the curriculum), are classical themes around which these empirical methods can be used, and in several curricula are already used. Students can be shown how to monitor their program's performance, using tools provided by the system in which they are operating, to confirm the more formal analyses done in class. They can also be given "black box" implementations of some specified problem like sorting, and asked to find out the computational complexity of the implementation, or of several competing implementations. Such activities make the study of algorithm analysis less "theory driven," which can positively affect the ability of many students to learn the material. Since the study of algorithms crops up in many parts of a computing curriculum (e.g., coverage of parallel computing, artificial intelligence, and graphics), this approach can be used repeatedly in different courses.

Beginning in intermediate level, software project-oriented courses, the use of measurement for project-management objectives is also useful. For example, students can record information about their time and effort in completing various software development activities, and track changes in these observations as the nature of the project, and their own maturity in writing software, changes. This will acquaint them first-hand with the difficulties of project cost and effort estimation, as well as giving them some insight into their own abilities and a means for budgeting their own time more effectively. It also should help stimulate discussions about the software development process.

Reviews are yet another form of measurement activity that is both appropriate and important to an undergraduate computing curriculum. Students should understand what it means to review various work products, and should have participated in reviews of, say, designs, code, and/or test plans. Records should be kept from these reviews.

A problem with performing data collection activities such as described in the previous paragraphs is that the data must not simply get collected, it must get used. Otherwise, the critical components of analysis and refinement, central to both science and engineering methodology, has not been practiced. Defect data, for example, can be used to discuss classes of faults and errors made during development, and can help motivate heuristics and developer behavior that might be useful in reducing the frequency with which certain problems occur. Performance data can be used to validate real-time constraints, and to approximate tradeoff points between alternative algorithms. Time and effort data often is harder to justify in an educational setting, because the length of a term places severe constraints on the scope of a software development project. Records kept in review meetings may need to be saved for later discussions analyzing or evaluating the review method. Course sequences involving team development activities are better suited to utilizing these kinds of data.

Measurement and experimentation are useful in aiding the understanding of other basic concepts. The mere visualization of recursion or deadlocks via experimentation may help overcome difficulties in assimilating notoriously tricky topics.

When discussing how to make software engineering into a more mature engineering discipline, it is often stated that we need to understand the strengths and weaknesses of various principles, tools, and methods. Measurement and experimentation come into play when these evaluations are to be done empirically. Therefore, it is tempting to try to incorporate laboratory experiences that focus on these strengths and weaknesses, and even to incorporate controlled experiments into the lab so that the differences between competing methods or tools can be assessed.

While these are good ideas in principle, care must be taken to ensure that students have the proper background to conduct such measurements and experiments. Evaluation is at the highest level of the educational objective taxonomy. To expect mastery at this level suggests mastery at the lower levels. Imagine trying to evaluate two design methods, for example. Among other things, this requires sufficient exposure to the methods that they have been applied to standard problems; analyzed for their properties, relationships, and unstated assumptions; and synthesized into the solving of new problems. In a typical undergraduate curriculum, there is not time to do all of these things, particularly with two different methods. It therefore is next to impossible to expect the student to appreciate strengths and weaknesses of the methods. It is possible, however, to experiment with various methods and tools (e.g., an expert system or design tool) to learn about their utility in solving a limited set of problems.

The statistical methods that are generally used to perform experiments by which various factors are compared, are frequently not taught to undergraduate level students. Many probability and statistics courses required of undergraduates do not cover analysis of variance, for example, and experiments frequently require more complicated experimental design due to constraints in the environment in which the experiment is being conducted. Either the instructor must compromise the use of proper statistical analysis so that a statistical method known by the student can be illustrated, or a method unknown to the student must be used in the analysis. Neither of these approaches is helpful at improving the student's knowledge of how to properly use experimental design and analysis in computing.

Finally, it is important to note that students in computing programs should be exposed to measurement and experimentation not only by incorporating these techniques into the major part of the program (i.e., the computing courses themselves), but also through courses taken to support the major. Traditional science, engineering, applied statistics, and other quantitative methods courses are useful requirements to a computing degree. In addition to building an understanding of the methods of science and engineering, such courses can serve to introduce students to disciplines in which there are important computational problems. Persons from these other disciplines may well be colleagues or customers when the student is on the job after graduation. The criteria for computer science accreditation published by the Computing Sciences Accreditation Board, for example, require a minimum of 2/5 of a year of such courses, beyond introductory probability and statistics.

3 Other Considerations

Our discipline would also benefit from a repository of materials appropriate for teaching experimentation and measurement to computing students. This would help faculty integrate the subject more quickly into their curricula. It is also timely to create such a repository, for with the publication of the recent ACM/IEEE-CS curriculum report, many academic computing programs are in the process of rethinking their curricula. The Software Engineering Institute already has begun collecting educational materials in software engineering; some of these may be useful for teaching measurement and experimentation. Some ACM SIGs in other areas also have begun collecting repositories of educational materials (not necessarily focused on measurement and experimentation) within their own areas.

References

[1] Bloom, B. Taxonomy of Educational Objectives: Handbook I: Cognitive Domain, McKay, New York, 1956.

[2] Denning, P. "Paradigms Crossed," CACM, 30, 10, October 1987, pp. 808-809.

Session 6 Summary
Technology Transfer, Teaching and Training

H. Dieter Rombach

Fachbereich Informatik
Universität Kaiserslautern
Germany

In session 6, the focus was on ways for utilizing the experimental paradigm for software technology transfer, especially for teaching students and training practitioners.

Manny Lehman presented in his keynote address a variety of different software engineering views and discussed the practical implications of each on technology transfer, teaching and training. He developed an experimental software engineering model with equal emphasis on product, process and quality issues. In his view, evaluation (e.g., the comparative evaluation of alternate methods) is a valid and essential software engineering task. It is obvious that switching to such a software engineering view requires substantial education and training.

Position papers addressed issues ranging from possible improvements of technology transfer processes (John Marciniak) to organizational issues of technology transfer (Dieter Rombach) and teaching curricula issues as related to experimentation (Stu Zweben).

The discussion focused on the following four issues:

1. Improvement in practice: How do we make improvements happen?

2. Organizational structure: What structures are needed to support technology transfer, especially what roles can universities and industry play?

3. Teaching curricula: How can we change our university curricula in order to instill the ideas of measurement and experimentation into students early on?

4. Training approaches: How can we train practitioners in the experimental paradigm of software engineering?

The discussion is summarized in terms of lessons learned in the last ten years, remaining key points of dissent, key issues left to be tackled over the next five years, and specific measurement studies suggested to the community.

Lessons learned in the Last Ten Years

Effective technology transfer is crucial to any engineering discipline. It is the vehicle to transfer research results into industrial practice and motivate research based on a better understanding of real problems. Good teaching and training has to complement any technology transfer approach.

When discussing issues 1 (improvement in practice) and 2 (organizational structure), the following lessons emerged:

- The choice of appropriate technology transfer approaches depends on context: Software technology transfer involves bridging the gap between the provider context (i.e. the context in which some technology has been developed and/or validated) and the consumer context (i.e., the context for which the technology is considered). Provider environments (e.g., universities) are different in terms of whether and how much validation they provide for candidate technologies. Consumer environments (e.g., companies) are different in terms of how well they understand their processes, or how well they know weaknesses of their current processes in measurable terms. Furthermore, the difference between small/midsize and large consumer companies was discussed in terms of the willingness/ability to invest in long-term technology transfer approaches (Günther Koch, Albert Endres, Dieter Rombach).

- The choice of appropriate technologies to be transferred depends on context: There are no silver bullet technologies. Each company has to identify its specific improvement needs, and select candidate technologies for improvement. This point was made by Frank McGarry who insisted that the NASA/SEL improvements (some of which are listed in the Preface) are only local not global truths.

- Technology Transfer is a two-way process: Technology transfer benefits both the provider and the consumer. Consumers utilize emerging research technologies to improve their business. Producers learn about real problems by working in the field (Les Belady).

- Technology transfer has to be a continuous process: Technology transfer must not be viewed as the last step in the research chain. Instead, technology transfer has to be kept in mind throughout the technology development process (Les Belady: "You prepare the soil in which you sow"). This was one of the essential aspects of the experimental paradigm introduced and discussed in Session 1.

- Laboratory environments are essential: Experimental software engineering research depends on access to real projects; yet real project environments are not the place for initial technology experiments. NASA's SEL was discussed as a successful laboratory environment to meet both needs. The collaboration between project people and researchers allows for effective technology transfer where experiments can be conducted at two levels: *experiments derived from constrained scenarios under statistical control versus case studies derived from real scenarios without statistical control.* More laboratory environments are being established (e.g., more SELs at NASA sites other than Goddard Space Flight Center; the Software Technology Transfer Initiative associated with the University of Kaiserslautern - STTI-KL). However, still more such laboratory environments are needed.

- Technology transfer requires appropriate organizational structures: Technology transfer doesn't work if delegated to product development organizations. Their priority is to deliver products of required quality on time. Therefore, it is not surprising that developers who are pushed for time are told by their managers to forget about technology transfer issues. It was agreed that a separation is required between responsibilities for product development and technology transfer (Manny Lehman: process development). The experimental paradigm presented by Vic Basili in session 1 seems to be an appropriate model because it suggests such a separation of concerns and responsibilities. Dieter Rombach presented the organizational framework for the Software Technology Transfer Initiative STTI-KL which is also based on Basili's paradigm.
  A second lesson is the need for involvement at all levels of a company, from technical staff to managerial staff (Manny Lehman).

- Technology transfer must be rewarded: Technology transfer is not being rewarded properly. Most practitioners view it as a no-win situation (Basili: probably because it is conducted as an add-on to other product development activities). At most universities, technology transfer activities are viewed as second priority behind pure research. Significant changes of academic and industrial software engineering views are needed.

When discussing issue 3 (teaching curricula), the following lessons emerged:

- Software engineering is part of most teaching curricula, but experimentation is not: Although there are still computer science departments which exclude or would like to exclude software engineering entirely (Marv Zelkowitz), most departments view software engineering as an essential building block of their curricula. However, the inclusion of experimental software engineering issues is still the exception.

- Teaching software engineering principles in theory is not enough, non-trivial examples are needed: There is a qualitative difference between teaching issues related to programming-in-the-small versus programming-in-the-large (software engineering). Examples of large systems are needed for teaching. These systems should come from industrial environments. The same argument applies to teaching of process and quality issues.

When discussing issue 4 (training approaches), the following lessons emerged:

- Training must be an integral part of any organization: John Marciniak questioned the value of short training courses given by outsiders without relating them to the specific problems and characteristics of a company. This view was supported by lessons from the SEL where training courses had been tailored to the specific SEL characteristics using concrete SEL examples (Vic Basili, Frank McGarry).

- A software engineering handbook is needed: A software engineering handbook is needed from a technology transfer, teaching and training perspective. It would be very helpful, even though the first edition cannot be perfect. It should contain an overview of existing principles, techniques, methods and tools together with existing documented experience regarding their application in different contexts. Such a handbook would enable the community to share its experiences.

Key Points of Dissent

- Feasibility of writing an engineering handbook today: There was some controversy about the value of an engineering handbook given our current understanding of the field. The majority opinion was that a first step had to be taken.

- Timing for introducing experimental issues into curricula: There was some controversy about whether undergraduate students should be exposed to experimental software engineering issues (e.g., measurement, empirical studies) or whether such topics should be reserved for graduate students. The majority opinion was to introduce experimental issues as early as possible. However, there was no clear model how to do it (see issue for the next five years).

- Feasibility of large-scale experiments: There was some discussion on the feasibility of large-scale experiments. The majority opinion was that large-scale experiments (better: case studies) are feasible. In any engineering discipline such large-scale experiments are useful and necessary.

- Development of formal models of technology transfer approaches: There was some controversy about the nature of software technology transfer processes and ability to treat them like other engineering processes. The majority opinion was that despite the fact that technology transfer has social facets (Walter Tichy), we should take an engineering approach to technology transfer (Walt Scacchi, Hausi Mueller). This means that formal process models should be developed, technology transfer processes should be studied and assessed, and better support technologies need to be developed.

Key Issues for the Next Five Years

As a result of the above discussions, the following key issues for the next five years were identified:

- Develop a first edition of a software engineering handbook

- Establish more experimentally oriented laboratory environments

- Establish corporate improvement programs as the umbrella/prerequisite for systematic technology transfer

- Include experimental issues in software engineering curricula, apply them and report on experiences
- Establish better models of technology transfer (as a two-way process, integrated into a continuous improvement program)

Specific Measurement Studies

Specific studies were suggested in the areas of:

- Comparative studies across environment contexts
- Evaluation of the effectiveness of methods/tools
- Measurement of the effectiveness of technology transfer and improvement approaches (e.g., What does it buy a company to move up one level in the SEI maturity scale?)
- Investigation of software evolution and system architecture aspects

Organizing Committee

Victor R. Basili
Institute for Advanced Computer Science
Department of Computer Science
University of Maryland
College Park, MD 20742
USA
Tel.: (+1) 301 405 2668
Fax: (+1) 301 405 6707
e-mail: basili@cs.umd.edu

H. Dieter Rombach
Universität Kaiserslautern
Fachbereich Informatik
AG Software Engineering
Postfach 3049
67653 Kaiserslautern
W-Germany
Tel.: (+49) (0)631 205 2895
Fax: (+49) (0)631 205 3331
e-mail: rombach@informatik.uni-kl.de

Richard W. Selby
University of California at Irvine
Department of Information & Computer Science
Irvine, CA 92717
USA
Tel.: (+1) 714 856 6326
e-mail: selby@ics.uci.edu

Giovanni Cantone
University of Rome "Tor Vergata"
Dept. of Electronic Engineering
Via della Ricerca Scientifica
I-00186 Rom
Tel.: (+39) 6672 594 495
Fax: (+ 39) 6202 0519
e-mail: cantone@tovvx1.ccd.utovrm.it

Michael Cusumano
Sloan School of Business Management
MIT
Cambridge, MA 02139
USA
Tel.: (+1) 617 253 2574
Fax: (+1) 617 253 2660
e-mail: MCUSUMANO@SLOAN.MIT.EDU

Norman Fenton
City University
CSR
Northhampton Square
London EC1V 0HB
UK
Tel.: (+44) 71 477 8425
Fax: (+44) 71 477 8585
e-mail: nf@cs.city.ac.uk

Academic Invitees

Lionel Briand
Institute for Advanced Computer Science
Department of Computer Science
University of Maryland
College Park, MD 20742
USA
Tel.: (+1) 301 405 2721
Fax: (+1) 301 405 6707
e-mail: lionel@cs.umd.edu

Warren Harrison
Portland State University
Laboratory for Software Quality Research
P.O. Box 751
Portland, Oregon 97207-0751
USA
Tel: (+1) 503 725 3108
Fax: (+1) 503 725 4882
e-mail: warren@cs.pdx.edu

Dan Hoffman
University of Victoria
Department of Computer Science
P.O. Box 3055
Victoria B.C. V8W 3P6
Canada
Tel.: (+1) 604 721 7222
e-mail: dhoffman@uvunix.uvic.ca

Ross Jeffery
University of New South Wales
Department of Information Systems
Faculty of Commerce
P.O.Box 1
Kensington, New South Wales 2033
Australia
Tel.: (+61) 2 697 4413
Fax: (+61) 2 662 4061
e-mail: rossj@cumulus.csd.unsw.oz.au

Chris Kemerer
Sloan School of Business, E53-315
MIT
50 Memorial Drive
Cambridge, MA 02139
USA
Tel.: (+1) 617 253 2971
Fax: (+1) 617 258 7579
e-mail: CKEMERER@SLOAN.MIT.EDU

Manny Lehman
Department of Computing
Imperial College of Science
180 Queens Gate
London SW7 2BZ
UK
Tel: (+44) 71 589 5111 Ex: 5009
Fax: (+44) 71 581 8024
e-mail: mml@doc.ic.ac.uk

Bev Littlewood
Center for Software Reliability
City University
Northampton Square
London EC1V HB
UK
Tel.: (+44) 71 477 8420
Fax: (+44) 71 477 8585
e-mail: b.littlewood@city.ac.uk

Jochen Ludewig
Universität Stuttgart
Fachbereich Informatik
Breitwiesenstr.
W-7000 Stuttgart
Germany
Tel:. (+49) (0)711 7816 354
Fax: (+49) (0)711 780 1042
e-mail: ludewig@informatik.uni-stuttgart.de

Nazim Madhavji
School of Computer Science
McGill University
3480 University Street
Montreal, Quebec
Canada H3A 2A7
Tel.: (+1) 514 398 3740
Fax: (+1) 514 398 3883
e-mail: madhavji@opus.cs.mcgill.ca

Anneliese v. Mayrhauser
Colorado State Unviersity
Department of Computer Science
Fort Collins, CO 80523
USA
Tel.: 001 303 491 7016
e-mail: avm@cs.colostate.edu
Fax: 001 303 491 6639

Hausi Müller
University of Victoria
Department of Computer Science
P.O. Box 3055
Victoria B.C. V8W 3P6
Canada
Tel.: (+1) 604 721 7630
Fax: (+1) 604 721 7292
e-mail: hausi@csr.uvic.ca

Markku Oivo
Technical Research Center of Finland
Computer Technology Laboratory
Kaitovayla 1
SF-90571 Oulu
Finland
Tel: (+358) 81 551 2111
e-mail:moi@tko.vtt.fi

Adam Porter
Institute for Advanced Computer Science
Department of Computer Science
University of Maryland
College Park, MD 20742
USA
Tel.: (+1) 301 405 2702
Fax: (+1) 301 405 6707
e-mail: aporter@cs.umd.edu

Walt Scacchi
University of Southern California
Dicision Systems Department
Bridge Hall 401V
School of Business Administration
Los Angeles, CA 90089-1421
USA
Tel.: (+1) 213 740 477782
Fax: (+1) 213 740 8494
e-mail: scacchi@pollux.usc.edu

Norm Schneidewind
Naval Postgraduate School Monterey
54Ss Administration Science Department
Monterey, CA 93940
USA
e-mail: nschneidewind@a.isi.edu

Vincent Shen
The Hong Kong University of Sci. and Tech.
Department of Computer Science
Clear Water Bay Road
Kowloon
Hong Kong
e-mail: shen@uxmail.ust.hk
Fax: 00852 358 1477

Walter Tichy
Universität Karlsruhe
Fachbereich Informatik I
Postfach 6980
7500 Karlsruhe
Germany
Tel.: (+49) (0)721 608 3934
e-mail: tichy@informatik.uni-karlsruhe.de

Marvin Zelkowitz
Institute for Advanced Computer Science
Department of Computer Science
University of Maryland
College Park, MD 20742
USA
Tel.: (+1) 301 405 2690
Fax: (+1) 301 405 6707
e-mail: mvz@cs.umd.edu

Horst Zuse
TU Berlin FR 5-3
Franklinstr. 28/29
1000 Berlin 10
Germany
Tel.: (+49) (0)30 314 73439
Fax: (+49) (0)30 314 21103
e-mail: zuse@tubvm.cs.tu-berlin.de

Stu Zweben
Ohio State University
Department of Computer and
Information Science
2036 Neil Ave.
Columbus, Ohio 43210-1277
USA
Tel.: (+1) 614 292 5813
Fax: (+1) 614 292 9021
e-mail: zweben@cis.ohio-state.edu

Industrial Invitees

William Agresti
MITRE Corporation
Navy & Information Systems Div.
7525 Colshire Drive
McLean VA 22102
USA
Tel.: (+1) 703 883 7577
e-mail: agresti@national.mitre.org

L. Les Belady
Mitsubishi Laboratories
201 Broadway
Cambridge, MA 02139
USA
Tel.: (+1) 617 621 7501
Fax: (+1) 617 621 7550
e-mail: belady@merl.com

Albert Endres
IBM Deutschland GmbH
Entwicklung und Forschung
Schnaicher Str. 220
7030 Bblingen
Germany
Tel.: (+49) (0)7031 16 3465
Fax: (+49) (0)7031 16 3545
e-mail: aendres@vnet.ibm.com

Stuart Feldman
Bellcore
MRE 2E-386
445 South Street
Morristown, NJ. 07960 1910
USA
Tel.: (+1) 201 829 4305
e-mail: sif@lachesis.bellcore.com

Norbert Fuchs
ALCATEL
Forschungszentrum
Ruthnergasse 1-7
1210 Wien
Österreich
Tel.: (+43) 222 39 1621/264
Fax: (+43) 222 391452
e-mail: se_fuchs@rcvie.uucp

Barbara Kitchenham
National Computer Centre Limited
Oxford House, Oxford Road
Manchester, M1 7ED
UK
Tel.: (+44) 612 286 333 ext. 2350
Fax: (+44) 612 282579

Günther Koch
2i Industrial Informatics GmbH
Haierweg 20e
7800 Freiburg
Germany
Tel.: (+49) (0)761 42257
Fax: (+49) (0)761 474312
e-mail: gk@dandsnx.uucp

Claus Lewerentz
FZI
Haid-und-Neu-Straße
7500 Karlsruhe 1
Tel.: (+49) (0)721 9654 602
Fax: (+49) (0)721 9654 609
e-mail: lewerentz@fzi.de

John Marciniak
CTA Inc.
6116 Executive Blvd.
Rockville, MD 20852
USA
Tel.: (+1) 301 816 1439
e-mail: marcinik@smtplink.cta.com

Frank McGarry
NASA/GSFC
Code 552
Room E231, Bldg. 23
Greenbelt, MD 20771
USA
Tel.: (+1) 301 286 6846
Fax: (+1) 301 286 9183
e-mail: fmgarry@gsfcmail.nasa.gov

K.H. Möller
SIEMENS AG
Otto-Hahn-Ring 6
8000 München 83
Germany
Tel.: (+49) (0)89 636 47660
Fax: (+49) (0)89 636 48281

Eric Sumner J.
AT&T Bell Laboratories
1000 E Warrenville Rd.
Naperville, Il 60566
USA
Tel.: (+1) 708 713 7660
Fax: (+1) 708 713 4982
e-mail: ees@graceland.ih.att.com

Kevin Wentzel
Hewlett Packard Laboratories
1501 Page Mill Road
P.O.Box 10490
Palo Alto, CA. 94303-0969
USA
Tel.: (+1) 415 857 4018
Fax: (+1) 415 857 8526
e-mail: wentzel@hpl.hp.com

Springer-Verlag
and the Environment

We at Springer-Verlag firmly believe that an international science publisher has a special obligation to the environment, and our corporate policies consistently reflect this conviction.

We also expect our business partners – paper mills, printers, packaging manufacturers, etc. – to commit themselves to using environmentally friendly materials and production processes.

The paper in this book is made from low- or no-chlorine pulp and is acid free, in conformance with international standards for paper permanency.

Printing: Weihert-Druck GmbH, Darmstadt
Binding: Buchbinderei Schäffer, Grünstadt

Lecture Notes in Computer Science

For information about Vols. 1–629
please contact your bookseller or Springer-Verlag

Vol. 669: R. S. Bird, C. C. Morgan, J. C. P. Woodcock (Eds.), Mathematics of Program Construction. Proceedings, 1992. VIII, 378 pages. 1993.

Vol. 670: J. C. P. Woodcock, P. G. Larsen (Eds.), FME '93: Industrial-Strength Formal Methods. Proceedings, 1993. XI, 689 pages. 1993.

Vol. 671: H. J. Ohlbach (Ed.), GWAI-92: Advances in Artificial Intelligence. Proceedings, 1992. XI, 397 pages. 1993. (Subseries LNAI).

Vol. 672: A. Barak, S. Guday, R. G. Wheeler, The MOSIX Distributed Operating System. X, 221 pages. 1993.

Vol. 673: G. Cohen, T. Mora, O. Moreno (Eds.), Applied Algebra, Algebraic Algorithms and Error-Correcting Codes. Proceedings, 1993. X, 355 pages 1993.

Vol. 674: G. Rozenberg (Ed.), Advances in Petri Nets 1993. VII, 457 pages. 1993.

Vol. 675: A. Mulkers, Live Data Structures in Logic Programs. VIII, 220 pages. 1993.

Vol. 676: Th. H. Reiss, Recognizing Planar Objects Using Invariant Image Features. X, 180 pages. 1993.

Vol. 677: H. Abdulrab, J.-P. Pécuchet (Eds.), Word Equations and Related Topics. Proceedings, 1991. VII, 214 pages. 1993.

Vol. 678: F. Meyer auf der Heide, B. Monien, A. L. Rosenberg (Eds.), Parallel Architectures and Their Efficient Use. Proceedings, 1992. XII, 227 pages. 1993.

Vol. 679: C. Fermüller, A. Leitsch, T. Tammet, N. Zamov, Resolution Methods for the Decision Problem. VIII, 205 pages. 1993. (Subseries LNAI).

Vol. 680: B. Hoffmann, B. Krieg-Brückner (Eds.), Program Development by Specification and Transformation. XV, 623 pages. 1993.

Vol. 681: H. Wansing, The Logic of Information Structures. IX, 163 pages. 1993. (Subseries LNAI).

Vol. 682: B. Bouchon-Meunier, L. Valverde, R. R. Yager (Eds.), IPMU '92 – Advanced Methods in Artificial Intelligence. Proceedings, 1992. IX, 367 pages. 1993.

Vol. 683: G.J. Milne, L. Pierre (Eds.), Correct Hardware Design and Verification Methods. Proceedings, 1993. VIII, 270 Pages. 1993.

Vol. 684: A. Apostolico, M. Crochemore, Z. Galil, U. Manber (Eds.), Combinatorial Pattern Matching. Proceedings, 1993. VIII, 265 pages. 1993.

Vol. 685: C. Rolland, F. Bodart, C. Cauvet (Eds.), Advanced Information Systems Engineering. Proceedings, 1993. XI, 650 pages. 1993.

Vol. 686: J. Mira, J. Cabestany, A. Prieto (Eds.), New Trends in Neural Computation. Proceedings, 1993. XVII, 746 pages. 1993.

Vol. 687: H. H. Barrett, A. F. Gmitro (Eds.), Information Processing in Medical Imaging. Proceedings, 1993. XVI, 567 pages. 1993.

Vol. 688: M. Gauthier (Ed.), Ada-Europe '93. Proceedings, 1993. VIII, 353 pages. 1993.

Vol. 689: J. Komorowski, Z. W. Ras (Eds.), Methodologies for Intelligent Systems. Proceedings, 1993. XI, 653 pages. 1993. (Subseries LNAI).

Vol. 690: C. Kirchner (Ed.), Rewriting Techniques and Applications. Proceedings, 1993. XI, 488 pages. 1993.

Vol. 691: M. Ajmone Marsan (Ed.), Application and Theory of Petri Nets 1993. Proceedings, 1993. IX, 591 pages. 1993.

Vol. 692: D. Abel, B.C. Ooi (Eds.), Advances in Spatial Databases. Proceedings, 1993. XIII, 529 pages. 1993.

Vol. 693: P. E. Lauer (Ed.), Functional Programming, Concurrency, Simulation and Automated Reasoning. Proceedings, 1991/1992. XI, 398 pages. 1993.

Vol. 694: A. Bode, M. Reeve, G. Wolf (Eds.), PARLE '93. Parallel Architectures and Languages Europe. Proceedings, 1993. XVII, 770 pages. 1993.

Vol. 695: E. P. Klement, W. Slany (Eds.), Fuzzy Logic in Artificial Intelligence. Proceedings, 1993. VIII, 192 pages. 1993. (Subseries LNAI).

Vol. 696: M. Worboys, A. F. Grundy (Eds.), Advances in Databases. Proceedings, 1993. X, 276 pages. 1993.

Vol. 697: C. Courcoubetis (Ed.), Computer Aided Verification. Proceedings, 1993. IX, 504 pages. 1993.

Vol. 698: A. Voronkov (Ed.), Logic Programming and Automated Reasoning. Proceedings, 1993. XIII, 386 pages. 1993. (Subseries LNAI).

Vol. 699: G. W. Mineau, B. Moulin, J. F. Sowa (Eds.), Conceptual Graphs for Knowledge Representation. Proceedings, 1993. IX, 451 pages. 1993. (Subseries LNAI).

Vol. 700: A. Lingas, R. Karlsson, S. Carlsson (Eds.), Automata, Languages and Programming. Proceedings, 1993. XII, 697 pages. 1993.

Vol. 701: P. Atzeni (Ed.), LOGIDATA+: Deductive Databases with Complex Objects. VIII, 273 pages. 1993.

Vol. 702: E. Börger, G. Jäger, H. Kleine Büning, S. Martini, M. M. Richter (Eds.), Computer Science Logic. Proceedings, 1992. VIII, 439 pages. 1993.

Vol. 703: M. de Berg, Ray Shooting, Depth Orders and Hidden Surface Removal. X, 201 pages. 1993.

Vol. 704: F. N. Paulisch, The Design of an Extendible Graph Editor. XV, 184 pages. 1993.

Vol. 705: H. Grünbacher, R. W. Hartenstein (Eds.), Field-Programmable Gate Arrays. Proceedings, 1992. VIII, 218 pages. 1993.

Vol. 706: H. D. Rombach, V. R. Basili, R. W. Selby (Eds.), Experimental Software Engineering Issues. Proceedings, 1992. XVIII, 261 pages. 1993.

Vol. 707: O. M. Nierstrasz (Ed.), ECOOP '93 – Object-Oriented Programming. Proceedings, 1993. XI, 531 pages. 1993.

Vol. 708: C. Laugier (Ed.), Geometric Reasoning for Perception and Action. Proceedings, 1991. VIII, 281 pages. 1993.

Vol. 709: F. Dehne, J.-R. Sack, N. Santoro, S. Whitesides (Eds.), Algorithms and Data Structures. Proceedings, 1993. XII, 634 pages. 1993.